Through the Knothole

Musings from Newport

Sue Hardesty & Nel Ward

FIRST EDITION
First Printing: 2023
ISBN: 978-1-63304-233-9
Cover: Ann Hubard,
Dreamstime.com
Book Design: Sue Hardesty
Editing: Kay Dubrow Grey
Typeset: Lori L. Lake

www.LaunchPointPress.com

A Launch Point Press Trade Paperback Original

Table of Contents

Dedication

To all the wonderful people who made this book possible

Foreword

Gleaning jewels from the chaff of social media is a crapshoot at best. This isn't it. Rather, think how stream of consciousness works, one chaotic thought tumbling over another, often jarringly unrelated as pages leap and tumble from curiously connected or diametrically opposed, quotes to shipwrecks and whales, murals, and snails, bits and pieces about Newport's famous Yaquina Bridge and Bay history, interspersed with more quotes, a story about the crow, fragments about family, the sad loss of the sea star, a few political rants, our favorite Newport buildings, and the naming of famous research ships. Etc.

Our look back over a decade of social posts is divided into four chronological parts. Part I covers the years from 2010 through 2018, largely focusing on local events and history with a few digressions into sea life. The next three parts are divided into 2019, 2020, and 2021 with a bit of 2022 tacked onto Part IV, concluding with the Epilogue. Otherwise called a dipping book, anywhere you open is the beginning. Not all the posts are in chronological order. To avoid repetition, some are incorporated in one location such as "Fourth of July" and "Blessing of the Fleet."

In 2019, we included more posts about politics because they made a huge impact on our life—clashes with loved ones, fake pandemic cures, growing violence demonstrating indifference to others, etc. We labeled these posts "Politics" and highlighted them in red. Feel free to skip them. For more information about our political writings, check out Nel's blog:

https://nelsnewday.wordpress.com/

With the postings, we incorporated photographs and pithy comments that struck our fancy, such as "If someone gave you a box that contained everything you have lost in your life, what's the first thing you'd search for? Copyright issues required us to delete many of these from the original, but those in public domain are scattered throughout the book.

We began these musings on social media over a decade ago when we advertised a cookbook we wrote with our friend, Lee Lynch. Those postings led us into writing about anything that took our fancy, many of them based on a view from our window, a "knothole" peek if you will, of our small coastal town and those who live among us. The book is comprised of jumbled up dibs and dabs related to our lives in the best place on earth—Newport, Oregon.

Sue and Nel

love

Introduction

Musings from Newport

For such a small town, Newport has it all. Even job offerings are surprisingly diverse. There's a boss who wants to know if you are a talker because he's looking for a storyteller and entertainer who is good with groups. Another needed a diver with a dry suit, full mask, and air tank, to herd sharks. We needed a Surimi (mincer of pollock to make a gelatinous paste used as crab substitute). And a Brew Master. A Relief Master for a research ship. If you're into research, a job was open for tracing pollutants with stable isotopes. I can't explain that one.

As a favorite tourist destination, jobs are endless in motels, restaurants, bars, and other related touristy places.

We also have government jobs along with medical jobs in our new hospital and animal clinics.

Then there's Hatfield's new, one-of-a-kind tsunami/earthquake proof building, housing brilliant scientists in marine research, providing valuable services to our country. Some say that the combined facilities of National Oceanic and Atmospheric Administration (NOAA), Oregon Museum of Science and Industry, Oregon Coast Aquarium, U.S. Fish and Wildlife Service, U.S. Geological Survey, U.S. Department of Agriculture, Oregon Department of Fish and Wildlife, and the Hatfield Marine Science Center from Oregon State University presents Newport as the Woods Hole of the Pacific. And we get to watch it all.

Along with research ships, the bay is always filled with other boats—fourteenth largest fishing fleet in the U.S., and hundreds of leisure and sailing boats taking advantage of sunny days. Two marinas and the Yaquina Bay docks host these boats, large and small.

Speaking of physical entertainment, we have the best under-roof activity center including an Olympic size swimming pool, water games, a running track, basketball and volleyball courts, and an exercise room. If you're not on the beautiful beaches picking up seashells, agates, and fossils or visiting our castle and our two lighthouses, you could bob in and out of stores and galleries or just stand and stare at the famous murals on our working bayfront.

Then there's the arts. Our Performing Arts Center (PAC) has two stages and multiple resident companies, known as "PAC rats." Theater, dance, and chorus groups join the Newport Symphony Orchestra, a teachers' association, and an international film series. During the COVID pandemic, it even hosted a drive-in movie theater. Performances in music concerts, plays, and dance productions on our stages have featured such famous actors as the late David Ogden Stiers and Harry Morgan.

Writers in our midst include famous authors of children's books, lesbian fiction, mysteries, and more. Newport also has a publishing house and several writing groups, one offering a reading series featuring well-known writers.

Among the artists, Newport's former mayor Sandy Roumagoux is internationally known, and the late Michel Gibbons, a local artist with a Toledo gallery, supported Oregon artists and helped rejuvenate the small art town six miles east of Newport. Rick Bartow—Native American singer, sculptor, painter, ceramicist, and more—saw his magnificent cedar sculptures installed at the Smithsonian's National Museum of the American Indian before he died in 2016.

We have three traditional gallery spaces in the Visual Arts Center (VAC), accompanying the plethora of private galleries throughout the community, providing photography, painting, and writing classes. Local volunteer artists can also exhibit their work next to the VAC at the Yaquina Art Gallery and Gift Shop. Over a century ago, this building was a bathhouse for surf bathers.

Newport's interest in the arts dates back to the late 1800s when a state teacher's conference in Newport offered classes in music, mirth, art, science, and religion. Although the summer sessions were dropped in 1903, the tradition for creating a home for the literary, scholarly, and artistic was established and continues today.

We have several glassblowers around town holding classes. Then there's quilting, hiking, surfing, air ballooning, pet walking for the humane society, and more.

Combined with famous buildings and bridges plus the Pacific Ocean; mix in the absurd such as a castle on the coast of Oregon, stories of jumping-for-love off Jump-off Joe, historical happenings such as our colorful railroad magnate Colonel Hogg (once a pirate); and we have a complete cross-section of the world in this colorful town, a joy to witness.

In addition to all that, the Newport area has some of the most beautiful and colorful scenery in the world to just sit, enjoy, and contemplate. I did not know so many colors of green existed in the grand forests surrounding us. Or blues and grays in the sky and sea, and red in the sunsets. Even the ocean sands show off their glorious variety of colors from glittering white to basalt black. Tide-pools teeming with unusual living creatures keep me watching for hours. Air so clean I can taste it.

We especially treasure the people from this seaside town who reached out a helping hand before you knew you needed one, who look you in the eye, smile, and wish you a good day and mean it.

OREGON HISTORY

YAQUINA BAY

THE OLD YAQUINA BAY LIGHTHOUSE ESTABLISHED IN 1871 IS THE EARLIEST AID TO NAVIGATION, STANDING WITHIN THE RANGE OF THE FIRST RECORDED LANDFALL MADE FROM A SHIP TO THE SHORES OF THE PACIFIC NORTHWEST. CAPTAIN JAMES COOK MADE THIS LANDFALL ON MARCH 7, 1778. AT NOON HE NAMED CAPE FOULWEATHER. ON ACCOUNT OF THE HEAVY WEATHER HE WAS COMPELLED TO STAND OUT AT SEA AT NIGHT AND ONLY APPROACH THE LAND IN THE AFTERNOON SO THAT HE WAS UNABLE TO FIND ANY HARBOR ALONG THE OREGON COAST. NEWS OF COOK'S VOYAGE TO THE PACIFIC NORTHWEST STIMULATED THE AMERICAN INTERESTS IN THIS REGION AND AROUSED IN THOMAS JEFFERSON AN INTEREST THAT LED TO THE LOUISIANA PURCHASE IN 1803 AND THE DISPATCH OF THE LEWIS AND CLARK EXPEDITION.

Part I – 2010 thru 2018

History of Yaquina Bay, a Brief Overview

First known photo of Yaquina Bay, 1865-1866

We have the best seat in the world. Not only do we watch a living portrait unfold out our window every day, but we also watch history in the making. We can look back and see the historical changes for the bay area. From the construction of the Oregon Pacific Railroad in the late nineteenth century to the addition of the Hatfield Science Center and National Oceanic and Atmospheric Administration headquarters during the last decade, Newport has developed into a community of science research.

The current major tourist industry didn't develop until the railroad allowed passengers to cross the coastal hills from Portland and the Willamette Valley.

The tracks followed the north side of Yaquina River to Yaquina City where passengers switched to steamboats for the rest of their trip to Newport. Once there, many travelers boarded a boat to San Francisco, having saved hours of travel time, but others stayed in Newport, creating a permanent population of 120 by the 1890s.

Portland competitors fought the railroad company, sending it into bankruptcy, and new owners kept it going until 1937. Over time, the railroad railings disappeared to Toledo although a trip up the river can still find an occasional trestle.

During the 1890s, a major development of the bay added the two jetties to lead the Yaquina River into the sea. Jetties kept the ocean waves out of the bay and the sand on the beaches. Fishing boats could freely move into the ocean after the invention of the gas motor, the building of the jetties, and the dredging of the bay. A vital part of the Bay's growth came from the establishment of the Port of Newport in 1910.

In 1948, a private company floated in three concrete navy ships and sank the *Pasley* and the *Hennebique* to form a new dock at McLean Point. The third one, the *Aspdin*, broke its mooring and sank at the end of the south jetty.

A breakwater, or seawall, protecting commercial fishing boats was built in 1966, and Newport's Bayfront became a focus of the town for both fishing and tourism industries. The

South Beach Marina was finished in 1981. The Rogue Ales, a brewery, opened for business in 1991 on another patch of the Bayfront and put Newport on the international map.

Science exploration arrived in Newport in 1965 when Oregon State University leased 50 acres and opened the doors of the Hatfield Marine Science Center (HMSC). In 1992, the Oregon Coast Aquarium opened its doors and brought more tourists. On April 29, 2011, NOAA took the keys to its new 10 acres and buildings that cost $38 million to construct. It provides engineering, maintenance, and logistical support to NOAA's fleet of research and survey ships in the Pacific Ocean.

A walk along Bay Boulevard allows exploration of the fishing boats, working canneries, shops, restaurants, bars, fishing boats at rest, famous murals, and visits with interesting people.

Historic Trips from the Valley to Newport

Crossing the Coast Range between Corvallis and Newport was a huge struggle in the nineteenth century, but intrepid travelers found commercial ways to do it. In 1868, the mail route was completed between Corvallis and Toledo, when a stagecoach began the exhausting 12-hour trip into Elk City. After a night spent in the Elk City hotel, passengers boarded a steamer that ran down the river to a small wharf at Newport. In the early 1880s, entrepreneur T. Edgenton Hogg—formerly pirate, master in the Confederate States Navy, lifer in Alcatraz, railroad baron, and major swindler—decided to build a railroad and founded Yaquina City. Looking for another way to make his fortune, he decided Newport would make a much better major seaport than Portland. He also reasoned getting into Newport would be easier than

Yaquina Bay, 1875

crossing the Columbia River bar and wasting fuel and time traveling upriver to Portland. Better yet, coming from Willamette Valley through Corvallis would shorten the Chicago to Sacramento trip by 300 miles and to San Francisco by 40 hours.

Originally, Hogg planned to end his railroad at Seal Rock, ten miles south of Newport. In 1877, excited people platted the proposed town with resort hotels and public walking spaces. Instead, Hogg stayed on the north side of the Yaquina River, and Seal Rock planners went broke. Newport prospered after the Army Corps of Engineers surveyed Yaquina Bay and found it to be deep enough for the sea-going ships to enter and dock. Completed in April 1883, the Bayfront, protected by a bulkhead, was filled in and the first street in Newport, Front Street, also became a long pier.

The completion of the Oregon Pacific Railroad from the Willamette Valley to Yaquina City and arrival of the first train in March 1885 drastically cut travel time from Portland to San

Francisco. Imagine you travel on a train around the Bay and up the Yaquina River from the remnants of Yaquina City to Toledo and on to the rest of the world.

Watching one of those huge locomotives turning around in the roundhouse at Yaquina City must have been like watching an airbus take off today. According to old timers, “the little building near the shoreline was a saloon.” Yaquina City proper was dry so some ingenious soul set up his liquor facility offshore. Several customers fell into the “drink” after a few too many.

Hogg’s concept to take the railroad all the way to Newport might have worked if a group from Portland had not feared economic ruin. They not only bought up the land between

Newport and Yaquina City to stop the railroad from reaching Newport but also sabotaged Hogg’s ships intended to take travelers from Yaquina City to San Francisco. The 1887 crash of the sea-worthy ship, the *Yaquina City* into the south jetty, and the 1888 wreck of the *Yaquina Bay* on her first trip into the harbor ended service in the 1890s.

These disasters, along with accidents along the tracks and other financial problems, left Hogg broke. The railroad was ordered into receivership with only one bid by A.B. Hamond for $100,000. Hogg died of a stroke in 1898 on a streetcar in Philadelphia.

In 1919, a plan to complete the tracks from Yaquina City to Newport was finally abandoned. Tourists from the Willamette Valley continued to travel the railroad to Yaquina

City and catch the smaller steamboats for their last trek to Newport until the 1920s. Steamers landing daily in Newport from Yaquina City brought the town out to watch mail boats arrive, and people piled off the steamers looking for the draymen. Wagons picked up loads to be transported elsewhere, and the Bayfront even had a band to welcome all the activity.

Abandoned Railroad Trestles on the Yaquina River between Newport and Toledo

Boat service from Yaquina City ended by 1929, and the railroad line between Toledo and Yaquina City was abandoned in 1937. Although planks replaced the railway tracks on low-lying trestles to create a road, it was often impassable from slides. That led to the final demise of Yaquina City, once a thriving town of 2,000.

Yaquina City was not the only town lost in history. Oregon has documented over 300 ghost towns, more than any other state and all with interesting stories about their abandonments. Many were lost to fires, epidemics, greed, etc., leaving behind oral and written records, graveyards, and sometimes a few buildings.

Road construction created Highway 20 from Corvallis, and the "Roosevelt Highway," now called Highway 101, was built in the 1920s. The completion of the Yaquina Bay Bridge in 1936 opened up travel along the entire West Coast. Newport went from an isolated area of 52 trappers and homesteaders to a bustling town of over 2,000 in just 60 years.

Oregon State University Hatfield Marine Science Center Research Ships

The Hatfield Marine Science Center (HMSC), a research and education center, was named after Mark Hatfield, governor for two terms before he became the longest-serving U.S. senator from Oregon. A Navy officer and one of the first witnesses of the Hiroshima Atomic bombing, Hatfield was an outspoken critic of wars. With students, teachers, and researchers, the HMSC works with many state and federal agencies.

When we moved to our home across the bay in 2004, the Center had two operational research ships: the 184-foot R/V *Wecoma* (later replaced by her 177-foot sister ship the *Oceanus)*

and the 54-foot R/V *Elakha*. The 85-foot R/V *Pacific Storm* came in 2016. In 2023, the 200-foot R/V *Taani* will replace the *Oceanus*. Their research includes issues of acidification, harmful algal blooms, tsunami prediction, and declining fisheries.

Hatfield daily pumps an astonishing 1.6 million gallons of seawater through its facilities researching diverse sea issues: ecology of fish, birds, and marine mammals; impacts from wave energy, marine reserves, climate change, and aquaculture; undersea volcanoes, faults, and hydrothermal vents; etc. It uses the newest and most innovative research tools such as genomics, remote sensing, satellite tags for wildlife tracking, and remotely-operated vehicles (ROVs) for underwater exploration along with the older tried and true traditional ones of nets, waders, seawater tanks, and World War II-era hydrophones. Luckily, much of the student research can be viewed in the Hatfield's visitor center free to the public.

Hatfield's R/V *Wecoma*'s Final Voyage

On a late October day in 2013, I sat on my usual perch taking photos and saw the *Wecoma* being towed away. A break in her hull was beyond repair. For 35 years, the Hatfield research ship took scientists and students out to sea to learn about fisheries, climate change, undersea earthquakes, volcanoes, tsunamis, marine dead zones, and more.

She was stripped of everything useful before her final trip to Ensenada, Mexico, where she was cut up for scrap. I could not help shedding a few tears as I watched her disappear between the jetties into the ocean.

The R/V *Oceanus*

On January 25, 2012, *Oceanus* departed her 37-year home in Woods Hole to replace the *Wecoma* as the Regional Class oceanographic research ship operated by Oregon State University. The *Oceanus* underwent a major refit in 1994: a new deck house and new pilot house along with increased laboratory space and accommodations for scientists. She accommodates a crew of 12 and a scientific party of 19 for up to 30 days at sea.

With three winches and a crane, *Oceanus* often deploys oceanographic buoys and moorings for hydrographic surveys. She also does all types of chemical, biological, and geological studies.

The R/V *Pacific Storm*

The 85-foot *Pacific Storm* was transferred to Hatfield on July 6, 2016. In 2018, the ship received funding for high school and college undergraduate and graduate students to conduct research on a variety of nearshore projects. In the past decade, the *Pacific Storm* hosted 52 cruises, including an appearance in the 96-minute *National Geographic* documentary, "Kingdom of the Blue Whale," featuring the largest animals to have ever lived on Earth.

In addition to whale research, the ship deploys wave energy buoys, conducts seafloor mapping off the Oregon Coast, and drops and recovers undersea gliders. She was originally a commercial trawler donated to the OSU Marine Mammal Institute by Scotty and Janet Hockema and refitted for research. Donations paid for the fish hold to be converted into three bunk rooms, two toilets, and a shower and the outfitting of a research laboratory.

R/V *Elakha*

Among the many classes taught at OSU Hatfield, marine biology is viewed as the "capstone" course for biology or zoology majors. This introduction to marine flora and fauna emphasizes ecological patterns and processes through field work. One of the 54-foot *Elakha*'s jobs is to take students out for estuarine and coastal field sampling. Hauled out of the water by boat gantry cranes, the *Elakha* recently received a mid-life redo with a new motor and research equipment making her faster and safer than ever.

Like the small sea otter she's named after, the *Elakha* is smaller ocean research boat. Built in 2001, she has a winch, a small laboratory, a small galley, and sleeps four. Her 600-horsepower diesel engine allows a range of around 575 miles. She travels primarily along the Oregon coast, estuaries, and rivers, including the Columbia, sometimes going about thirty nautical miles out to sea where students drop and recover gliders and crab pots, do box coring, study plankton, deep-sea dive, and more.

Anyone with a research project fitting the university mission can rent the *Elakha.*

Note: Ships are called "she" like other traveling trains, cars, etc. Why? Because men owned them. However, tools, computers and such are referred to as "he" because men use them. Or so says the internet dictionary.

R/V *Taani*

Oregon State University's grant of $121.88 million from the National Science Foundation, the largest in OSU history, spearheaded the building of a new class of research ships for the United States Academic Research Fleet. The *Taani* will join the Hatfield in 2023. (To the right: An artist's rendering of the ship.)

Taani, the Siletz tribes' word for "offshore," will be just short of 200 feet with a payload of 66 tons (including permanent equipment) and berthing for thirty-three. It can last three weeks without going into port for a range of over 5,000 nautical miles.

"I don't want to protect the environment. I want to create a world where the environment doesn't need protecting. We have come to believe in a society based on insults, on lies, and on things that just aren't true. It creates an environment where deranged people feel empowered." – Colin Powell

NOAA Comes to Newport

In 2010, NOAA arrived at the Bay; I was fascinated with the construction across the river from me. After a competitive lease award process, NOAA signed a 20-year lease with the Port of Newport in 2009.

Otherwise known as MOC-P (Marine Operations Center – Pacific), this center serves as a homeport for two NOAA ships (*Rainier* and *Bell Shimada*) and supports five other ships homeported in California and Alaska. It provides administrative, maintenance, engineering, and logistical support to all of NOAA's Pacific fleet.

The Newport facility also houses the Marine Operations directorate, which oversees the Pacific, Pacific-Islands, and Atlantic marine centers and all NOAA ship operations.

The facility includes 40,852 square feet of office and warehouse space, a 1,300-foot-long wharf, and a small boat dock. The main buildings are built to Leadership in Energy and Environmental Design standards for environmentally sustainable construction.

Part of NOAA's job is to protect and research our major waterways, oceans, and the air we breathe. Its fifteen active survey and research ships have completed more than one-hundred missions over 4.3 million square miles of marine terrain collecting data essential to protecting marine mammals, coral reefs, and historic shipwrecks; managing commercial marine fish stocks; understanding climate processes; and producing nautical charts that help keep mariners safe.

NOAA ships also deploy and help maintain buoys that gather oceanographic and weather information and warn of tsunamis.

The following four panels illustrate the construction of NOAA headquarters, shop, and dock. Check the same road on the left in all four panels.

Before NOAA was built this site was a fish farm.

Bell M. Shimada *Fairweather* *Oscar Dyson* *Rainier* *Ruben Lasker*

Of these five ships in port, only the *Shimada* and the *Rainier* homeport in Newport. *Fairweather* homeports in Ketchikan (AK). *Oscar Dyson* homeports in Kodiak (AK), and the *Reuben Lasker* homeports in San Diego.

On June 5, 2010, the first ship to call Newport her new home, the R/V *Miller Freeman* arrived, hung around awhile, and disappeared. I learned later she had been decommissioned. The next day, June 6, the R/V *Bell M. Shimada* came home.

Terry Hillman, a reporter from the News-Times, said it best, sometimes using descriptions from a crew member: "As if on cue, the fog began to lift 'like a rising stage curtain' as the ship made her way between the jetties. It unveiled a small fleet of pleasure craft, charter boats, and commercial fishing boats, all filled with people waving American flags and cheering. Other folks lined the 'postcard-worthy bridge that perfectly defined the skyline of Newport' and the jetties that 'led us under the bridge like a red-carpet aisle, velvet ropes and all.' Ships horns and bells rang out... Through it all the F/V *Michelle Ann* spouted water from her main fire hose, a traditional sign of highest nautical honor. On 'that dreary, cloudy, foggy, no-good Sunday morning,' the town of Newport welcomed NOAA Ship *Bell M. Shimada* home."

R/V *Bell Shimada* Research Ship

In 2019, the *News-Times* reported our very own *Bell Shimada* was NOAA's Ship of the Year. Congratulations to the crew and those who watch after her. The article described the *Shimada* as the research ship that primarily deals with the ecosystem surrounding pelagic fish. I discovered this marine life has to do with the mid-water column in the ocean between the coast and edge of the continental shelf. These fish usually swim in the area above the sea floor and below the water surface. Pelagic fish include small forage fish (sardines, anchovy, squid, and krill) hunted by larger pelagic fish (albacore, sharks, salmon, tuna). The smaller fish feed on plankton, stay in schools, and often migrate long distances.

As the primary NOAA ship to cover the West Coast, *Shimada* is a FSV (Fast Supply Vessel) class of acoustically quiet stern trawlers, allowing scientists to track fish populations without disturbing behavior. Most important is the sonar system which accurately measures the biomass of fish such as albacore, sharks, salmon, groundfish, sardine, hake, and other coastal pelagic species. Along with tracking fish population, the *Shimada* tracks marine mammal and bird populations, conducts oceanographic research, observes weather, measures contents of a water column, and deploys and recovers floating and bottom sensors, acoustic receivers, vertical nets, and hundreds of floating and bottom sensors measuring water temperature and land movement. On a recent trip, *Shimada* worked with our Oregon Coast

Aquarium to collect measurements of changing ocean conditions within the Northern California current. She can work with vehicles that tow, dive, dredge, and core the ocean bottom. The *Shimada* has also sailed more than any other ship in the entire NOAA fleet.

Bell Shimada, the Man

I enjoy learning the source of names. Like Beverly Beach, north of Newport was named after a little girl's doll. Or Yachats, a Native American term, means "dark at the foot of the mountain." Idaho Point was originally Point Virtue. And the three concrete boats bought to build the dock at Newport's International Port were named after men involved in developing concrete.

The *Shimada* was named after Bell Masayuki Shimada, an American fisheries scientist noted for his study of tuna in the Pacific Ocean during the 1950s.

Born January 17, 1922, in Seattle (WA) of Japanese immigrants, Shimada studied math and science until his parents were taken to a Japanese internment camp in Idaho on April 29, 1942. A senior in college, he could either join his folks or enlist in the army. Because he spoke Japanese, he trained in intelligence and went to Hawaii as a translator/interpreter. In August 1945, he was transferred to Tokyo where he collected and synthesized economic and infrastructure data on the effects of strategic bombing until he was discharged from the military in February 1946. Shimada left Japan and returned home where he graduated cum laude in marine science at the University of Washington. From 1948 to 1951, Shimada worked for Pacific Oceanic Fisheries Investigations in charge of observing research ships and finished his doctorate in 1956.

In February 1952, Shimada moved to the Inter-American Tropical Tuna Commission in La Jolla (CA) where he did his famous work researching tuna distribution in the Pacific Ocean.

Shimada died in a plane crash near Guadalajara, Mexico, on June 2, 1958.

When I was a kid, I remember my teacher scolding me, "Nobody's going to pay you to stare out a window!" I wanted to ask her about truckers, bus drivers, pilots, deliverers, and all the other jobs requiring looking out a window. Even window washers. Then there's me. It is because of my living room window that I wrote this book. Who knows what great things we envision looking out a window? Not that this book is a great envision. You know what I mean.

– Sue Hardesty

Concrete Ships

A huge, majestic propeller stands sentinel outside the Pacific Maritime Heritage Center on the Bayfront. It propelled the SS *C.W. Pasley* named after Sir Charles William Pasley (1780-1861), a British military engineer who wrote textbooks and experimented with improving concrete. Under the wartime emergency program near the end of World War II, she was one of twenty-four ships built by McCloskey and Company. The decks and hulls were made entirely of concrete with six-inch-thick rebar-reinforced walls.

The SS *Joseph Aspdin* was also named for a Brit (1778-1855) who created "Portland cement." On April 12, 1948, the ship broke loose from its moorings and floated out of the river on a high tide, grounding on the North Jetty at the entrance to the bay. Ten days later, the *Aspdin,* known as the ship that committed suicide, broke in half and sank. The wreck lies at the end of the jetty under 40 feet of water. It can be seen with a dangerous dive through twisted rebar and strong currents.

The third ship was the SS *Francois Hennebique*, named after a French stonemason (1842-1921), a successful engineer who pioneered the use of reinforced concrete. The ship had been launched and delivered to the army in 1944 for use in the Southwest Pacific, but her two large guns were never used.

The twenty-four concrete ships were built at a rapid rate, one launched per month. Two of the ships were sunk as blockships in the Allied invasion of Normandy. Nine more were sunk as breakwaters for a ferry landing at Kiptopeke (VA). Ten still float in a giant breakwater on the Powell River in Canada. They form the breakwater protecting the logging pond of the Powell River Company pulp and paper mill. Nine of these ships were built by McCloskey, and the tenth ship, the SS *Peralta*, is the last remaining World War I concrete ship afloat. And of course, three of them can be found in Yaquina Bay.

Rebuilding The International Terminal

When the *Pasley* and the *Hennebique* were floated to their current location in 1948, they were sunk by blasting holes in their sides and bottoms. Over time, the *Pasley* shifted and rolled, causing structural failure and cracks in her hull. Oil leaks polluting the bay closed the wharf in 2001.

The renovation of the terminal at McLean Point began in 2010 when the *Pasley* was refloated and dismantled and the *Hennebique* partially dismantled. Much of the *Hennebique* hull remains under the terminal; the bow can be seen, outlined in the tarmac. The concrete from the hulls was cleaned and ground up to be reused as paving material and fill for the cleaned-out places inside the Hennebique. The metal rebar was recycled. The new terminal opened for business in August 2013.

In one large shed at the terminal, three workers braid nylon rope into large fishing nets. It's worth the watch.

Blessing of the Fleet

On a sunny spring day, I spent the afternoon sitting on my porch watching the Blessing of the Fleet. This happens every first Saturday in May when leaders of diverse religious denominations get on a Coast Guard boat and sit under the Yaquina Bridge blessing the circling fishing boats. It is a wondrous sight.

"Where ignorance is our master, there is no possibility of real peace."

– Dalai Lama

Research Ships

The research vessels coming into Yaquina Bay have a hierarchy topped by NOAA (National Oceanic and Atmospheric Administration), operated by the U.S. scientific agency within the Department of Commerce. The **ONR** (Office of Naval Research) owns another twelve major research ships. An organization within the U.S. Department of the Navy, it coordinates, executes, and promotes the science and technology programs of the U.S. Navy and Marine Corps through schools, universities, government laboratories, nonprofit organizations, and for-profit organizations.

The ONR turns their operation over to **UNOLS** (University-National Oceanographic Laboratory System) who loans or assigns these research ships to marine educational institutions such as **WHOI** (Woods Hole Oceanographic Institution), operating *Alvin*, R/V *Neil Armstrong*, R/V *Knorr*, and R/V *Tioga* research ships; Scripps Institution of Oceanography, operating R/V *Sally Ride* and R/V *Roger Revelle;* the University of Washington, operating R/V *Thomas Thompson;* and the Hatfield Science Center operating the *soon to arrive, R/V Taani*. UNOLS is a group of U.S. academic institutions and national laboratories to coordinate research ships used for federally funded ocean research.

WHOI is the widely cited, largest independent oceanic research institution in the U.S., known around the world for groundbreaking oceanic research, including famously, the discovery of the wreck of the *RMS Titanic*.

Private enterprise also owns research ships. A wealthy offshore oil magnate, Kjell Inge Røkke, built the *REV Ocean*, a 600-foot research ship twice the size as any one before it.

[**Update**: The completed ship now operates in the North Sea. The Norwegian who made his money from taking oil and gas from the ocean says he will find solutions to overfishing, ocean acidification, climate change, etc.]

Historic Snow Fall

On March 13, 2012, I woke up to a rare snowy morning. Some areas had only powder, some roads were cleared, and some back streets were a mess with downed trees and slick conditions. LINCOLN COUNTY SCHOOLS CLOSED TODAY came over television. Highway 101 at Cape Foulweather was closed. People were told to wait for the stuff to melt. They should have traction devices or a 4X4 if they had to go out. People who can, should stay in, enjoy the morning, and maybe get out later on today. I went out. I needed milk and walked to the store. Rather, I slipped and slid and ended on my butt several times. It was pretty funny. That's all there is for 2012.

Note: The record snowfall in Newport was eleven inches in December 1972. Records along the Oregon coast date back to the late 1800s.

My Friend, the Crow

In addition to Yaquina Bay and the town of Newport surrounding the bay, nearby beaches are not to be missed. Nothing is better than walking a beach, especially beaches on the Oregon Coast. One of the first beaches I loved was Ona Beach, a few miles south of Newport. My favorite activity was feeding the crows peanuts and the sea anemones fishy cat food.

One day I ran out of peanuts to feed my crow friends. I gave them the fishy cat food. Looked good to the crows.

Happily, for me, they kept having babies every year and flew them in for lessons on how to eat peanuts. Cutest of all is when Mom pecks the squawking baby's head to shut it up before it tells everyone in the neighborhood the peanuts have arrived.

Sea Star Extinction

On this birthday, July 11, 2013, my present to myself was walking my favorite beach at the end of Quail Street in Seal Rock. Watching the surf slamming and shooting up over rocks is mesmerizing. Next was exploring the everchanging tide pools. Until they weren't. I never expected to actually observe the loss of a key species on this earth from global warming.

Every day colorful sea stars disintegrated before my eyes, melting into a smear on the rocks. Scientists predict its extinction within months. Although it's taking years, they weren't wrong. Anyone who watches this terrible sight and still believes we are not the cause needs to wake up fast and do something before we are next. The sick sea stars are in the left photo; the right photo taken at the same time is the last healthy sea star I ever found.

Now there are none.

"The significant problems we face cannot be solved at the same level of thinking we were at when we created them." – Albert Einstein

"The fog comes on little cat feet. It sits looking over harbor and city on silent haunches and then moves on." – Carl Sandburg

The Boss: I watched the Coast Guard tow a boat and caught this guy bossing the job.

NOAA *Fairweather* Survey Ship

Nel and I were fortunate to be invited by one of our vacation rental guests to board and tour the *Fairweather*, homebased in Ketchikan (AK). Shelley's job was to draw maps in areas not surveyed for ships since the 1930s to check changes in the waterways.

Although the *Fairweather*'s main job is to conduct hydrographic surveys for nautical charting, she can perform many other activities from fisheries research to buoy support.

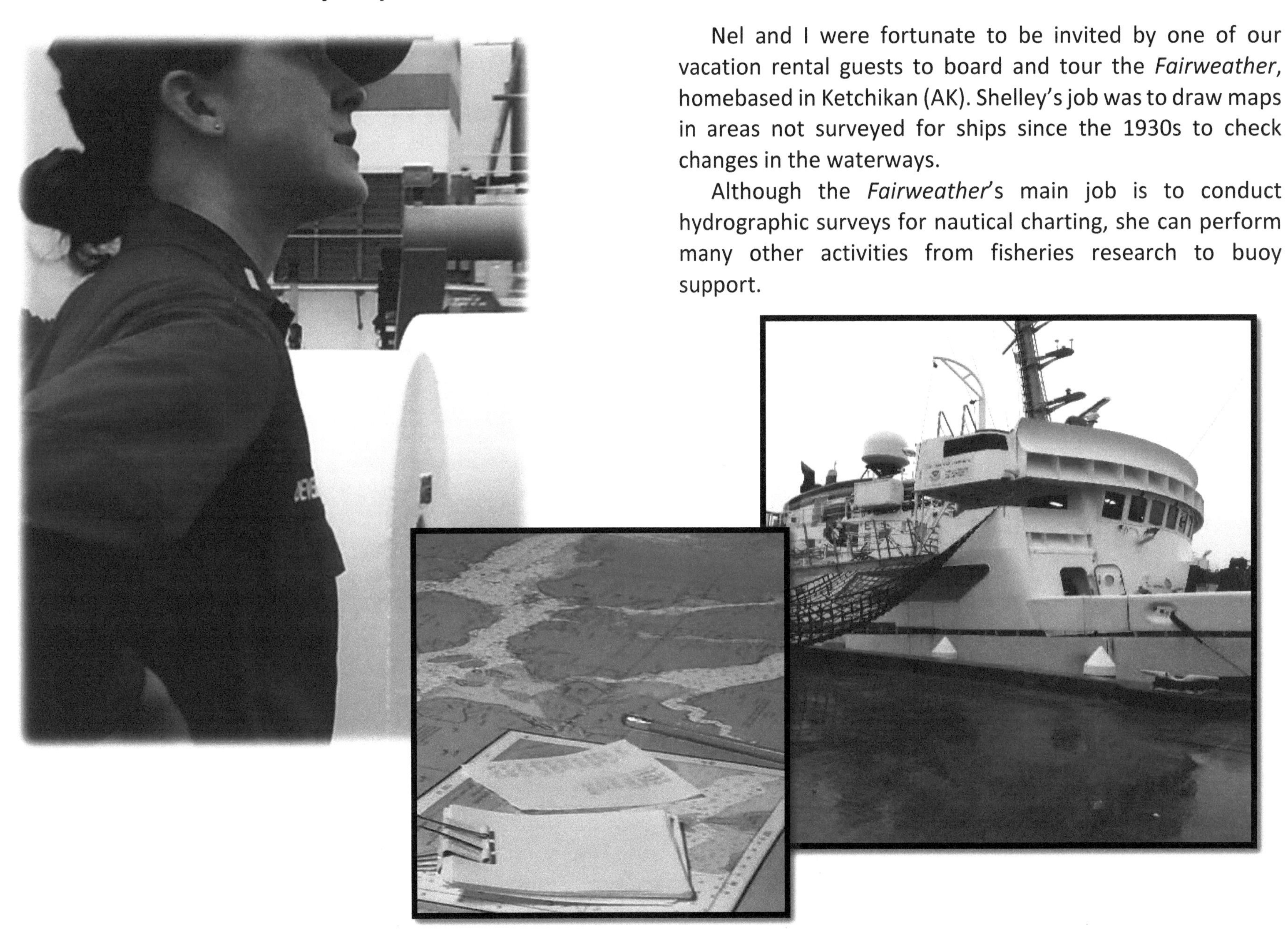

Keiko, the "Killer Whale"

One of Newport's more famous visitors, among famous research ships such as the *Atlantis/Alvin* and the *Marcus Langseth* research ships and movie personalities such as Paul Newman and Henry Fonda is Keiko, the large-toothed dolphin called a "killer whale." Captured in 1979 in Iceland waters as a two-year old, the orca was sold to a Mexico City amusement park in 1985. Renamed Keiko, "Lucky One" in Japanese, he starred in the movie *Free Willy,* but the warm waters of his small tank caused his poor health.

Donations provided for Keiko's new facility at the Oregon Coast Aquarium, and UPS airlifted him to Newport on January 7, 1996, where he experienced cool seawater for the first time in 11 years. He stayed at the aquarium for almost three years, learning to hunt live fish and regaining his health for a return to the wild. Again, UPS flew him to Klettsvik, a bay in Iceland. Upon landing, the C-17 Globe-master's landing gear failed, causing a million-plus dollars in damage, but Keiko was not hurt.

In the summer of 2002, Keiko was freed with a VHF tagged to his dorsal fin for tracking. A month later, he showed up in Norway's Skålvik Fjord looking for human companionship and happy to give children rides. He lived for five years in the wild, never finding a home. In a tragic end, he died in Norway's Taknes fjord, lonely and gasping from pneumonia, a continent away from his friends and home. Keiko was buried on December 15, 2003, in a pasture near the shoreline. Ultimately it cost $50 million, and he was never really free.

Keiko in Reflection

While looking for some forgotten item, I ran across photos I took some twenty odd years ago of Keiko. A friend gave me the honor of climbing to the top of Keiko's tank to watch him be trained to survive before his release back into the wild. He was taught to find and eat live fish, eating fifty pounds a day. The trainers explained that he would catch them at first but rather than eat them, he returned the fish to the trainers. His behavior that dark cloudy afternoon was so human-like he stole my heart. I watched him play with his trainers, show off for us, beg for affection, and sulk when denied what he wanted. To look him in the eye and touch him was an experience I shall never forget.

I also found the article about my good friend and deep-sea diver, John Crowe, who helped capture Lolita, the orca in Florida who has worn her teeth away begging to be released. John said he only cried three times in his life: one was when they captured Lolita and killed her mother. "A baby crying for her dead mother," he said, "was heartbreaking." He spent the rest of his life trying to free Lolita but died with the job still undone. Lolita has been in captivity since 1970.

I am on the side of the fishermen who risk their lives day after day, generation after generation, keeping families together and strong to put good food on our tables. The ocean's rape comes from big fishing businesses coming into communities with their franchises, chains, and huge facilities, resources, and paltry hourly jobs, gutting and gobbling local natural resources, destroying local businesses and towns by underselling as they take huge profits never recycled back into the communities they rob.

Yaquina River: Spring brings these large dolphins to Newport area looking for baby whales. Sometimes they travel several miles up Yaquina River. After they passed in front of my window—an incredible sight—I watched a sea lion sitting on a dock watching the orcas. Hollering his head off in complaint, he seemed to be hiding, perhaps waiting for the orcas to return to the sea.

Red Crab

Back in the day when I was a bit faster, it was great fun to go crabbing. When I was younger. A full-sized male Dungeness crab crawling out of the trap and scooting sideways across the dock at full speed, waving pincers was enough to scatter everyone, mostly me. Even so, throwing a crab pot in, waiting awhile, and pulling it back up is much easier than shoveling for clams.

Our bay has three major edible species of crabs: Dungeness, commercially caught for the most meat; the very destructive invasive green crab, a native from Europe that arrived on the West Coast in the late 80s; and the important red rock crab, whose survival is a sign of a healthy ecosystem. The red rock crab is so aggressive that everything crawling on the bottom, especially the unwanted green crab, better get out of the way. As a scavenger, its primary prey includes worms, mussels, snails, clams, abalone, barnacles, oysters, and each other.

Then there's this other red crab, a phenomenon unlike anywhere else on earth, found only on Christmas Island where up to 50 million land crabs live in burrows under forest debris, eating most anything from fallen leaves, seedlings, and fruits to dead animals and even each other. Add 30 years in life expectancy, that's a lot of crab.

When the annual rainy season begins, these guys migrate to the sea to breed and lay eggs, many traveling as far as 100 miles, in mass by the millions. Fifty million crabs coming out of the forest, crossing roads, stopping traffic, crawling along sidewalks, crossing grass, invading homes, into, under, and over anything for three weeks.

On top of that they're not even edible. As soon as the eggs (100,000 per female) are released into the sea, turning the surf water black, the babies hatch at once and get swept out to sea where they stay around a month before these 0.2" babies crawl out to began their nine-day march, again, up, over, under, and into everything on their way to the forest. One day, cleaning out a computer, a homeowner found three dead baby crabs.

If crabbing interests you, there are places around town you can rent a trap, buy bait, and public docks you can crab from. Just remember, when you pull up your trap up and dump it on the dock, be ready to run.

Planet Earth has five great oceans and 113 seas. They represent 72 percent of the surface of the globe and 70 percent of the air we breathe. Together they've been an endless source of inspiration for humankind.

Sea Star Disaster

The sea star keeps surviving. Barely. As a keystone species, it is an organism in the ecosystem critical to the survival of other plant and animal life. Without keystone species, ecosystems collapse. For example, sea stars eat sea urchins that gnaw kelp plants from top to bottom. If too many spiny urchins gather at the base of a kelp stalk, they can chew right through the holdfast (or root), setting the whole plant adrift. Like clear-cutting a forest. The life forms that hide in the kelp canopy—fish, crabs, shrimp, otters—disappear as well.

Along with sea otters, sea stars also keep mussels at a safe level. Mussels, the ocean's great filter, take in massive amounts of floating plankton (the main food source for small fish and crustaceans) and scrub the water clean.

> **Seventy percent of the air we breathe comes from the ocean and is produced by plankton which also removes carbon dioxide from the air. Along with the importance of our rainforests, the health of the oceans is even more important for breathable air survival.**

Newport Belle Paddleboat

On a cloudy afternoon, I watched a tugboat pushing the *Belle* paddleboat to its mooring. She had been up the river to get her bottom cleaned and repainted. In the photo (above right), she returned to her berth to paddle no more. Instead, she is a bed and breakfast in Yaquina Bay. Nel and I spent the night on her when she was in Winchester Bay and had a great time. Always wanted to live on a boat. And now I have.

I read the *Belle* was for sale for a mere $374,000. She is a river-worthy, US Coast Guard-registered boat, 97-foot-long

with a beam of 24 feet, with nearly 3,000 square feet of living space on three decks. This remarkable replica of the famous river sternwheeler paddleboats has five guestrooms, owner's suite, and quarters for the crew. Former owner Sherry Porter said she bought the boat from a man who spent two years (1993-94) building it as a B&B to run the Coquille River. He didn't much care for people, so he sold it to Sherry.

The *Belle* made me curious about other boats paddling on the Yaquina Bay. Only one, the sidewheeler *Oneatta,* ran the bay for a short time in 1872 before she was transferred to the Columbia River.

Our Publications

Nel and I began collaborating on books in 1971 with a textbook called *Electric Media,* a practical hands-on media guide for high school students. Using media production—movies, videos, slide-tapes, etc.—students learned how media sways opinions. With positive national reviews, the book sold around the world.

We wrote our next book, *the butch cook book,* with our friend Lee Lynch. In it, we edited recipes submitted by self-identified butch lesbians from many countries. The book won a *Huffington Post* contest for the most unusual cookbook of the year and played a cameo part in the movie *The Perfect Family,* starring the brilliant Kathleen Turner. Her desperate-to-look-mainstream character uses our own *butch cook book* for a perfect moment of unspoken cultural divide with her pregnant lesbian daughter, played by Emily Deschanel, who also appeared on the TV drama *Bones.* We chuckled at the language when academics analyzed the cookbook as an influential reflection on a community of women.

The cookbook began as a joke about how lesbians can't cook, but that quickly changed because we received really tasty recipes. We delegated jobs among the three of us. Lee used her vast network to collect the recipes. Nel and I researched, I wrote introductions and obtained rights to copyrighted material, and Nel edited, with commentary on the offerings. She also shopped for ingredients and cooked each recipe which Lee and Sue gladly ate. Mostly. It was through advertising the cookbook that our foray into social media actually began.

Dr. Nel Ward Receives Boa Award for Roundtable Work

Nel and I kept writing after we finished the cookbook. I wrote fiction, two short stories and four novels published during the next few years, and occasionally hawked them on social media.

I also reviewed books (sometimes posting reviews in social media), for the American Library As-sociation (ALA) GLBTRT Reviews Committee Nel had created.

Always active, Nel co-founded both the Rainbow Project (now the Rainbow List), an annual listing of best LGBTQ books for youth, and a companion list for adults, Over the Rainbow, for the American Library Association GLBTRT, now renamed the Rainbow Round Table. During this time, she chaired the Rainbow List and the ALA Stonewall Committee, receiving a "Boa Award" in 2014 for her endeavors. Of course, I bragged about it everywhere.

It's the eleventh of July 2018 and guess what?

My cat Latte and I share a birthday today. She is two and my twin brother and I are much older. Happy birthday to the three of us.

Weird thing about her eyes—they change color at the drop of a hat from light green to light blue to light yellow to gray. She's supposed to be a Burmese. I don't think so! Can't say I care either.

Traveling

I do enjoy day trips near Newport to places such as wineries, covered bridges, lighthouses, Spruce Goose Museum, Oregon Gardens State Park, Shore Acres State Park, Bush's Pasture Park, tulip farms in the early spring, and boat races in Toledo. Especially fun are the cardboard boat races in Toledo although they usually sink before the finish line. And another favorite, the sea lion caves. After ten non-stopping stories down on the elevator, I was stunned by the formation of the cave, like looking up into a turning page where the molten rocks had split open from the bottom. Nel was also impressed. One look up, and she was back in the elevator and gone.

A favorite short trip is along Bay Boulevard paralleling the Yaquina River to photograph train trestles left from the early nineteenth century, a nostalgic experience on a warm February day.

I also love trains. As a kid growing up, our big treat of the day was to drive to the train tracks after supper and watch the 7:10 pm train pass by. Beg a penny to lay on the track to be squished and then disappear with the train and its mournful warnings, no matter how long I looked. I was 68 years old before I got to ride on one. We drove over to Albany and caught the train to San Diego, clickity-clacking all the way, food provided along with a not-so-soft bed. Surprising were the massive snowbanks and heavy forests we traveled through into California. Many of our views through towns in lower California were back yards, fascinating to check out.

Fourth of July

A gorgeous light show, both from humans and nature. When the NOAA dock was built, the town firefighters put our July 4th fireworks onto a barge at the Newport Inter-national Terminal and brought it down the river to anchor below where we live. The view from our deck had a light cloud cover as the barge arrived at sunset.

Suddenly the sky turned blood red, washing across everything, turning the water, boats, landscape, clouds, into a gorgeous glowing red. In the south appeared a red rainbow that stayed until the dark washed it all away, and the sky lit up all over again.

Diesel Spill

A commercial fishing boat at one of the Yaquina Bay fishing docks forgot to turn off a diesel fuel transfer pump and dumped 700 gallons of fuel into the bay.

Fortunately, the spill was on the inside of the sea wall. Any fuel missed by the containment booms and sorbents as it goes down the river and out to sea won't be floating by the Aquarium and Hatfield water intake valves that pipe into the tanks of living creatures.

Hatfield's Earthquake/Tsunami Building

My deep-sea diving friend John Crowe went all over the world and had seen what tsunamis can do. Hearing any warning about the smallest tsunami, even a two-inch wave, he packed his camper and headed east, over the hills.

Whenever I look over the river at the spot of land supporting the NOAA headquarters and the HMSC campus, I think about watching John's taillights and all the people working and exploring on that flat area exposed and vulnerable to any tsunami. The big one can come within fifteen minutes after a warning. At least the Hatfield campus

doesn't have to worry again. Expected to handle over nine hundred students and adults in the classrooms and labs, this uniquely designed building will withstand a 9.0 earthquake and following tsunami. Stairs, elevators, and outdoor access ramp lead to the roof. Construction began September 2018.

A deep-soil-mixing auger drill (right), standing 100-feet tall, drills 100 feet deep into the mud and sand, mixing in cement as it goes and forming hundreds of pillars on which the building will stand.

From our windows, we can see both the impressively tall auger and the four tall yellow "towers" on the left. They are huge cement truck trailers tilted up onto their bottoms with huge tires on their lower right. They pour massive amounts of cement into the auger holes.

It has occurred to me that the pieces of my life I have most enjoyed were not on my Bucket List

The *Star Legend* Luxury Yacht

This luxury cruiser, the *Star Legend,* came into the Yaquina River International Dock. Anyone who can afford to pay $185,000 a week can take it out. The yacht has six cabins and fourteen crew members.

M/V *Enhydra*, Amazing Visitor to Our Bay

According to Dave Gallagher of the *Bellingham Herald*, the M/V *Enhydra*, a 128-foot-long, 600-passenger ferry ship, was launched at 7:00 am, August 14, 2018. The ship has a molded beam of 30 feet and will be the first aluminum monohull, lithium-ion battery electric hybrid ship. Built for San Francisco's Red and White Fleet, it sailed into Yaquina Bay at 8:43 am, September 3, 2018.

Enhydra is specifically designed for harbor tours of San Francisco Bay and the Golden Gate Bridge with vivid views of the bay and cityscape from each of the three decks. The second level offers a full wrap around viewing deck with access to the enlarged bow foredeck, and the top deck, completely open, and offers lots of outdoor seating. The new lithium-ion battery electric hybrid system provides a silent, emission-free operation.

The Lady Washington, Ship Ahoy!

The *Lady Washington* and the *Hawaiian Chieftain* won't be coming to Newport anymore. A conflict with the Port of Newport led to cancellation of both the *Lady* and its companion ship *Hawaiian Chieftain.* Fishing folk and other businesses complained that the ship's two-week stay in the summer kept them from necessary dock and parking space and triggered loss of income. The South Beach Marina is too shallow for the *Lady,* and the International Terminal is too remote. The original *Lady Washington* was built in New York City in the spring of 1776 at the request of General George Washington. After the Revolutionary War, she was refitted as a trading ship and sailed around Cape Horn and became the first U.S. ship to land on America's Northwest coast in 1788. She was also the first U.S. ship to stop at Japan, Honolulu, and Hong Kong. The *Lady* continued to trade in the Pacific until July 1797, when she went down in the Philippines at the mouth of the Mestizo River.

Built in 1989 in Washington state, this full-scale duplicate of *Lady Washington* has appeared in the films *Pirates of the Caribbean*: *The Curse of the Black Pearl, Starship Enterprise, Star Trek Generations, Treasure Planet*, and *The Great American West*. On TV she was in *Blackbeard* and *Once Upon a Time*.

The *Hawaiian Chieftain*, a copy of the two-masted sailing ship built of steel in 1988 in Maui, was rigged like nineteenth-century trading ships although she has a modern triple keel and shallow draft hull drawing only five feet, five inches. The shallow draft makes her highly maneuverable in shallow waters. The *Chieftain* was originally designed for cargo trade among the Hawaiian Islands.

I miss watching these two ships sail under the Yaquina Bridge on their way to do battle in the Bay—smoke and loud bursts rising from cannon fire and close-quarters maneuvers as the two majestic ships face off against one another. It reminds me of those slow summer childhood days of swords made from tree branches and pirate hats from folded newspapers.

The past became real the day I climbed aboard the *Lady Washington* and felt the planks under my feet and stepped around the two three-pounder guns. With the wind in my face and the sounds of a loud voice ordering crewmates to HEAVE with every pull of six miles of rigging rope, I was even more in awe as all 4,442 square feet of the massive sails lifted and unfurled, flapping in the wind above me.

As exciting as it was to watch everything around me unfold, I thought about how special it must be to become part of this crew of twelve. It's too late for me, but maybe not for you. You can join this crew of buccaneers for a two-week experience living and working aboard a tall ship out on the open sea. Check it out for yourself:

https://historicalseaport.org/sail-training/

The R/V *Sally Ride* Research Ship

I am in awe. This weekend, July 18, 2018, I watched the *Sally Ride*, my favorite ship next to NOAA's *Oscar Dyson*, come in to tie up at the Hatfield Marine Science Center. *Sally Ride* is assigned to the Scripps Institution of Oceanography at the University of California and homeported in San Diego. This 238-foot ship is one of the most technologically advanced research ships in the world.

Her main job is to welcome all students, especially girls, in STEM (integration of science, technology, and engineering) studies.

"You've been criticizing yourself for years and it hasn't worked. Try approving of yourself and see what happens." ~Louise Hay

History of the Coast Guard

The Coast Guard motto—"Semper Paratus"—means "Always Prepared." Well, almost always. I watched the USCGC (630) *Alert* chug into our port and tie up to the NOAA dock. One of her jobs is patrolling our maritime boundary in U.S. coastal waters of Washington, Oregon, and California.

This cutter heading out under the bridge is one of three in this class stationed in Oregon and Washington. Seems a bunch of equipment failures, thirty-five of them the first 19 days on this counter-narcotics patrol, forced this tired 49-year-old cutter back home to Astoria.

These cutters are responsible for homeland security and fishery law enforcement, drug and contraband patrols, marine safety, search and rescue, and environmental protections. Some even had a pad for helicopters.

Over the years, the Coast Guard has had hundreds of cutters in many classes such as patrol, endurance, icebreakers, buoy tenders, and response cutters.

America's oldest maritime defenders were the cutters.

It was President George Washington who, on August 4, 1790, signed the Tariff Act authorizing the building of ten cutters to stop smuggling. As the country grew, the cutters merged with the U.S. Life-Saving Service and was renamed the Coast Guard, the only U.S. maritime service enforcing laws and saving lives at sea.

The first steam engine cutter was the *Charles B. Penrose*, built in 1906. She wasn't much of a patrol cutter because she couldn't travel far and only had a crew of four. Actively serving in the Gulf of Mexico, she sank in a storm off Pensacola in 1905. She was refloated and stayed in service until the government sold her for $610 in 1924.

Over two-hundred cutters were active when Prohibition started, and fourteen had been 110-foot wooden submarine chasers.

Because of Prohibition, a new cutter class called the Six Bitters (slang for "six bits" meaning 75 cents) was known as rumrunner "chasers." The only presently active sailing cutter is the *Eagle*, built in 1936 as a trainer for German naval cadets and is now homeported at the Coast Guard Academy in New London (CT).

I get a kick out of films when a Coast Guard cutter shows up to save the day. One of them, *Overboard* with Goldie Hawn and Kurt Russell, was filmed in the Newport area. This crazy story is about an heiress who makes fun of a carpenter, cheating him out of money for his work. When she falls overboard and ends up with amnesia, he claims her as his wife and takes her home to care for his four untamed boys. She gets her memory back and returns to her yacht, jumps off to escape a murderous husband, and gets rescued by—wait for it!—a Coast Guard cutter.

Coast Guard airlifts injured woman from cruise ship off Oregon Coast

Coast Guard rescues 5 off rugged Oregon coast
Coast Guard rescues 4 from overturned boat in Newport
Coast Guard rescues 3 in Yaquina Bay
Coast Guard rescues 2 from cave south of Yachats
Coast Guard rescues surfers in Newport, Oregon
Coast Guard rescues man after boat capsizes

Coast Guard Storm Warning Flags

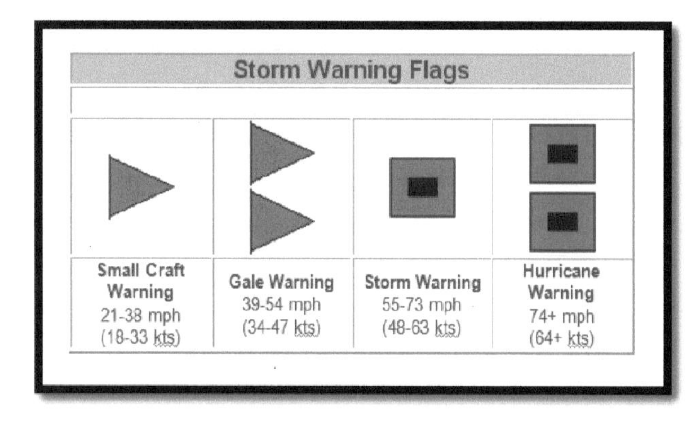

The Coast Guard flies warning flags for mariners at the station on the entrance to the Bay.

Lighted Christmas Boats

On the first Saturday of December, our fishing town welcomes the winter holiday season with a parade of boats lit with vibrant, multicolored lights. About twenty boats line up and circle the bay three times, stopping to bow to the waiting judges on one of our docks on the Bayfront. People book passage or find spaces to watch the show. I still enjoy remembering the images from last year's lighted boats, wondering what colorful creative sights will cross our view this year.

So many shapes on fishing, sailing, and tourist boats. So many good memories like a small fishing skiff with a real live Santa standing behind a lighted reindeer, shaking his reins to spur on the reindeer. It keeps me smiling for days.

Even our NOAA ships join the fun with strings of lights. I can't make up my mind on a favorite.

Well, maybe the choo-choo.

Loss of the Sea Star

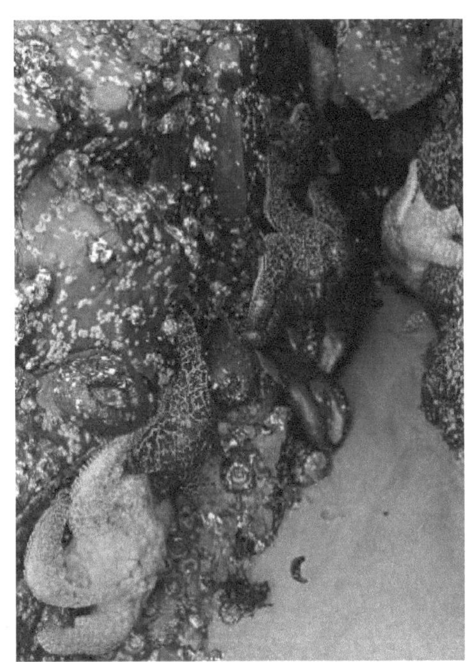

A report from the Coastal Ocean Research Institute has cited the disease called the "sea star wasting syndrome" from Mexico to Alaska. Like the perfect storm, this disease developed in elevated sea water temperatures combined with an imbalance of microbiome or likely several microbe pathogens.

The abundance of juveniles in 2014-15 gave hope for a resurgence, but they disappeared in weeks. UVM author Melanie Lloyd said, "If this disease was happening in humans, it would be the making of a Stephen King novel."

This little sea creature has no fins, or brain, or teeth, or even bones. It circulates sea water through their systems instead of blood, but they are still tough guys of wonderous colors and shapes. Remark-ably, they have eyes at the end of each arm, can produce millions of eggs at one time, replace lost arms, and change gender from male to female at will. They can even create glue with their feet.

Hummingbirds:

People say hummingbirds migrate, but not the Anna. This little guy finds a home and stays. This Anna has been with us for three years. I recognize him from the wiggle in his tail

when he feeds. He is joined occasionally by the migrating Rufous.

The hummingbird comes in second to my favorite, the crow. It was a hard choice. My favorite crows rank in smarts next to homo species, maybe even smarter when solving problems and making tools. In third place is the pair of gangling blue heron that fly by my window every day, trailing those large feet behind them, going back and forth from their nest in the pine trees below me to their feeding ground in our protected estuary.

I'm also fascinated by the scurrying sand pipers sprinting ahead of me in and out with the surf. And the Canadian geese that squawk overhead as they head north in the spring and then back again in the fall. I was told they mate for life and when a mate is lost, they leave a space in their formation in commemoration which always makes me sad.

Yet the hummingbird has my heart. The tiny acrobatic creature flies like a helicopter, dashes after bugs, hovers over a flower or my feeder to drink the nectar, wings backwards to avoid an attack, and rises high in the sky to dive-bomb at a stunning speed of sixty miles an hour in a flirting dance for their potential mate. They remind me of the small dog yapping syndrome, fighting the world for their bitty place in it.

Those that migrate fly high in the frozen atmosphere across the Himalayans or cross the vast gulf waters between Texas and Mexico, often traveling more than 3,000 miles without stopping. I feel proud if I can make it a mile to the store.

Nel brought me a hummingbird guide, and I found that only two of the 340 world-wide species visit our Oregon coast, the rusty-red fearless Rufous and the Anna, our only non-migrating hummingbird resident.

The male Anna has a metallic green back, grey breast, red crown, and gorget, and the female has a green back, grey breast, red spots on the throat, and white tips on the outer tail feathers.

Like the ankle-biter, they are a highly aggressive little sucker and will guard my feeder for hours, chasing away any visitor. The only answer I found was to hang a few more feeders and drive my bullies into exhaustion.

Idaho Point up Yaquina River

Sylvia Beach Hotel

A favorite building in Newport is the Sylvia Beach Hotel. The dilapidated, leaky, old goliath had been used as a cheap place to live for years. Childhood friends Goody Cable and Sally Ford bought the run-down building in 1984 and began the difficult task of renovation. Renamed the Sylvia Beach Hotel, they invited their friends to each choose an author and decorate a room at their own expense, including the author's complete works. In exchange, they could have an annual free week stay for five years. The hotel became world-famous.

I would have picked Laurie King for her Mary Russell and Sherlock Holmes series if they had been written at the time. I am also fond of many of the original authors featured in the 21-room hotel such as Agatha Christie, Ernest Hemingway, F. Scott Fitzgerald, Tennessee Williams, Mark Twain, Herman Melville, Willa Cather, Robert Louis Stevenson, Oscar Wilde, Edgar Allen Poe, William Shakespeare, and Dr. Seuss. To add to the ambiance, guest rooms have no telephones, televisions, or radios. And no smoking.

Even the restaurant in the bottom of the building is unlike any other restaurant I've ever seen. Appropriately called the Tables of Content, restaurant-goers select only their entrée. The scrumptious full-course dinner served family style every evening requires a reservation. Going early gives diners the chance to look at the rooms. Open doors are an invitation to enter. The west side of the third floor is the library where you can pet a cat. Or two.

Built in 1913 as the Cliff House, Peter Gilmore bought it in 1921 and renamed it the Gilmore House. In the 1921 photo below, wood planks covered the street.

The name Sylvia Beach comes from the American expatriate in Paris who opened Shakespeare & Company in 1919, a bookstore and lending library with English-language books. Her place attracted the great expat writers of the time such as Fitzgerald, Eliot, Pound, Hemingway, and Gertrude Stein. Beach also published modern literature that no one else would touch, such as James Joyce's *Ulysses* in 1922.

While searching for bookstore location, Sylvia Beach met Adrienne Monnier, who owned a bookstore and helped Beach move in across the street. They lived together for 36 years. Beach refused to sell a Nazi soldier a copy of James Joyce's *Finnegan's Wake.* He left but threatened to return. She immediately moved all her books upstairs, but she still spent six months in an internment camp. She never reopened her bookstore and died in Paris in 1962.

Newport Lighthouses

Every lighthouse has a different story to tell. Like the one on Prince Edward Island, the first to hear the tragic cry from the *Titanic.*

Yaquina Bay Lighthouse: My favorite lighthouse is one of two in Newport a mile apart as the crow flies. Built in 1871 it led a short life, decommissioned in 1874 and replaced by the much taller Yaquina Head Lighthouse finished 1873. Although the bay lighthouse was 161 feet above sea level, some say it

was built in the wrong place because boats couldn't see it until they were too close to the land. Others say it wasn't needed so close to the bay entrance after the South Jetty was built.

Believed to be the oldest structure in the town, it is now the only existing Oregon lighthouse with built-in living quarters. And the only historic wooden Oregon lighthouse still standing. The first and only lighthouse keeper had a wife and nine children with another on the way when they moved into the tiny two-bedroom house. And on a hill. A tall hill.

After many bumpy years of serious neglect, the dilapidated lighthouse was remodeled in 1972 and restored to full glory with a steady white light that shines from dusk to dawn. Some say the lighthouse is haunted. In 1899, a local teenage girl wrote the now-famous short story about the ghost of a girl named Muriel who haunted the place. Her tale was complete with secret passageways and a cave beneath the lighthouse that may or may not have contained pirates—and other imaginative stuff that seemed a prequel to the Goonies movie. Other paranormal books included the girl ghost.

Yaquina Head Lighthouse: The other Newport lighthouse, listed as Oregon's tallest lighthouse at 93 feet tall, stands on a narrow point of land jutting due west nearly one mile into the Pacific Ocean. Construction took over 370,000 bricks and almost a year. Its oil-burning wicks were lit August 20, 1873, shining a fixed white light from sunset to sunrise that can be seen 20 miles out to sea.

Now the fully automated first-order Fresnel lens and 1000-watt globe run on commercial power, flashing a unique pattern of two seconds on, two seconds off, two seconds on, and fourteen seconds off for 24 hours a day. (Note: Every lighthouse has a different on-off lighting sequence so they can be recognized separately at sea.)

The rumor that the lighthouse may be haunted comes from the compasses going haywire when ships come close. Science attributes the problem to magnetized iron in the land under the lighthouse throwing off readings. The lighthouse has a great interpretive center and a handicapped ramp down the hill from the parking lot to accessible tide pools, complete with water creatures. If you don't want to wander, just sit and listen to the waves washing in and out and the sea birds squawking overhead.

Cleft of the Rock Lighthouse: Oregon has two privately owned lighthouses. Pelican Bay Lighthouse can be seen from Brookings; Cleft of the Rock Lighthouse is part of a private home two miles south of Yachats. It isn't open to the public but can be seen from a pullout at Highway 101's Mile 166 on the northwest corner of the Cape Perpetua National Scenic Area. James Gibbs, a former keeper in the 1940s at the isolated and dangerous Tillamook Lighthouse, built this as his home in 1976.

After he retired from government lighthouse keeper in 1972, he became editor of *Marine Digest* and authored the *Lighthouses of the Pacific; Tillamook Lighthouse, A True Account; Sentinels of Solitude: West Coast Lighthouses; Twilight on the Lighthouses;* and more maritime and shipwreck books.

He also coauthored *Oregon's Seacoast Lighthouses* and was considered one of the best authorities on West Coast shipwrecks and lighthouses. Gibbs died in 2010.

"Go 24 hours without complaining. Not even once . . . then watch how your life starts changing." – Lara Nelson

Rogue Ale Brewery

This Newport business helped put the town on the map. The brewery is in South Beach, but it has restaurants both there and on the Bayfront. They not only brew their own beer but also grow the hops on their own farms, construct their own aging barrels, bottle their own brew, and truck what they sell. From the farm to the customer, they do it all!

In 1987 Jack Joyce, Rob Strasser, and Bob Woodell were approached by friend Jeff Schultz, a dedicated home brewer, to start a brew pub down south in Ashland (OR).

Named for the Rogue River, the pub grew fast enough to send Jack searching for other places to open. One early, cold, and blustery February day in 1989, Jack found himself stuck in a rare snowstorm on Newport's historic Bayfront, unable to climb the slippery streets back to the top of the hill. Lucky for him a remarkable woman by the name of Mohave Niemi (known as Mo, founder of Mo's Famous Chowder Bowl) pulled him into her restaurant, fed him a bowl of her famous chowder, and listened to his dream of adding another Rogue Pub.

Mo showed him a vacant space in a large building on the Bayfront she would rent him at a very fair price. She had only two stipulations—give back to the fishermen and forever hang a picture of herself naked in a bathtub at the pub. (I can tell you it is still there, straight ahead and slightly right as you walk up the stairs to the restaurant). A copy of the photo also hangs in every Rogue Meeting Hall.

Building renovation, starting in February 1989, enticed John Maier to leave Alaska Brewing to work for Rogue. By May, the pub opened for business, attracting a good many locals who came and stayed to volunteer help with projects around the pub. To this day brass plaques on the bar immortalize these early participants.

Rogue brewed its ales in the Bayfront Brewery garage until it transported "Howard," the 15-barrel brew system in the back of the Bayfront Public House, across the Newport Bay Bridge to a larger facility in South Beach. The Rogue House of Spirits opened for business on June 10, 2006. Home to Rogue's distillery and cooperage, this building soon became the world headquarters of Rogue Ales & Spirits when flooding forced the Ashland location to close. Rogue has produced more than 100 different ales; among their award winners are Amber Ale, Chocolate Stout, Nut Brown Ale, Robust Porter, Black Ale, Smoked Beer, Imperial Stout, Oatmeal Stout, and Red Ale.

A walk-through grain silo welcoming customers to the brewery was added. Jack Joyce says he saw an ad and had a truck pick up the silo although Jim Cline, VP of beer sales, credits himself with finding the silo on a long-haul truck where the owner with an unclaimed silo willingly sold it to Jim cheap to get it off his truck. Jim said, "I told Jack, 'I just bought a silo. Jack basically said, 'What the ... are you doing buying a silo?! I've got four of them sitting on my lot!' and I said, 'I got it for $400.' And he said, 'Brilliant!'"

They painted the silo a fire-engine-red, much to the dismay of the Port of Newport. The port manager said, "It does not match the color scheme of the port, and it sticks out like a sore thumb." Whether it was Joyce's bright pink pickup parked on top of a shipping container in protest or the letter-writing protest campaign, the victory for keeping the silo red was commemorated in the News-Times as, "Rogue's Big Red Erection." But the silo's problems weren't over yet. For a few hours, the painter misspelled Rogue as "Rouge."

Hilan Castle

As much as I love living over the bay and watching bay activity, I do miss Nye Beach. The view from the kitchen window of our B&B was a castle—perched up on the hill, fancy as you please, a real honest-to-god living castle. Atop the three medieval stories were crenellated parapets like on real towers and battlements. Skinny windows in castle-like threes had stone mullions and transom bars. The icing on the cake—or castle—was the exterior finish, gray shiplap shingles made to look like building blocks.

Instead of using the fine Scottish name, locals just call it the Castle. Charles Roper built it in 1912 for his Canadian wife, Theresa, who wanted to have that style for her home. He documented Lincoln County in the 1910s and 1920s with his photography studio on the castle's top floor. Roper was elected mayor of Newport in 1922, and Theresa wrote and illustrated romantic history books using local Native American objects in her illustrations. According to local lore, they lost the castle in the Crash of 1929.

I saw the inside of the castle only once when I went there for a poetry reading. It was like stepping back almost a century. Everything seemed to be preserved—kitchen cabinets and counters, original trim on the doors and windows, hardware including door-knobs and hinges, old porcelain light fixtures, old wooden plank floors with worn patterns through years of use.

Theresa & Chas. Roper.

See it for yourself. If you take the back road through Newport to Nye Beach, look up when you reach Alder and you will see a real live castle clinging to the side of the hill. In America. In Oregon. In Newport.

Aquarium Village

A trip to Aquarium Village in South Beach is worth the time for the weirdness both inside and out. This cache of whimsey, boutiques, and unusual galleries including local artists, tshatshkes, jewelry, edible goodies, and cafes, plus happenings and fun is located right next to the Oregon Coast Aquarium.

Nessie, the famous Crown Lizard sea monster of Yaquina Bay; a statue of Keiko the "killer whale" of the movie *Free Willy*; and life-sized pirates scattered about among the castles, riverboats, and ships such as *The Brigantine,* a pirate ship brought from a Nevada casino and on display in the Yo Ho Indoor Bounce building welcome visitors. The New-port Interactive Zoo lets people feed and pet a goat, chicken, llama, pig, emu, turtle, a snake or two, and a dog. And don't forget to visit the super circus with a Wild West show. Or the Escape Rooms Newport, an immersive live adventure game that leaves a group locked in a room for an hour and forced to solve a series of puzzles and riddles using clues and strategy both mentally and physically challenging to get out. (They actually let people out in an hour if they fail.)

Studios include mural painters, leather workers, pottery makers, a wood gallery with the name of If I Wood and graphic artistry such as Jac Genovese Studios. Even a didgeridoo designer by the name of Tyler Spencer who not only builds the didgeridoo but also teaches you how to play it. For tshatshkes, try 3 Gypsy's Boutique, Pirate's Plunder, Rooster's Rocks, Rare Finds Gift Shop, and Black Pearl Treasures & Gifts. The Hot Shop and A Glass Blowing Studio both sell glass items and teach glassblowing. Hungry? Try Fishtails Café, Molly's Food Follies & Bakery, or Bojomama's Toffee & Baking Company. Although you would be hard pressed to notice, they are all built in storage area units!

Jump-Off Joe

When we moved to Nye Beach decades ago, we walked our two standard poodles almost every day on the nearby beach. At one end was an outcropping of rock the locals called Jump-off Joe.

The first story I heard was about a Native American named Joe so heartsick at the loss of his girlfriend that he jumped to his death. The second one I heard was that Joe was cornered on top of the rock and jumped to avoid capture. History explains that travelers in the 1880s, using the beach for a road, had to jump over to continue on. I prefer the first story.

I was a little nervous walking through Joe's arch because it wasn't stable. The first arch had disappeared many years before. Kind of like climbing Mt. Everest—because you can. Until one day I looked down the beach at a pile of rocks, and Jump-off Joe was gone. Overnight! This huge hunk of rock with this incredible arch walkway was just gone.

Shipwrecks

Peter Iredale: Because I came from the Wild West, you might expect me to play cowboys and Indians as a kid. In fact, we played pirates on the high seas. Buccaneers to the end. Of course, we had no boats, or swords, or eye patches, or pirate hats, or hooks and peglegs. Or water. Only plenty of imagination. So you can imagine why the first thing I wanted to do when I moved to Newport was to see a shipwreck.

There is something eerie about shipwrecks, at least, those that have not yet been completely taken by the sea. Most shipwrecks along our Oregon Coast have long disappeared into a home far, far away because it doesn't take long for the surf and sand to bury everything. The *Peter Iredale* is approaching that status, disintegrating at an alarming rate.

She can be seen at Clatsop Spit on the north end of the Oregon coast at the Fort Stevens State Park. She was another one of over two-thousand vessels attempting to cross the bar called the "graveyard of the Pacific" in the Columbia River and never making it.

The *Iredale* ran ashore October 25, 1906. This English-built four-masted steel barque sailing ship was on its way to Portland (OR) to pick up a load of wheat for her return trip to England. She arrived at the mouth of the Columbia River during heavy fog and wind. Waiting for the pilot boat, she was blown around and forced aground at Clatsop Beach. When she hit the beach, three of her masts broke from the force of the impact, but no one was seriously injured.

Captain Lawrence ordered the ship abandoned and fired rockets for help. A team of men from the Point Adams lifesaving station quickly arrived to the rescue and, despite danger, saved the twenty-seven crewmen along with a couple of stowaways. Once on shore, the captain saluted his ship and said, "May God bless you and may your bones bleach in these sands." Lifting a bottle of scotch, he turned to his crew. "Boys," he said, "have a drink."

The Blue Magpie: A famous loss at the Newport bar occurred on November 19, 1983. The three-hundred-thirty-four-foot cargo ship on its way to Vancouver to pick up a load of lumber was caught in a severe storm for hours. The captain was desperate to get to shelter and headed for the Yaquina jetty. Convinced his ship was breaking up and too scared to listen to the Coast Guard warnings to not cross the bar, he disobeyed directions and proceeded.

The *Magpie* was shoved into the jetty, flipped around, and broken up into three pieces by the fourteen-foot flat-sided waves. The good news was that all nineteen members of the crew were safely picked up by the Coast Guard helicopter. The bad news is that 3,000 gallons of diesel fuel and 70,000 gallons of crude oil escaped, causing the largest spill on the Oregon coast. The disaster killed hundreds of seabirds. Only divers can see the wreck now. For a video dive on the wreck, watch this:

https://www.youtube.com/watch?v=yDveGpb6ZBE

J. Marhoffer: Remains of another shipwreck on the coast can be seen where it blew up at Boiler Bay, a short ride north of Newport, in 1904. Three years after this oil steam schooner was built in Grays Harbor, Washington, her engine room caught fire. Before the fire could be extinguished, the room exploded in flames, forcing evacuation of the ship. Before jumping, the captain turned the *Marhoffer* toward shore where she crashed in a massive explosion.

A huge boiler was left behind from the explosion of the *J. Marhoffer* steamboat.

Debris scattered so high in the air that metal pieces came back down and impaled on the cliff edge where they stand today; only the boiler, best seen at low tide, remains in the rocks below. All hands, including the dog thrown overboard earlier and the captain's wife, escaped the ship. Only one casualty occurred when one of the boats flipped while landing and drowned the injured cook.

New Carissa: Do I have a whale of a tale for you! Blowing up the whale at Florence made a huge mess, but this time the explosion to sink a ship was a bit more destructive. This one started near Coos Bay, a hundred miles south of Newport, and ended at Waldport, a small town fifteen miles south of Newport.

One stormy February night in 1999, the freighter *New Carissa* was told to stay out in the ocean because the Coos Bay bar was too dangerous to cross until the storm abated. Unlike the *Magpie* crossing the Yaquina Bay bar, the captain of the *New Carissa* told his crew to lower the anchor for the night. According to the incident report from the Coast Guard, the anchor's chain was too short, and the winds pushed the ship towards the shore. By the time the crew reacted, it was too late, and the ship grounded three miles north of the entrance into Coos Bay. The good news is that all twenty-three men aboard were rescued with no injuries. The bad news is that the ship began to leak diesel fuel, spilling 70,000 gallons onto the water and beaches.

The bizarre was just beginning. This freighter is 640 feet long. Picture a football field and double it. Add a twelve-story building sitting on those two football fields. Or a 45-foot, eight-ton dead sperm whale on the beach with a half-ton of dynamite dug in below it. Setting the freighter afire to get rid of the spilling diesel had much the same result as blowing up that whale. It was not only a disastrous failure, but it also broke the ship apart, dumping great amounts of fuel which were still spurting after several days of trying to burn it off. The fuel in only one of the four tanks was burned, and more storms halted more attempts to syphon the rest of the fuel. The leak became Oregon's second major environmental disaster, the spill of 70,000 gallons of fuel killing over 70,000 sea birds.

The next strategy to rid Coos Bay of the ship was to tow the larger bow section of the *New Carissa* to sea and sink it. After several days, a tugboat finally pulled the larger section off the beach and out into the ocean. In one of the worst storms of the winter and 40 miles later, the towline snapped. Now the *New Carissa* was running free, blown by the wind at about six miles per hour right onto the beach just south of the Alsea River in Waldport.

Nel and I joined the queue driving south on 101 just to get a glimpse. We weren't allowed to stop, but the sight as we slowly passed by was overwhelming. The gargantuan ship invaded massive amounts of space and blocked out the sun. The next day the ship was loaded with plastic explosives and towed for three days and 280 miles out to sea. That explosion was the second failure. Next, a Navy ship firing 70 shells into the New Carissa failed to sink it. Finally, the *USS Bremerton* submarine sank the ship with a torpedo. The stern, however, was still stuck on the beach. It stayed for another nine years until it was cut up and hauled away in 2008. Cleaning up the mess required almost a decade and millions of dollars.

Commercial Crabbing

In all the years that I have lived above docks filled with fishing boats, I enjoy watching the opening of the crab season the most. Starting in early November, the boats fill to the rafters with crab pots usually stored on the riverbanks. If crab season opens on time, they can drop their crab pots 64 hours earlier, but they must wait until midnight of December 1 to retrieve the filled pots from the ocean.

The exodus of nearly two hundred boats, leaving docks suddenly empty, look like a string of ants as the boats go to claim their space. Just as suddenly they come home again, waiting for until they can go back out again. Gone again until they return to port, full of crabs.

During the next three months I can see their lights far out to sea as they head for home with, hopefully, a full belly. The unloading begins with bags of ice and huge crates in a semi-circle to be filled by the crane unloading the boats. They don't slow down until after Valentine's Day and prices start to drop.

Although a crabber needs a commercial fishing license, a Master license, US Coast Guard licensure, first aid/CPR certificate, and special equipment like boots and gloves, a strong back is more important than formal education. Crabbers get up at 4:00 am and work without stopping for 13 or more hours in wild and crazy storms with swells 20 feet or higher, bitter cold weather, and sideways heavy rain slapping them in the face. Full crab pots weigh up to 800 pounds and have to be pulled up, over and over as workers dump up to 150,000 pounds of crab in the hold. The pay may help make up for the hard work—$25,000 to $100,000 salary for three months work, depending on experience, crabs caught, and their prices which can wholesale for around $4.25 or more a pound. Boats usually fill their hold several times during a season.

Some years, however, crab boats are still tied up to the docks at Christmas, mostly without pots, because the crabs are too small or suffer from domoic acid. I sometimes wonder if it's time for crabbers to find other jobs, especially those who like to live on the sharp edge. Like one crabber described, "It's one of the last things where you can wake up in the morning and you have no idea what's going to happen. It's the last cowboy-ish thing to do."

Maybe he could drive a truck on ice roads. The average pay for that is $2,000 round-trip for about 20 hours driving without stopping or resting because sinking through the ice is as real as it gets. Or he could be a storm chaser and get a TV station to pay $500 for storm footage. In addition, passengers will often pay as high as $3,500 for the trip. I think I would forget about the film and hire a bus.

Problems also include greedy fishermen over-crabbing, pollution from farm run-off, and a small group of wealthy men controlling the coast. The one I support: global warming of the ocean waters causing low oxygen to strike a big swath of "hot spots" off the West Coast. The result is extreme hypoxia, killing the crab and anything else. Once the low oxygen was only on the seafloor, but no more. The NOAA Coastal Hypoxia Research report that it's climbed up to half of the water column. One crabber dropped 120 pots and brought up four live crabs. Another pulled up gobs of dead crab and a few miles away pulled up gobs of healthy ones. This phenomenon has become so common in the last few years we now have a hypoxia season. Fire Season, Hypoxia Season, what's next? Annihilated Season?

There is hope. As NOAA researches the effects of hypoxia, OSU Hatfield Center is dropping 40 "dissolved oxygen" sensors on crab pots to determine how rapidly hypoxia develops and where. Oregon bill (H.R. 6267) will attempt to deal with ocean acidification. And a lawsuit was filed in San Francisco County Superior Court where commercial crabbers in Oregon and California are suing 30 fossil fuel companies, accusing them of raising ocean temperatures, causing algae blooms that have shortened the crab season the past three years and likely will continue to do so. "We believe it's a substantiated claim that harm has been done by one industry to another and the industry that caused that harm should pay," said Noah Oppenheim, the association's executive director. He went on to say that "climate science has advanced to the point that the connection between fossil fuel use and domoic acid closures is "crystal clear." Crab is the most valuable single species commercial fishery in Oregon, with an average harvest of 16 million pounds per season, all caught with Oregon's fleet of 984 boats.

[**Update**: 2022 was an outstanding year. Not only was the season on time, the first since 2014, but the catch exceeded all of 2021 in the first month with a whopping 12.8 million pounds valued at $63.1 million.]

The two best days in a fisherman's life are the day he bought the boat and the day he sold it!

Sport Crabbing

Commercial crabbing is restricted to nine or fewer months, but recreational crabbing is year-round for people with fishing licenses. The best time to crab is supposedly at high and low tides because they float into the bay at high and out at low. The public is welcome to crab from the shore, places such as the South Beach pier under the Yaquina Bridge. I've had great fun crabbing at the Bayfront from Abby Street and Bay Street piers even if we had to throw back most of them. All females must be returned to the water. Males have to be at least five and three-fourth inches at the widest place of their bodies. They also need to be kept in a dry bucket to keep them alive; they can breathe air for a while, but water runs out of oxygen in the bucket and kills them. People can also rent a boat, usually with crab rings, at the Bayfront. Chicken parts, especially necks, are great bait.

I no longer spot any colorful round, ball-like floats in the bay indicating a crab pot. People on the boats seem to throw out pots with the rope attached to the boat, wait a few minutes, and pull the pot in. Other boats seem to putt along with someone hanging out with a net. They may have a trotline, a long rope with bait attached every four to six feet.

As the boat slowly travels, the line comes out of the water with crabs hanging onto the bait. The person holding the net better be fast before the crabs let go when they reach the surface.

This boat has crab pots stacked, ready to throw. It's a sunny warm day, great for crabbing. What I want to know is, what is that bundled up thing up front with the strange green eyes?

Who's driving?

Clamming

A good clamming place is on the river side of the seawall at low tide. Especially fun if you rent a boat and putt-putt to the exposed sand. The lower the tide, the longer you get to stay. It's hard work, but we collected a variety of clams, took them home, and ate them.

The last time I clammed before going to the seawall was when I went down to Agate Beach with my skinny shovel and handy-dandy bucket to dig for razor clams.

After a long time of digging, I drove down to the Bayfront and bought two dozen, brought them home, soaked them a few hours in cornmeal to get the sand out, and pretended I was successful all on my own.

We had a tasty meal that night. The B&B guests admired my prowess until I had to admit, "About these clams . . ." followed by a chorus of "Oh no, you didn't!"

The Famous Exploding Whale

Fifty miles south of Newport is Florence with a vast expanse of sand dunes along the ocean with sand dune buggies bouncing up and down them. Nel and I would drive down there to the small movie theater, now closed. A friend who moved there had a little creek running behind her house.

Whenever I think of Florence, however, I remember the story of the exploding whale. Town fathers came up with the bright idea of blowing up a rotting sperm whale to get rid of it. Whale flesh flew for 800 feet. KATU-TV photographer Doug Brazil and reporter Paul Linnman caught the scene in 1970. Watch it here! So fun.

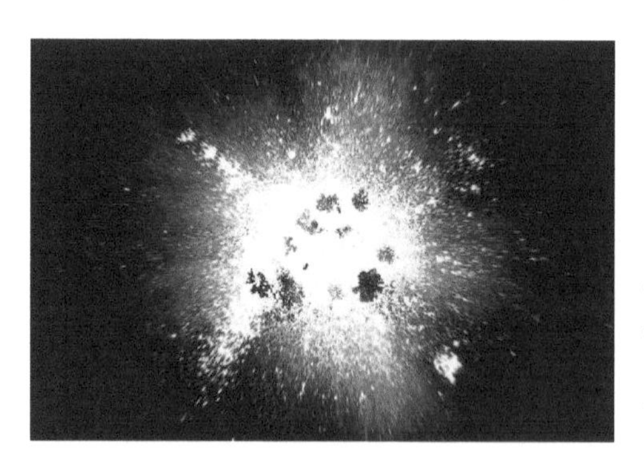

https://www.youtube.com/watch?v=YK7gFTgA0FQ

Fishermen Superstitions

I'm curious about fishing superstition. After all, everybody seems to have superstitions. Some of mine I consider just for fun. Some I take seriously, like knocking on wood three times. Or on my head if wood is remiss. Why take any chances? And then there are the cultural superstitions such as my Western cowboy culture where you never throw a hat on a bed. This led me to wonder about superstitions in my adopted fishing community.

Superstitions can be a big part of daily life at sea. On a fishing boat, never eat a banana; never whistle as it brings storms; never turn the deck hatch over (it turns the boat over at sea); never spit into the wind as wind is the breath of God. (Personally, I don't spit into the wind because it comes right back at me.) Never eat any meat but fish for the first meal at sea; never set top sails first as this offends the Gods; never set sail on a Friday; never say "pig"; never launch a boat without a blessing; and never bed a woman the night before you set sail.

A woman on board makes the seas angry and is an omen of bad luck. Sailors who wear earrings or have tattoos won't drown. If a St. Elmo's fire (electrical discharge) occurs in the rigging, throw something valuable overboard; when leaving port, empty all your pocket change overboard because if you pay early, you won't pay later; never change the name of a boat, even if it's sold, because it brings bad luck; feeding the harbor ducks brings good luck.

Considering the danger both the fisherman and the cowboy can face, God bless them. I pray each superstition they obeyed is the one that saved the day.

Hagfish, Ugly Is As Ugly Does, May be One of Our Most Valuable Useful Rejects

Among the edible fish you might expect to catch on the Yaquina include bass, chinook, steelhead, cabezon, perch, rockfish, greenling, salmon, sturgeon, herring, and crab. Oh, yes. And a real slime-ball called hagfish. True, they are edible and highly sought after in places if you don't care what you stick in your mouth.

A pure clump of protein, a hagfish could be a great substitute for eggs. Especially if you like scrambled. These ugly creatures are a big delicacy in Japan and other Asian countries. Koreans even consider the hagfish an aphrodisiac.

If you're really trying to fish, beware. Hagfish can devour your fish before you can reel it in. What's really revolting is picking up these little suckers. When they feel threatened, they secret snotty slime by the buckets. Averaging twelve inches long, they can expand by 10,000 times in a fraction of a second and repel predators such as sharks by throwing clouds of suffocating slime over their heads. With an amazing rotation in and out of a knot twisting from head to tail, the hagfish cleans itself, scraping the slime away. Mixed with water, the slime quickly turns into a sticky thick gel with hundreds of thousands of extremely strong protein threads a hundred times smaller than hair and a hundred-thousand times softer than Jell-O.

Don't ask me how to count the threads or measure slime softness. Or even Jell-O softness!

Considered one of the ugliest of sea animals, the hagfish has an eel body, a boneless skeleton with an actual skull (classifying it as an animal), up to fourteen pairs of gill pores, five hearts, strong jaws with sharp teeth, and no scales. And they're blind as a bat. Traced back to fish evolving in the Paleozoic era, the hagfish is a scavenger found mostly on soft mud bottoms. It feeds off dead or live fish by entering through any orifice. They are caught by traps built from olive or pickle barrels with one-way entrance holes for them to enter.

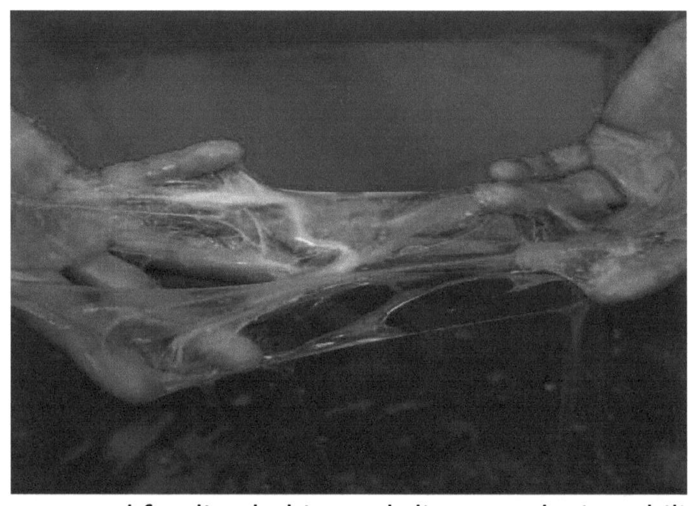

The unusual feeding habits and slime-producing abilities of hagfish make them both the most "disgusting" and the most useful of all sea creatures. Their soft skin is easily processed into leather goods and sold throughout the world. Hagfish slime may be used in biodegradable polymers and space-filling gel—even stopping blood flow in accident victims and during surgery plus covering burn victims, ballistics, firefighting, anti-shark spray, and diver protection. The tough, stretchy fibers can also be used for fabric in clothes.

My favorite story about the hagfish has to do with an extremely rare, intact carcass of a giant blue whale that had washed up near Gold Beach in 2015. Until this event, there hadn't been a documented case of a blue whale beached in Oregon since Lewis and Clark made their historic journey to the coast more than 200 years ago where they saw Native Americans salvaging edible parts from a blue whale. The blue whale is the largest animal to have ever lived, even larger than the largest dinosaur.

The whale at Gold Beach was hit by a ship and too ill and weak from starvation to survive. The body was shipped here to Newport where scientists at Hatfield Marine Science Center removed 58 tons of flesh from the bones. With the help of a technical dive team from the Oregon Coast Aquarium, they sank the bones in huge nets and weights in Yaquina Bay and left them for three years while hagfish scrubbed the bones. All 365 bones were brought to the surface including a skull weighing 6,500 pounds and taken to a nearby warehouse. Once reassembled by volunteers, the skeleton will go on display at the new marine studies building.

My second favorite story happened in Newport. According to our local paper, on July 14, 2017, a truck full of hagfish destined for South Korea from one of our fishing boats slammed on its brakes and lost its hagfish load on July 14, 2017. Animals were strewn across a stretch of highway, covering the road and a pitiful car in slime. It was funny at the time. Luckily for the driver, the car was a rental.

Astoria

Watching these mammoth ships go by on their way on their travels to and from the ocean is awe-inspiring. We would stay in the Cannery (motel to the left in photo below) and watch them out our window. The ships travel about ten miles inland to Astoria from the mouth of the Columbia River where it pours into the Pacific Ocean.

"Your kindness
causes ripples
that are felt all
over the world."
- Sara

Part II – 2019 – Year of Crazy

It was the best of times
It was the worst of times

I swear the year 2019 was salted more than usual with extreme crazy. Weather-wise, in January we had a massive rare and deadly cold storm going through Texas. May brought a tornado outbreak. The spring witnessed Midwest flooding, and massive summer drought was followed by lethal fires in the west. Hurricane Dorian came in August, followed by a bomb cyclone in October. Through it all was political explosions.

> **"I could stand in the middle of 5th Avenue and shoot somebody, and I wouldn't lose voters."**
> **– Donald Trump**

In politics, Donald Trump continued wiping out any and all political traditions that safeguarded our democracy. His reign exacerbated the extreme nasty behavior in politics. At the height of his arrogance, he even tried to buy a country. At taxpayer expense. Iceland refused. He invited the Taliban to Camp David and demanded Congress designate Antifa (Anti-fascist) a domestic terrorist organization. It's the only group he went after. Does that mean he considers himself a fascist?

When it came to making a mark on America, Trump had a lot of help. I tried to avoid politics in social media, but I got

overwhelmed by the continuing massive avoidance from the right about the political corruption of their own: Bush launched two disastrous wars that created ISIS, crashed the housing market, destroyed millions of jobs, and turned Clinton's surplus into a $1.4 trillion deficit. And instead of blaming Bush, Republicans lost their minds and blamed Obama and nominated Donald Trump. You can't make this shit up!

Republicans compare Trump to Jesus Christ. Well, if we nail him up and he returns in three days, I'll sing hallelujah!

Crazy wasn't all tragic. Valentine's Day at the El Paso Zoo was a hoot if you like that sort of thing. Have an ex you hate? Fun, fun, fun! You can name a sad cockroach after your ex and watch it get ripped to pieces by a bloodthirsty meerkat. Or—what the hell—marry the cockroach. A guy named Yuma who claimed he was 100 percent in love, dated a "hot" cockroach named Lisa for a year. Or at least he did until she died. Then he ate her. True stories. I kid you not.

That was last year. This year cockroach-naming after your ex will be expanded to a variety of zoo birds and primates. Considering the zoo buys around 1.5 million insects a year, you can buy and name as many as you wish. And as a special treat, El Paso's Zoo director Joe Montisano will even eat a cockroach for every $1,000 raised. I do hope he washes it first. Maybe even boil it a very long time.

January 2019

Politics:

Guns

I don't have a problem in general with guns; I grew up in the "Wild West" on the Arizona desert where we had some sort of rifle or shotgun behind every door. We literally hunted to eat. Usually rabbit, quail, and white wing. I refused to eat rattlesnake no matter how hungry I was. Sometimes when they were wounded, they bit themselves.

Luckily, nobody in our household was particularly interested in playing with guns. Or had an anger problem. This was not the case with many of our friends. Some used a gun to end their lives. Too many others died from an accidental discharge, usually by children playing with a gun. Yes, I know that guns don't kill people. And I do know that people kill people. And that is the problem. People who don't keep their guns secured or have mental and anger problems should not have access to a gun. Period! End of discussion!

"Guns don't kill people. People kill people." Really? We want mandatory safety courses for people, not guns. We want more thorough background checks of people, not guns. We want stricter negligence penalties imposed on people, not guns. If you're stupid enough to think activists are pissed at guns, you're too stupid to own one.

Same old argument since 1776. Once again, gun-owning laws are bandied around among my friends and in public forums. I wonder why anyone would want an assault rifle considering we average more than one mass shooting for every single day. So I sent this letter to our newspaper. No one responded. I'm not sure if it was that bad or if there was nothing left to say:

"Even though there was a time when hunting was necessary for our survival, that is no longer true. By the time a hunter buys the gun and ammunition, hunting permit, clothing, camping gear, a truck to get in the hunting ground and to carry the carcass out, gas, time off work, cleaning, butchering, and freezing the carcass, the cost is far more than the savings. The point is, hunting is no longer necessary; it is a sport. I'm sure the hunters had a great time and found it worthwhile even though I still suffer as I think of the life draining out of beautiful brown eyes that are the color of my nephew's. I also concede that hunting for sport should continue as we are still the best predators on earth and some species still need to be culled. Or so they say. My problem is when we start gearing up to hunt each other. Why else would anyone buy an assault rifle or pistol that is specifically meant to kill other humans? Am I the only one out there worried because we still want to kill one another, and we do nothing to stop this serious failure in the human condition?"

"So, if guns kill people, then pens must misspell words, forks make people fat, and cars drive drunk."

Politics:

More Terrorists Enter Through Canada Than Mexico

I moved from the Southwest to the Northwest and find a trip to Canada very doable. But nobody ever talks about immigrants crossing our northern border. I found that the U.S. Customs and Border Protection agency has apprehended more people with suspected terrorist backgrounds or links to terror organizations entering the U.S. from Canada than from Mexico. Why not? Crossing this border is easy-peasy, especially on back roads where border patrols either don't exist or monitor only part time. Including Alaska, the Great Lakes and the Atlantic, Arctic, and Pacific coasts, the border is 5,525 miles long, the longest international border in the world. Longer than the Great Wall of China. The border with Mexico is only 1,954 miles long. Maybe Trump's building his wall on the wrong border.

We were humans together until religion separated us, race disconnected us, wealth classified us, and politics divided us.

Bayfront Murals

The Newport City Public Arts Committee has been charged with preserving murals popping around town, beginning with those on the Bayfront lining SW Bay Boulevard from Hatfield Drive to the Coast Guard station, each expressing a maritime story unique to Newport. Many of the paintings depict fishing boats calmly docked or being

repaired while others display them dramatically fighting storms and rough waters to bring another fresh catch into port. Many of these images represent the rigorous and often dangerous life led by local fishermen and remind visitors of the historical significance of ocean fishing.

My experiences with murals began one fine August afternoon in the year 1994. I was wandering around on the bayfront and stopped to watch a man on a scaffold hanging off a large cannery building with a paint sprayer in his hand. It took a few days before a large whale with a scar on its back slowly took shape. Because of this marking, she was well-known among the few hundred California gray whales that return year after year to winter along our central Oregon Coastal waters. She was beautiful. I heard he followed her around the ocean for two weeks before he started the painting that nearly never was.

This whale of a story explains why murals of marine life are splashed all over Newport's bayfront. A young painter by the name of Robert Wyland approached the cannery owner and asked if he could paint the wall. The doubting owner immediately shut him down. He had no idea what would go up on the huge, HUGE space for all to see. The young man brought back examples of his artwork, and the impressed owner immediately agreed. History was made in our very own small town.

This was Wyland's fifty-ninth painting on large walls around the world. On July 9, 1981, Wyland painted his first wall, a gray whale and calf in Laguna Beach (CA). On June 14, 2008, he did his one-hundredth and last mural, a 24,000-square-foot, half-mile-long series in Beijing, China, called "Hands Across the Oceans." All in all, more than a billion people have seen one of his murals in 84 U.S. cities, Hawaii, Canada, Japan, Australia, Mexico, Brazil, and China.

Wyland's appreciation of marine animals began when he was fourteen years old visiting Laguna Beach where he saw several California gray whales heading to their nesting grounds in Mexico. Seventeen years later, he moved to Laguna Beach. Since the beginning of his travels around the world, his unique paintings, sculptures, and photography have had a positive impact on marine life conservation. His Wyland Foundation even became a partner with NOAA, and he has been a host on "Wyland's Ocean World" on the Discovery Channel, "Wyland: A Brush with Giants," and other shows. Considered the foremost marine life painter today, his art appears on specialty license plates in Florida and California as well as on U.S. postage stamps commemorating Intergovernmental Oceanographic Commission's fiftieth anniversary celebration. According to many sources, he's considered one of the most influential artists of the 21st Century, with artwork in museums, corporate collections, and private homes in more than one hundred countries

This is one story I can't verify. Many people around town say his purpose behind his whaling walls is to support conservation measures protecting these majestic animals. Others say that Wyland also painted Whaling Walls as an interesting homophone referring to the Wailing Wall in Jerusalem. He is purported to believe in the 1,000-year millennium following Jesus's second coming when little creatures will come down to earth looking for the friendliest places to collect the good souls to take back to heaven. Believing sea creatures are the friendliest life on earth, Wyland painted his massive murals to attract the heavenly creatures in areas where he spends much of his time. He wanted to make sure these creatures could find him.

Why do we have one in Newport? One story is that his mother liked to vacation here, and he painted it for her. I don't know if either or both stories are true nor do I care. But if you see me down on the Bayfront visiting old Scarback, I might be going on a trip, and you're welcome to come along. Wonder what those creatures dropping out of the sky really look like?

Spruce Goose

Occasional day trips are my favorite way to travel. I'm a train person, but nothing is more impressive than the sight of the Spruce Goose.

Why it's called the Spruce Goose I don't know because there is not a smidgen of spruce in it. Or goose for that matter. Planes tend to scare the crap out of me, especially times when the government is shut down, but I think I would have climbed in the old goose even for its one-minute flight on November 2, 1947, before it was hidden in a giant hangar for the next thirty years.

Formally called the Hughes H-4 Hercules, intended to transport military troops and supplies during World War II, it wasn't finished in time. The largest plane ever built, it never flew again, although the builder, billionaire Howard Hughes, always kept it maintained and ready to go. I am grateful for my imagination when I climbed in and around this magnificent beast, heard the roar of the eight huge engines in take-off, and felt the shudder of the plane as we soared above the earth. People enjoying the goose at the Evergreen Aviation and Space Museum in McMinnville (OR) can also have a good time visiting the nearby wineries.

Talk about Traveling!

I think of history as the volcanic eruption in 79 AD that buried the city of Pompeii in ashes. Maybe signing the Declaration of Independence. Or dropping of the bomb on Hiroshima. I remember that one all too well, watching the film over and over at the movie theater of the bomb's devastation and its aftermath. At school, we practiced hiding under our desks when we all knew it was useless. For the first time in our small lives, every person and thing alive on earth were vulnerable with no place to hide. Then there were the small historical happenings such as this one for the homeowners of these houses.

In Waldport, 20 miles south of Newport, heavy rains in February 1996 saturated the land and caused a large

landslide with two houses and the land under them down the hill onto Cedar Street.

A young man whose mother lived in one of the houses told me the city insisted she get it moved. In turn, she insisted the city do it because the house and the land it sat on were now in the middle of a city road, making it city property. She did retrieve her personal property from the house, but insurance may not have paid off. Insurance policies usually don't pay for anything it calls "an act of God," a fact I learned when a friend lost his house to a summer flood that filled a canal over its banks.

Waldport—meaning "forest port" in German—got its name in a post office mix-up. It applied for the name Alsea, the Native American tribe living on the coast, at the same time as a town forty miles up the Alsea River applied for Waldport. Someone in the USPS flipped the names.

"In America, they call it 'lobbying.' Everywhere else in the world they call it 'Bribery and Corruption.' "

- Roslynne Levine

Politics:

Lobbyists

If you believe making money is more important than the well-being of your fellow man, then become a lobbyist for businesses. They pay big bucks to get legislatures to vote their way. That's how big business took over the government so that they could collect our tax money and change protective laws to gain more profit for them. "The Revolving Door," people moving back and forth from government job to industry to government job to industry, remains wide open although presidents have tried to close it. Donald Trump didn't. In 2019, for example, he appointed 281 lobbyists to his administration. Every time we elect a business shill instead of a statesman who respects the rule of law, we are one more step away from "of the people, by the people, and [especially] for the people." Individual companies spend tens of millions of dollars each year in lobbying to make sure it stays that way.

I was determined to find something to smile about even if it was scatological.

What do you think you're doing?

How do you explain to a total stranger that the hundred-plus-years-old and very tired, cracked toilet sitting in your front yard is your birthplace?

In short, my twin brother came first and my mother, not aware another baby was coming, told my dad to take her to the bathroom to get rid of the afterbirth. I came out instead.

I drink from there!

Of all the parts of a house I enjoy the most building or rebuilding, it's bathrooms Usually the sinks.

Where else can you be as creative? We hunted in several large warehouses before we found this potbellied stove to fit our sink.

I even love hanging very weird whatevers in my bathrooms. Have you ever watched how someone you just met comes in your house and sees something but doesn't quite know how to ask the question? You know, the "WHAT THE HELL IS THAT?" question.

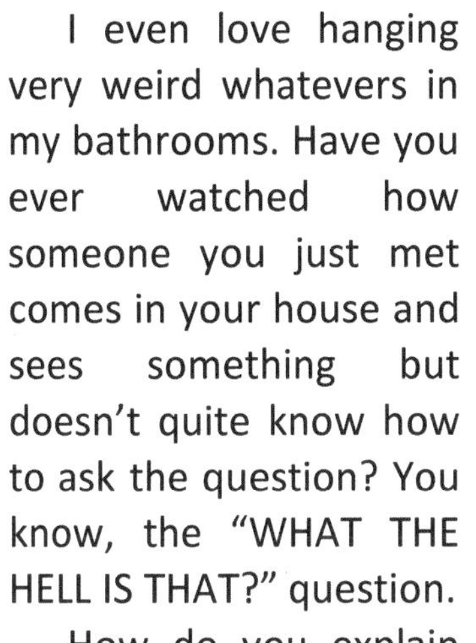

How do you explain how the sad, warped hundred-plus-years-old picture of a child on a pot is a keepsake, the only one you have from any of your grandparents?

Then there's a decadent soak in a special jet tub with bath gels and smelly herbs floating about to purify. Seems like some of our utmost important functions in life happen in the bathroom, so why not have a bit of humor surrounding us? I do admit that in all the bathrooms I've been acquainted with I've seriously neglected the toilet. After all, that is where I began.

We Raise Our Voices

For those of you who have children around you, I recommend this book for them: *We Rise, We Resist, We Raise Our Voices* for kids 8 to 12. With their photos and brief bios at the end of the book, over 50 artists and authors for youth contributed to these thirty encouraging messages for children of color distraught by the racist behavior from Donald Trump while he was in the White House Oval office. Editors, publishers of Just Out Books, began by describing the segregation during their youth and their decision to share encouraging advice on surviving the challenges of the current times. "Kindness Is a Choice," a letter from Jacqueline Woodson, the 2015 Young People's Poet Laureate, tells her children to ask themselves each morning, "What choice am I going to make today?"

Nel wrote: "Through vivid colors and poignant images, the stunning artwork joins both poetry and prose to create hope in a time that has grown much darker for minorities. In a personal way, the anthology encourages children faced with hatred and racism to learn from their history when young people 'changed this world for the better.'"

March 2019

"The planet does not need more 'successful people.' The planet desperately needs more peacemakers, healers, restorers, story-tellers, and lovers of all kinds."

— Dalai Lama

Purple Sea Urchins

An article in the *Register-Guard* by Gillian Flaccus and Terence Chea was discouraging. Purple sea urchins, tens of millions of them, devour 90 percent of the giant bull kelp forests on the California coast. You know how it looks when a forest gets cleared of every tree and only the woody debris is left behind? Like forest animals left without a home to protect them, all that's left be-hind in the ocean are purple sea urchins.

Recently the 350 million purple sea urchins counted on one Oregon reef were a 10,000 percent increase in six years. The urchins have taken over because their biggest enemy, the sea star, is reaching extinction status from wasting disease caused by the warming of ocean waters.

[Update]: Since 2014 the temperature rise in sea water has produced a wasting disease killing our sea stars. Due to this loss, along with the loss of sea otters, the natural predators of the purple urchin, thousands and thousands of sea urchins have invaded the west coast including Newport's shores, destroying kelp beds, forming an Urchin Barren. Now, nothing is left but urchins and rocks.]

Webcams

My favorite webcams are the ones filming my personal world. The webcam at the Newport Embarcadero displays the marina, NOAA, and Yaquina Bridge as well as linking to other sites with views from all over the state such as the Aquarium, both universities, and many cities, plus a camera that watches the surf hit the rocks. It's also a good cam for checking on wind in the area. Look out for the rooster tails (when white froth is flying west from the east winds). Things can turn cold and nasty fast. Other cams watch sea life such as the sea lions in the bay and octopus at the Hatfield Marine Science Center:

https://worldcam.eu/webcams/north-america/oregon-usa/14354-newport-embarcadero-marina

The Hatfield Oceanus research ship filming their ocean trips from the deck:
http://webcam.oregonstate.edu/oceanus

From the Yaquina Bar Coast Guard, especially interesting for the dangerous waves jumping the jetty:
https://www.weather.gov/pqr/barcams

The mother lode of webcams for Oregon covering the state:
https://www.northwestwebcams.com/oregon-web-cams.php

ODOT TripCheck: https://tripcheck.com/ for roadside images with information about Oregon traffic congestion, incidents, weather conditions, services and commercial vehicle restrictions and registration. Always something interesting going on.

Other webcams covering the Newport area include NOAA docks, Coast Guard yard, Yaquina Bridge, and the cage trapping sick and injured California sea lions:
http://webcam.oregonstate.edu/sealion

Oregon State University's new marine studies building at Hatfield Marine Science Center houses our marine science education and research capacity as it also serves as one of the first vertical evacuations tsunami sites in the United States:
http://webcam.oregonstate.edu/msisouth

A really great weather site: https://www.windy.com/?44.648,-124.051,5

Whale Watching

Whale Watching month comes around twice a year in late December and late March, and do I have a job for you! All you have to do is count whales. For no pay. A program called "Whale Watch Spoken Here" stations volunteers at twenty-four locations along the coast. Started in 1978 by Don Giles and colleagues Bruce Mate and Denise Herzing, these three determined that the major migration of the whales occurred twice a year, during winter holidays and near the last week in March. Wanting to share this experience, they created the whale-watching program. You don't have to be a whale expert, but you do have to attend one weekend of training. For further information or a registration form, go to:

https://orwhalewatch.org/

A frequent visitor is the California gray whale. About 18,000 of them travel in easy view of the coast on their spring migration from their breeding grounds in Baja California, Mexico, to home in Alaska. In December, they reverse the process. Around two hundred whales drop out of the migration to find a home in our central coast waters. Of these, about sixty have been identified and are recognizable year after year. Some even have names from scientists who follow them. You can meet Old Scarback on the Bayfront in Wyland's famous mural.

If you're on your own, these watching places are within easy driving distance from Depoe Bay to south of Yachats:

- *Boiler Bay State Scenic Viewpoint, south of Boiler Bay turn-out, also a place to view shipwreck remnants.*
- *Whale Watching Center in Depoe Bay and its sea wall.*
- *Cape Foulweather pullout for an infrequent clear day.*

- *Devil's Punchbowl State Natural Area in Otter Rock where you watch the bowl fill and empty, fill and empty . . .*
- *Yaquina Head Outstanding Natural Area and its interpretive center.*
- *Don Davis City Park in Newport (above), great on blustery days.*
- *Cape Perpetua Interpretive Center, a view 35 miles out to sea.*
- *Sea Lion Caves Turnout south of tunnel on Highway 101. Don't forget to visit the caves!*

If someone asked me what my hobbies were, I'd have to say whale watching is not on the list. If you asked why, I might ask, "Is that like, I don't know, counting sand pebbles on a beach?" I suppose whale watching would take Coleridge's "the willing suspension of disbelief" for me to know with absolute certainty that beneath that occasional waterspout popping up way, way out there on a wave, is a magnificent gargantuan animal. Maybe better said is that I like to watch other people watch.

I do have a favorite spout, however. Drive south to Yachats and park on the right at the last curve before the bridge. On the east side of the highway is a hump of grass with a metal whale flute at the end sticking out of the ground. In the center of the hump—wait for it—and thar she blows. A buried water pipe spurts every minute. Every time it spouts, I roll in laughter until I hurt. Best time ever.

If you really want to see what's under that spout way out in the ocean, get on a charter boat. This can give you an up-close-and-personal look. You may find it exciting to spot a spout, but nothing is more fun than watching whales spy hop, sticking their heads straight up out of the water as though they are looking around or checking out the surf as they go close to the coastline. Or examining the boats. The breach takes their bodies out of the water before they fall with a splash. They may breach to knock off parasites. Or maybe just because it's fun.

I got on a charter boat once, and a whale came right up alongside the boat staring up at me. I swear that whale looked me in the eye and deliberately sprayed straight into my face the hot, hottest air of the most godawful stink of dead fish I ever smelled and that took several showers to get rid of. I know she had a good laugh at my expense for the rest of the day. Travel at your own risk. The Depoe Bay boats take less time to get out into the ocean, but Marine Discovery Tours gives a "whale" of a tour.

Waking Up to SNOW!

That rare occurrence—snow on the coast. Drifting and swirling on a breath of air, it was spectacular. It's been so warm and wet this winter that our spring had already sprung, and the early freeze wilted my daffodils. As sad as it could have been, my mood changed when I recalled the last six lines of a William Wordsworth poem, reminding me again that attitude is all.

For oft, when on my couch I lie
In vacant or in pensive mood,
They flash upon that inward eye
Which is the bliss of solitude;
And then my heart with pleasure fills,
And dances with the daffodils."
- William Wordsworth

Horsetail

I had never seen this plant until I moved here—probably because I grew up on the Arizona desert. Nothing was green there for long, and most plants never were green.

Turns out it's the oldest living plant on earth with the common name of horsetail. Another "ah ha" moment for life in Newport. A plant almost as old as life itself. Imagine that.

I thought it was called horsetail because it looked like an upside-down horse's tail, but instead, it got that name for being a popular food for horses in Sweden. Its silica content with a reedy exterior is also a great metal polisher and cleaner.

Even more, it was a favorite of folk medicine to stop bleeding and treat ulcers, kidney stones, wounds, and skin inflammation. North American tribes found horsetail acted as a diuretic to aid kidney function. It was also used to treat rheumatism, gout, acne, coughs, asthma, brittle hair, and fingernails as well as act as a blood purifier. Horsetail may even be a remedy for senility.

Modern science is beginning to support some of these old wives' tales formerly considered superstitions. Horsetail contains fifteen types of bioflavonoids helping diuretic action, and the high silicon content strengthens ligaments, hair, fingernails, bones, and connective tissue. Other helps for slowing senility are the horsetail's tannins, alkaloids, potassium, caffeic acids, phenolic acids, aluminum, phytosterols, manganese, and saponins.

Now that old age lurks, or lurches, I'm thinking about making a tea, or better yet a stew, maybe mixing the horsetail with a few nice herbs with a little chopped tomatoes and onions to stave off falling apart for a year or two longer.

Damn, if I could only remember where I found them. And manage to get there.

Vaccinations

You say you don't know what's in the vaccine as the reason you refuse to get it. Do you have any idea what's in what you eat, like hotdogs? Or how about eating a chemical in Silly Putty, found in many fast foods. Then there's shellac, also known as Confectioners Glaze, that is on any glazed candy such as jelly beans and candy corn.

Don't forget ammonia, also known as pink slime: companies spray meat with it to kill bacteria before packaging. And how about eating silicon dioxide found in powdered foods to stop clumping?

Then there's "natural flavoring" which is beaver's butt anal gland secretions often including urine. Or carmine, a red food coloring from boiled beetle cochineals. And bromine, a toxin used in flame retardant, also often used in sodas. One of my favorites, titanium dioxide, a whitening chemical used in sunblock and paint, that's also used in salad dressings, icing, and coffee creamer. Don't forget phthalates, a chemical used in pesticides, sprayed on fruits and vegetables.

And you still worry about what's in the COVID shot that has kept millions from extreme illness and death?

"May the wind always be at your back and the sun upon your face, and the winds of destiny carry you aloft to dance with the stars." – George Jung

Want to Sail?

Newport has a really cool club founded in 1947, called the Yaquina Bay Yacht Club (YBYC), that encourages water sports preserving the traditions of navigation and seamanship. Members of all ages share a love of all things water. I watch sailboat races every Wednesday late afternoon in the bay below us. They start each year on March 27 and last all summer until Indigenous People's weekend, concluding with a bang-out final regatta for two days. Every time Wednesday comes back around, I compensate "damn, time to get trash out of the house" day with "wheeeee, it's sailboat racing day!"

Yaquina Bay, August 26, 2006

The Yacht Club is the place to go if you want to learn or resume sailboat racing, keelboat sailing, small boat or junior sailing, power boat navigating, rowing, paddling, crabbing, fishing, and kayaking. If they don't teach or do it, they know who does. Member or not, you can race with them every "casual racing" Wednesday for a small fee.

Occasionally on racing day, I would like to be young again. And attend the BBQ burger dinner after. Other annual Yacht Club regattas coordinate with the Seafood & Wine Festival, Loyalty Days Parade, Newport Marathon, Toledo Wooden Boat Show, the Bridge-to-Bridge Race, and the December Lighted Boat Parade.

Politics:

The Blast Heard around the World

In a closed room, during a congressional hearing.

Microphones everywhere. At a House Natural Resources subcommittee hearing, a new congressman, Joe Cunningham from South Carolina, blasted an ear-splitting 120-decibel airhorn that filled the committee room and my ears. The audience of about fifty gasped and whispered, and a fetus moved in a pregnant woman's womb. Cunningham proceeded to question a Trump hire for NOAA fisheries, Chris Oliver, also an oil-drilling supporter. He approves of seismic air guns for oil drilling and swears they do no harm. This was a man who had worked for bigtime corporate fisheries in Alaska.

In addition to managing commercial fisheries, his job with NOAA is to manage productive and sustainable domestic fisheries, including some aspects of marine aquaculture, work to recover and conserve protected resources such as whales, sea turtles, and corals. Here's the edited version of the conversation when Cunningham asked Oliver what he thought of the sound: "Would you consider such a sound 'disruptive' if it was repeated every 10 seconds?"

Chris Oliver replied, "If I were close to the sound, probably."

"What if you depended on sound for hunting your food and for communication? Do you think it would be disruptive?"

(Oliver was non-committal for the next few questions.)

Cunningham asked, "What if that seismic air gun was 16,000 decibels louder than 120 decibels you just heard? And blasting every 10 seconds. Would you consider the sound 'disruptive' then?"

If it takes only 200 decibels to kill us dead, what will 16,000 decibels do to sea life? Especially since that many decibels send acoustic waves through water up to 2,500 miles which last for weeks. Maybe even Oliver got the message. Will he change his mind? Likely not. His Trump-appointed boss and new head of NOAA, Neil Jacobs, NOAA's new chief, will expedite Trump's plan. Jacob's former boss, Trump-appointed Secretary of Interior Ryan Zinke was the man who introduced Trump's five-year plan opening over ninety percent of the U.S. coasts to oil drilling by the end of the year. Every East Coast state governor objected, and the plan is in the courts as well as under investigation by Congress.

[**Updates:** 2021 – A lawsuit is challenging seismic oil, gas testing in Gulf of Mexico. 2022 – The Biden Administration halted new drilling in a legal fight over climate costs.]

Supermoon

If you missed the supermoon, you missed a gorgeous sight. It only happens when the moon comes full once every fourteen months. I was nine years old when I saw the first one out on the desert—no other lights for miles. It was huge and yellow, enlarged by the dust in the air, and seemed to take over the sky.

The R/V *Sikuliaq* Research Ship

Maybe she came in to unload the scientists she picked up a few days ago. Or maybe adding more. Belonging to the University of Alaska and homeported in Seward, she's a real beaut.

Built in 2014, the $200 million ship, pronounced "see-KOO-lee-auk," was named for the Iñupiaq word meaning "young sea ice." Housing up to 26 scientists and students for as long as 300 days at sea, she can cut through ice up to three feet thick, especially necessary during heavy ice months of March and April, in a search of information on global warming. One thing, she discovered a newly formed partnership between an alga and bacteria producing much needed nitrogen in the Arctic Ocean.

"The biggest problem is we do not listen to understand. We listen to reply."
– Stephen R. Covey

Walking Tall – Good Cop/Bad Cop

Throughout my life, I have been inundated by the media's version of cop icons. You know what I mean. The smiling friendly cop on the beat who helps old ladies across the street, the old-fashioned Western sheriff who shoots it out with the bad guys at high noon, the highly trained storm-trooper who saves the hostages, the laid-back detective who finds the killer, and the one I remember the best, good old boy backwoods Walkin' Tall Sheriff Buford Pusser. The Tennessee sheriff who single-handedly cleaned up his small town of corruption and crime.

Released in February 1973, the movie *Walking Tall,* based on Pusser's life, was a surprise runaway big-time hit. No other movie has left me with a lasting imprint like that one. A level of violence I had never seen before overwhelmed me. I was shocked, disgusted, intrigued, appalled, fascinated, repelled, and terrified with emotions that have slammed back and forth in me to this day. The movie made so much money that it was followed by a TV movie, a short TV series, and a remake with two more sequels.

A whole new breed of cop was born. I call it Gestapo fascism. It is realistic gut-wrenching violence that not only ends tragically but also shreds our constitution. A sheriff in a small southern town, Pusser is a wooden-club-wielding mad man destroying public property as he beats a man to death in the name of justice and law while he breaks law after law. And the theme of the movies? I quote from Jim Knipfel's article, "There's just somethin' wrong about a law that protects the guilty and don't care about the innocent." This "ass-kicking" movie appealed to those who were fed up with the slow and perhaps ineffective ways law responded to bad guys who "were not getting what they had coming."

I remember when we wanted nice guys as cops, at least in small town America. They were our neighbors, our friends, the people we went with on picnics. Kind of like our kindly priest helping his parish, the cop walking the beat helped those in need.

Somewhere, our admiration of the kindly cop changed to what I call the "Walking Tall" syndrome, meaning violence is good, and in the real world the bad guy is really the good guy. We've admired other anti-heroes, the ones before and after *Walking Tall* who depended on violence to solve their problems such as Steve McQueen in *The Getaway* (1972), John Wayne in *True Grit* (1969), Clint Eastwood in *Dirty Harry* (1971), and Bruce Willis in *Die Hard* (1998).

Admiring the bad guy is nothing new. Like when God orders Samuel to "kill both man and woman, infant and nursing child, ox and sheep, camel and donkey." We could go back to the beginning of time and find solving problems with violence has always been the natural order of things. I prefer Martin Luther King's take on violence: "Returning violence for violence multiplies violence, adding deeper darkness to a night already devoid of stars. Darkness cannot drive out darkness; only light can do that. Hate cannot drive out hate; only love can do that."

"Yesterday, upon the stair,
I met a man who wasn't there.
He wasn't there again today.
I wish, I wish he'd go away."
– William Hughes Mearns

This is one of my favorite photos, because I've seen so many stairs washed out in my walks on the beach. I took this one at Nye Beach. I think some owners must get tired of repairing and let the pile be taken by the sea. I am also reminded of some of my dead-end trips. Fortunately, I always found a way back.

OMSI

A fun place for kids is Camp Gray, OMSI's (Oregon Museum of Science and Industry) facilities built on twenty acres in South Beach. The camp teaches 5,000 children over the course of a year. And I thought 150 kids a year was exhausting! The camp can sleep up to 156 kids in separate bunk rooms in cabins with individual toilet and shower stalls. And it feeds them three meals a day. On top of that, 150 kids get turned loose outside for their classwork. It's an exciting, freeing environment for children to explore areas such as fossil beds. I have a friend who tells me the butter clam fossils are over two million years old. And I thought I was old.

Kids also explore tide pools, (I wonder if they know anemones eat dry fishy cat food), learn to use compasses, and build fires. And they investigate life in coastal forests, dissect squid, paddle up a creek in a raft built by the student, discover edible plants, and check out dune ecology. Plus go on a night hike. I'm not sure where they go, but it's night so who cares?

In my 30-year teaching career, I found students learn best with considerable hands-on activities, even in academia. It's the most effective way to teach how to observe and collect data for processing and making decisions. It's the kind of education that stays with you and you can actually use again and again.

In addition to beach access, OMSI restored the dunes, trees, and native plants on the 20-acre camp property for an outdoor classroom. Add hands-on science labs, and access to OSU's Hatfield Marine Science Center, Oregon Aquarium, and NOAA for a great educational experience.

Camp Gray's main goal is to get kids interested in looking for jobs in marine science, technology, and engineering fields. It offers scholarships for the camp that provides jobs for teens and adults: cooking, teaching, playing outdoor games, driving a bus, sweeping a floor, etc.

The camp was named after John Gray who helped with the purchase of the land. Born and raised in Oregon, Gray built the Sunriver Resort in Bend, Salishan on the Oregon Coast, Skamania Lodge in the Columbia Gorge, and John's Landing in Portland. His daughter is Janet Webster, a librarian at Hatfield for many years and a philanthropist like her father.

OSU Marine Hatfield Science Center at Sunset

John Nye

A friend asked me to look into the old-timer pioneer names about town, like the reason for the name Nye Beach. (Below right: Nye Beach bathers, 1920) According to the U.S. Census from 1832 to 1911: "John T. Nye was one of the earliest settlers in Newport. He took up a homestead along the beach and was instrumental in the development of the area. His property is now occupied by motels and houses."

Nye was just thirteen years old when his father, Michael Nye, died in 1844. He became an apprentice tailor in his home state of Ohio, presumably to help support the family, and worked at the business until 1859 when he crossed the plains with a team of oxen. At Pikes Peak County, he turned around and returned to Atchison, Kansas. On his second attempt, he stopped in Salt Lake City, Utah, where he traded his oxen for horses. Nye finished his trip to Corvallis with no major incidents and stayed there for the winter of 1860. In spring, he headed for British Columbia's Rock Creek mines before going back to Corvallis. The Civil War caused him to enlist as a tailor in the Union Army with the First Oregon Volunteers. For 19 months he was at Fort Vancouver, Fort Yamhill, and Camp Polk. Leaving the army in 1863, he first worked as a general store clerk. Following that he worked on building roads including Highway 20. Heading west in 1865, he took out a claim on present-day Nye Beach; his cabin, the second house in Newport, was located at Brook and Third Streets. He even did some mining in Nye Creek, next to his cabin.

For nineteen months, he lived in Nye Beach but kept his claim until he sold it in 1880 to developer Sam Irvin. Meanwhile he traveled to Indiana in 1871 to marry Olive Kist, namesake for Olive Street. They lived in Corvallis for three years before coming back to a 160-acre homestead east of Newport near Fruitvale Road and Highway 20. They raised eight children, and the Nyes lived there until John died. Olive spent the rest of her life on a nearby farm with her son Andrew.

Quail Beach Entrance

This ocean access doesn't have a name. I call it Quail Beach, for the street south of Seal Rock leading to the ocean. East of Highway 101, Quail Street turns into Seal Rock Loop.

Beach access here is also one of the places where jutting rock formations on the beach forced old Highway One to go to the top of the cliff. Among the rock obstacles blocking beach travel was the expanse of tide pools, the best in miles for their size and teeming marine life. Sometimes so empty of people, beaches can feel strange and freeing.

The Crow—My Favorite Animal

After feeding peanuts to crows on Ona Beach, I find they have become my good friends. Not only do they delight in playing, but they are also so smart! The world has 1,371,500 total species. Out of those, 384 use tools, and 42 can make or modify tools. Only five species can make multiple kinds of tools: humans, chimpanzees, orangutans, capuchin monkeys, and New Caledonian crows. Only two species can make hooked tools — humans and New Caledonian crows. Next to humans, the crow is the smartest species, bar none. They also believe in quid pro quo. Next time one hops up to you asking for a drink of water or a piece of your apple, give it to him, and he might bring you a valuable trinket in exchange.

Funny Place Names

In addition to John Nye, Sylvia Beach, Rogue Ale, Hilan Castle, Spruce Goose, other places in Oregon have fascinating backgrounds. *OregonLive* had a fun piece by Jamie Hale with stories behind the names of Oregon state parks taken from the *Oregon Geographic Names*. Hale wrote the "parks not named for people reflect our culture in more nuanced ways: a doll, a cook stove, a shipwrecked boiler. By diving into the history of these names, we can uncover small slices of Oregon history, deepening our understanding of how these lands became public in the first place."

The doll? Beverly Beach, five miles north of Newport, for the favorite doll of a child of the family who founded Beverly Beach. The shipwrecked boiler? Boiler Bay, 25 miles north of Newport for the *J. Marhoffer* in 1910.

Others named for people include Carl G. Washburne Memorial State Park, a highway commissioner from 1932 to 1935, and Jessie M. Honeyman Memorial State Park, an advocate for roadside beautification and scenic preservation.

Hug Point got its name from travelers "hugging" the rocks to get around the point before U.S. 101 was built. Devil's Lake, in the middle of Lincoln City, was named after a local tribal legend about a giant fish or marine monster that lived in the lake. Neptune was the Roman god of the seas, thus the name for a viewpoint just south of Cape Perpetua because of the huge winter waves.

Thirteen miles south of Coos Bay, Shore Acres State Park was once home to a palatial estate built in 1910 by shipbuilder and lumberman Louis J. Simpson. The opulent three-story mansion burned to the ground in 1921 but was rebuilt even bigger than before. In 1942, the Simpsons sold the land to Oregon, which eventually tore down the neglected home and established a state park.

Movies Come to Newport

Filmmakers have used Newport's shores over the decades for complete or at least parts of over 25 films and TV shows.

The famous *Sometimes a Great Notion* (1970) was based on a book by Oregon author Ken Kesey. The film was shot within a 30-mile area around Newport, Toledo, Kernville, and other areas along the Siletz River. The Stamper House, which Universal Studios originally built as a movie set, was sold and finished. It still stands across the Siletz River several miles upstream from Kernville.

Other well-known movies/TV shows with Newport influence are *The Ring,* a 2002 horror movie filmed at Yaquina Head Lighthouse; *Prom Night,* another horror film opening with Yaquina Bridge; and *Benji the Hunted* (1987), in which a dog is lost in the wilderness. In *Hysterical* (1983), filmed at the Yaquina Head Lighthouse, a writer who plans to write a novel and moves into a lighthouse haunted by a female spirit. And a part of *Overboard* (1987), filmed in Depoe Bay, about an heiress falling off a boat, developing amnesia and believing she's married to another man with five children.

Other movies from this vicinity: *Homecoming III* (2004) and *Raiders of the Lost Clam to the Future* (2021). Episodes from TV dramas and documentaries: "Fatal Devotion" (2012) from *Final Witness* about Christian Longo murdering and concealing his wife and three children, *Twisted Fates* (2012), the music video *Gentri: Home* (2017), disasters in *X-Ray Earth* (2011), horror stories from *Razilee and Elijah Part 3* (2021), *We Stay Econo* (2019) about weird things happening to Econo Guy in a motel, strange phenomena in *All Cats Are Grey* (2011), people driving million-dollar motor homes in *Motor Mansions* (2005), "The Mystery of Pirate's Cove" (1977) from *The Hardy Boys/Nancy Drew Mysteries,* "Message in a Bottle" (1984) from *Knotts Landing,* "New Breed Vets with Steve Irwin" in *False Eye,* "Eagle Cap Extreme, Newport Fishmonger" (2020) in *Oregon Field Guide,* "Sea Rescue" (2013) and "Missions of Mercy" (2017) in *Up, Up and Away,* "On Location" (2020) in *Trail Blazers*, and *Dungeon Cove* (2016) in *Deadliest Catch.*

What would you do if you weren't afraid?

R/V *Rachel Carson*

I can be awed by the names we give our ships, especially the research ships such as the one that moored at the Hatfield this morning. The *Rachel Carson* research ship, belonging to the University of Washington's School of Oceanography, aids UW researchers and students in exploring waters throughout Puget Sound and along nearby coasts. Originally named the *Aora* and built in 2003 at Macduff, Scotland, the *Rachel Carson* began as a fisheries research platform.

A second *Rachel Carson*, now scrapped, once worked on the Great Lakes. A third, a mooring buoy maintenance ship, belongs to the Florida Keys National Marine Sanctuary.

Rachel Carson, known as the "mother of environmental movements," was the first person to tell the world how badly pesticides, especially DDT, and chemical fertilizers were poisoning our environment. Over time, she warned, we will end up with a bleak, black world. A U.S. marine biologist, Carson wrote several environmental books, such as the famous *Silent Spring*. Her book provided the impetus behind the creation of the Environmental Protection Agency, and President Jimmy Carter also posthumously awarded Carson the Presidential Medal of Freedom, the highest civilian award, in 1980.

"There is something infinitely healing in the repeated refrains of nature —the assurance that dawn comes after night, and spring after winter."

–Rachel Carson
(May 27, 1907 – April 14, 1964)

Thank you, Rachel.

March 2019

The R/V *Atlantis* Research Ship

The *Atlantis* came in—tug and all. A tug pilot is rarely needed to bring a ship into our port, and most tugs come from Coos Bay 100 miles south of us. I am more surprised to see the *Atlantis* a long way from her home port at Woods Hole Oceanographic Institution in Massachusetts. She may be the most famous research ship today because of her submersibles and underwater robots. One of them, *Alvin*, is the only deep-diving research submersible that can carry humans to the sea floor.

Atlantis 1 was the first American ship built for marine biology, geology, and oceanography research—a 142-foot ketch rigged ship who sailed from 1931 to 1966. The Atlantis space shuttle was named after *Atlantis 1*.

The new *Atlantis*, in addition to the grand title of a top research ship, has six science labs, sonar seafloor mapping, satellite communications, winches, cranes, and specially designed hangars to house *Alvin*, a human-occupied submersible, the remotely operated vehicle *Jason*, and the towed vehicles *Argo II* and *DSL 120*. One of my former students told me how long he stayed miles below on his latest trip. I was proud of him even though I get chills just thinking about where he went to work.

I do love hearing about the vital and fascinating discoveries such as fish living in a nearly barren oxygen world finding new ways to produce oxygen, hidden faults, a lost uranium fuel rod, and missing planes, ships, and submarines missing since World War II. And the *Titanic*!

"Thinking is difficult. That's why most people judge." – Carl Gustav Jung

Alvin

The ability of this submersible makes *Alvin* and *Atlantis* much in demand. When they visited Newport in September 2016, Nancy Steinberg wrote that "most locals were unaware of the star in their midst." On November 26, 2018, *Alvin* made its 5,000th dive during an expedition to the Guaymas Basin in the Gulf of California.

In 1964, her first untethered dive measured thirty-five feet. Now she plunges to 14,764 feet with dives lasting ten hours. *Alvin* can maneuver, hover, rest on the sea floor, collect data and samples, produce maps, and take and take photos. In one sea floor discovery, *Alvin* and the autonomous underwater vehicle *Sentry* found gas-filled volcanic rocks that "pop" when brought to the surface.

Alvin was named after Woods Hole engineer Allyn Vine, a contraction of his name. He was the first to envision a deep-sea research ship for people when he was a graduate student in the 1930s.

"There are only two days in the year that nothing can be done. One is called yesterday, and the other is called tomorrow. So today is the right day to love, believe, do, and mostly live." - Dalai Lama

Frank Luke

The first weekend of May always brings Loyalty Day to Newport, one of only two U.S. cities left celebrating our opposition to Communism. In Arizona, one of our heroes was Frank Luke, Jr., a fighter pilot against the Germans in World War I long before twentieth-century fears during the Cold War.

Near my old Arizona home is Luke AFB, an airfield for as long as I can remember. Every time a jet flew over me, I felt overwhelmed. My fascination with the power of jets, however, doesn't include the time I bought my five nieces and nephews walky-talkies. We were out in the fields talking to each other until this voice from the heavens said, "Get off those damn radios now!" After a few surprised "What?" the voice explained he was in a jet above us, and we were interfering with communication with his base. Needless to say, once we finally accepted that the angry voice was not God, we slunk back to the house in giggles until our fright was gone.

Another time a jet from Luke came in low over our heads and crashed a block from us, exploding debris everywhere. We ran as close as we could, hoping no one was hurt. Luckily, the plane only gouged a short path in a wheat field, and nothing was injured. The pilot had parachuted to safety.

Luke AFB was named after another Loyalty Day kind of hero, Second Lt. Frank Luke, Jr. who died in 1918 when he was 21 years old. He was the number two United States ace in World War I when he achieved eighteen aerial wins fighting over France. Luke was shot down on September 29, 1918. He survived the crash but died in a shooting fight with German soldiers, killing several of them before they killed him. Luke posthumously received the Medal of Honor.

When housing developments invaded the land near Luke, a new homeowner wrote, "Whom do we thank for the morning air show? Last Wednesday, at precisely 9:11 A.M, a tight formation of four F-16 jets made a low pass over Arrowhead Mall, continuing west over Bell Road at approximately 500 feet. Imagine our good fortune! Do the Tom Cruise-wannabes feel we need this wake-up call, or were they trying to impress the cashiers at Mervyn's early bird special? Any response would be appreciated."

He did get a response. Lt. Col. Grant L. Rosensteel, Jr. answered, "Regarding 'A wake-up call from Luke's jets': On June 15, at precisely 9:12 a.m., a perfectly timed four-ship fly-by of F-16s from the 63rd Fighter Squadron at Luke Air Force Base flew over the grave of Capt. Jeremy Fresques. Capt. Fresques was an Air Force officer who was previously stationed at Luke Air Force Base and was killed in Iraq on May

30, Memorial Day. At 9 a.m. on June 15, his family and friends gathered at Sunland Memorial Park in Sun City to mourn the loss of a husband, son, and friend.

"Based on the letter writer's recount of the fly by, and because of the jet noise, I'm sure you didn't hear the 21-gun salute, the playing of taps, or my words to the widow and parents of Capt. Fresques as I gave them their son's flag on behalf of the President of the United States and all those veterans and servicemen and women who understand the sacrifices they have endured. A four-ship flyby gives a display of respect the Air Force for those who sacrificed their lives in defense of freedom. We are professional aviators and take our jobs seriously, and on June 15 what the letter writer witnessed was four officers lining up to pay their ultimate respects.

"The letter writer asks, 'Whom do we thank for the morning air show?' The 56th Fighter Wing will make the call for you and forward your thanks to the widow and parents of Capt. Fresques, and thank them for you, for it was in their honor that my pilots flew the most honorable formation of their lives."

Found Art

When I was a kid, my mom prospected the Arizona desert with her handy-dandy rock axe, while my dad spent a good deal of his leisure time walking the Butterfield Stage-coach Trail collecting artifacts that were thrown, dropped, or lost off the passing stagecoaches. We got so little rain that tracks and debris remained for decades. Over the years he ended up with quite a collection. One day he brought home a chain and welded all the artifacts to it. He hung the chains over the windowsills in our living room. One of my uncles came along looking for supper, stared around at the hanging chains, and commented, "Huh. I noticed someone finally cleaned the yard, but did you have to bring the garbage in the house and hang it on the living room walls?"

Others find a purpose for found beach trash in wild displays from the "Washed Ashore" art creations. Some objects are huge, some are cute, and others can be considered disgusting. This group has created it all, popping up in such places as the display hanging from the ceiling in the abandoned elephant area at the San Francisco Zoo. From a distance, it's beautiful. Closer, people see it's made from shoes, Styrofoam cups, frisbees, and a thousand other pieces of trash.

Ann Hubard wrote: "The huge, tufted puffin is about seven to feet tall and made of plastic that has washed up on the shore. It is both sobering and a fascinating art piece. There is a Washed Ashore Museum in Bandon with art made of only plastic that has washed ashore to make us pay attention to all the plastic out there."

The Yaquina Dredge

As I focus on events outside my window, I realize I concentrated on research ships coming into the bay. This morning the USAV *Yaquina* tied up at the NOAA dock, one of two dredges in Oregon owned by the Army Corp of Engineers—the *Yaquina* (the name of an Oregon Native American tribe) and the *Essayons* (meaning "Let Us Try"). Merchant Marine crews operate both hopper dredges, homeported in Portland (OR). These specialized sea-going ships work like vacuum cleaners, dredging and transporting silt from ocean bars, fast flowing rivers, and isolated harbors to open-water disposal areas.

The *Essayons* works on larger entrance bars, rivers, and harbors on the coasts of California, Oregon, Hawaii, Alaska, and, in emergencies, the Mississippi River with bigger volume sand deposits. Its size makes the *Yaquina* particularly well-suited for dredging the small, shallow coastal entrances and smaller, shifting sand deposits in river channels.

Assigned to Newport, the *Yaquina* occasionally appears in our Yaquina Bay; she quietly floats in and circles about the bay, in and out of the jetty, until she finishes her job. Just as she came, she quietly slips away with no recognition of how vital she is to the survival of this bay. Like the importance of the keystone species such as the sea star or the bee who buzzes about pollinating, providing food and shelter for bugs who, in turn provide food for birds, who ...

As impressed as I am with our research ships and fishing boats that grace our bay, the *Yaquina* makes it possible for them to be here. She annually removes approximately 300,000 to 500,000 cubic yards of sludge from the Yaquina River's 40-foot entrance, a 30-foot channel in the bay, and the turning basin. Whatever the season, brave fishing folk risk their lives to bring back seafood for millions of people, locally processing commercial halibut, salmon, herring, sardines, albacore, shrimp, hagfish, etc., including offbeat seafood products such as urchins and slime eels, bringing more millions of dollars in salaries.

The fleet is also a leader in Oregon's crabbing season. In 2019, Newport had the highest harvest value in Oregon. Its fishing industry provided over 2,000 jobs with 331 fishing boats, bringing in 124 million pounds of seafood valued at $60 million.

On the recreational side, an estimated 50,000 anglers and whale watchers boarded Lincoln County's charter and tour boats in 2021. Boats go out either on the ocean or along riverbanks for the same fish sought commercially while people dig along the seawall for clams.

Oregon Coast Aquarium

Our world-famous aquarium hosts World Oceans Day in June, and too good to pass up. The one in 2010 honored the fiftieth anniversary of Dr. Seuss' *One Fish, Two Fish, Red Fish, Blue Fish* with giveaways, posters, and activity books. Annual activities are children's story time with sea otters, sharks, and other fish as well as ocean crafts and face painting. Visitors walk through acrylic tubes in the awesome "Passages of the Deep," surrounding them with ever-changing deep-water marine animals.

The theme "Wear Blue and Tell Two" means we can all reach out with two interesting facts about the ocean or two ways we can personally help prevent or clean up ocean pollution. This year's program also focused on our personal impact of garbage on sea life with a challenge to get involved with the Seven C's Pledge cleaning up our ocean:

1) Commit to making a difference
2) Conserve at home
3) Consume consciously
4) Communicate interest and concerns
5) Challenge ourselves daily
6) Connect to community
7) Celebrate our ocean

Blue Heron in Yaquina River Estuary

Dungeon Cove

Watching the crab boats come and go while hearing the name "Dungeon Cove's Graveyard of the Pacific" always reminds me of a sweet little inlet somewhere up the coast until I watched the *Deadliest Catch,* the five-part television series of Newport fishermen tossing out crab pots into the high seas. The National Institute of Occupation Safety and Health cite Dungeon Cove as having the most deaths on the West Coast and third most fatalities in the nation. Between 2000 and 2010, an average of nine commercial fishermen died each year.

Case in point, while the filmmakers were busy around Newport and on its docks and boats, the F/V *Eagle III* and the F/V *Sara Jo* met with disaster at the mouth of Coos Bay. Three of the four on board the *Eagle* died when she was rolled by a rogue wave. *The Sara Jo,* trying to collect the *Eagle's* crab pots, capsized with one dead and two injured.

The *Deadliest Catch* filmmakers first took on the king crabbers in Alaska's Bering Sea in a series that ranked in the top 20 cable shows and earned 16 Emmys during its eleven seasons.

Captains participating in Newport's series on *Dungeon Cove* filming are John Law of the F/V *Lady Law*; Gary Ripka of the F/V *Redeemer* and his son Kenny of the F/V *Western Breeze;* and Mike Retherford of the F/V *Excalibur* and his brother Chris of the F/V *Winona J*. Jim Burns of the F/V *Galway Bay* homeports in Coos Bay. The F/V *Western Hunter* was used as the "chase boat" while filming at sea.

Crabbing is the last "free-for-all" commercial fishing with no quotas for totals as long as the crabs are male and at least 5¾ inches wide. It pays to be first to the docks with a belly load to sell. All the activity, out to the ocean to drop the pots and return to pull them in, starts in early December during the dead of winter storms while boats navigate around sandbars, massive waves, and dangerous currents in the Dungeon Cove. The deck can be stacked with up to five hundred pots, each one weighing up to one-hundred and twenty-five pounds, skewing the boat's center of gravity. As boats slough through massive waves and tread the bar, their rocking and rolling can send pots helter-skelter.

In Newport, crabbing has tended to be a family business, generation after generation. Captain Jonny Law's daughter Alyssa Mae works hard separating crabs in the hold, while son Maddox practices at the helm to be a future captain. Captain Gary "the Ripper" Ripka and his son Kenny have a lot of respect for each other, and Gary wants nothing more than to see his son continue the family legacy. Captain Mikey Retherford and his brother Chris Retherford grew up fishing with their dad. By 21, Mikey Retherford was running his own boat, and he's training his teenage son to be part of the family business. His wife and manager, Kelley, says, "It's a family business from start to finish. Actually, it's a family life. We love the ocean. We love the business. We love the fish. It's a dream come true, being able to be a family and work together."

Warming of the Earth

We all know the earth is warming, so far by 1.9F degrees since industrialization in the late 1800s, mostly in the past few decades. The tipping point is another .9F degrees, with a 44 percent chance of that happening in the next five years. The past eight years have been the warmest on record since recordkeeping began in 1880. Last year tied with 2018 for the warmest.

Ground-based measurements are collected by NOAA and other legitimate sources from ships, ocean buoys, and weather stations from around the world and validated by NASA satellites. Data are compared to a base temperature averaged from the years 1951 to 1980. This base formula also included other weather factors such as La Niña and El Niño for accuracy.

Pacific Trash Patch

Some hopefuls look forward to the Great Pacific Garbage Patch, twice the size of Texas, being sucked up into a big vacuum. Halfway between Hawaii and California, this pile of 1.8 trillion pieces of floating trash, mostly plastic and weighing around 79,000 metric tons, was discovered in the 1980s. Thus far, the sucking vacuum hasn't been a success. Perhaps the super-enzyme degrading plastic bottles will whittle down our huge trash piles.

Politics:

Gini Index

According to Wikipedia, "the Gini coefficient (/ˈdʒiːni/ JEE-nee), also known as the Gini Index or Gini Ratio, is a measure of statistical dispersion intended to represent the income or wealth inequality within a nation or a social group ... as a measure of inequality of income or wealth." The share of income held by the top 1 percent was as large in 2005 as it was in 1928 during the "Roaring Twenties" before the 1929 crash almost 100 years ago. The return to that high inequality began in the 1980s. The wealth gap between America's richest and poorest families more than doubled from Reagan's reign in the 1980s to 2016. Reagan started this increasing inequality with his tax cuts, and George W. Bush made them much worse in 2001 and 2003. These presidents also had the highest debt of any other president with Trump hot on their heels.

[Update: During the first three weeks of the pandemic, America's super-rich saw their wealth rise by $282 billion while more than 30 million Americans applied for unemployment. Jeff Bezos (founder of Amazon and the world's richest person) and Mark Zuckerberg (founder of Facebook) saw their combined fortunes grow by nearly $60 billion during a two-month span, Bezos' wealth jumping by 30 percent and Zuckerberg's wealth by an incredible 46 percent. During the same time, 38 million Americans lost their jobs.]

"The saddest aspect of life right now is that science gathers knowledge faster than society gathers wisdom." – Isaac Asimov

Samuel Clemens' Yard Art

One quiet Sunday morning found me cleaning out drawers. In a box, I came across two photos that flooded me with a memory of a past summer. In 2006, a local artist painted a replica of da Vinci's *Mona Lisa*, forty feet by sixty feet in the dirt of a hillside three miles east of Newport. She caused big-time problems as gawking drivers frequently brought the traffic to a standstill. Headlines in the nation read, "*Mona Lisa's* smile stops traffic in the U.S."

Mona Lisa's image was so big a person could crawl in the cave-like nostril and take a nap. It had pupils the size of the artist's head and fingers the width of the artist's body. The artist Samuel Clemens (no relation to Mark Twain) said, "I was worried about the detail because the hill isn't smooth. It isn't like a piece of paper. As it was, I lost a little smile at the corner of her mouth, and one of her eyes is in undulation."

Eventually the rains came, and plants covered Mona Lisa. The next summer, however, Clemens painted a reclining nude of his wife based on his drawing of her when they first met. He used a cut-out from environmentally friendly latex and finished in 24 hours. Same traffic problems.

The artist's story matches his work in being interesting. Eight years earlier, he bought an abandoned dairy farm and cleared a large hillside from weeds, bushes, and blackberry brambles before starting on his paintings.

The Mona Lisa and his wife's paintings are long gone, but I still have photos—and memories.

I had a college professor once who said images are the furniture of the mind. How do you furnish yours?

Oregon Beaches State Highway

In Oregon, people can't own beaches or deny others access. If you've ever tried to gain access to California beaches or dodge around all the sand buggies whizzing about the Washington coasts, you would thank Gov. Oswald West (1873-1960). Despite a corrupt government, he persuaded Republican legislators to adopt our beaches as a public highway. They didn't even know what they did.

Born in Canada, West ended up in Oregon with his six siblings and parents. After a Portland hotel fire nearly put the family into poverty, they moved to Salem. West's father took up cattle for a living, and Oswald spent his school years driving cattle through town. He quit school at sixteen and drove a butcher's delivery wagon before he changed directions to work for a bank as a messenger and then a teller where he witnessed many land frauds. In 1903, Governor Chamberlin appointed West to the Railroad Commission. He investigated frauds before becoming a state land agent when he watched men involved in frauds running for political offices. That's when he decided to run against them. And won.

In June 1912, West took the train to Yaquina City and ferry to Newport for a celebration. Heavy, blowing rains washed away the outdoor decorations, but seventy-five of Newport's finest, about ten percent of the population, heard the speeches by Mayor George Wilcox, railroad man John Scott, and Governor West. Much to their surprise, his speech was about women's right to vote. When West was ten years old, he had heard a speech from Abigail Scott Duniway who asked him, "Don't you consider your mother as good if not better than an ordinary saloon bum?" West answered her, "Sure I do."

Seven months after his speech in Newport, West wrote a sixty-word bill designating all Oregon beaches as a public highway. It wasn't an odd request: many beaches at low tide were already used to travel the Oregon coast. But West knew that once he created a Highway Commission (before we even had highways), the beaches would never be open to private enterprise and land fraudsters to exploit.

A Republican legislation tried to change the law in 1947 by changing beaches from "highway" to "recreation areas" with permits to move anything from the beaches. West faced a highway commission meeting and said, "As long as God gives me strength, nobody is going to remove a shovelful of sand, a shovelful of rocks from those beaches."

People give Gov. Tom McCall credit for free access to Oregon beaches because of his media push for the 1967 Beach Bill. In Cannon Beach, a hotel owner blocked the dry beach by his place, declaring it available only to his guests.

West's law was for wet sand. Legislators paid attention to McCall's helicopter trip to the coast and expanded public ownership to the beach's vegetation line. Anyone enjoying Oregon's free and undisturbed beaches need to thank both West and McCall.

"I enjoy a glass of wine each night for its health benefits. The other glasses are for my witty comebacks and flawless dance moves."

Hunting Elephants in Oregon

"Hunting elephants in Oregon country is a delightful sport." Or so wrote John Horner, author of *Days and Deeds in the Oregon Country*, published in 1928. Years ago, near where the Oregon State Agricultural College stands, a woman told her husband to go clean out the spring because the water was bad. Bones were dug up including teeth. The wife made this delightful description of them:

"The teeth were many thousands of times bigger than ours, interesting when we think about toothaches, many causes of acute misery. We should multiply our toothache by a thousand or by ten thousand to get an idea of tooth troubles to an elephant." Then the workmen dug up a tusk. According to Horner, "It was very big, but then tusks are just teeth overgrown. Overgrown eye-teeth are called tushes, and teeth much larger than tushes are called tusks. In the language of the old-time schoolmaster, one might say: Positive, tooth; comparative, tush; superlative, tusk."

The discovery set off an elephant hunt along the Willamette River with a hundred college student cadets and cadetines (girls), along with a mayor. According to Horner, the mayor and the elephant took the same trail to the river except the elephant took the trail to get a drink. The cadets, arriving at a spring, dug a hole as large as a freight train car and found more elephant bones. Everyone joined in the fun of the dig except a "fine-looking pioneer who was in deep study. He bore the appearance of one who depends more upon opinion than on books—a custom not uncommon among old-timers." When asked what he thought, he answered, "I can't understand how a great hill of flesh ever crawled under that spring."

Elephant finds along with mammoths, mastodons, ground sloth, Cayuse pony, three-toed horse, and more were brought out of gravel beds, moraines, marshes, and streams. Geological evidence indicates the land west of the Cascade Range was a "zoological garden where elephants and mastodons, the first plowmen of the Oregon country, used their great tusks in upturning roots for food. Those were the days of elephant-and-palm climate when huge animals now extinct, lived here in great numbers." The largest tusk found was by a girl, fishing, who thought it was a snag.

Horner ends his elephant hunt story describing the dreams of the young elephant hunters. "The hunt was exciting, gleaning a lesson in natural history from first sources in elephant land. With the world for a classroom and the sky for a canopy, everything was so interesting that, occasionally, a boy pinched himself to determine whether he really was on the earth or over in dreamland."

NOAA Research Ship *Rainier*

The *Rainier* arrived for the winter. She and the *Bell Shimada* are the two remaining out of the original NOAA five ships homeported in Newport. The other three ships originally homeported in Newport, along with the decommissioned *Hi'ialakai* still docked here, have been sold into the private world. NOAA describes the *Rainier*, named for Mount Rainier in the state of Washington "the most productive hydrographic platform in the world." She mainly makes geodetic surveys of the ocean bottom.

The *Fairweather* and *Rainier* on March 22, 2018, the day NOAA hosted a party and ship tours at Newport to celebrate the ships' successful fifty years of service to the United States.

With her sister ship, the *Fairweather*, the *Rainier* surveys the world, especially the ice melt along the Pacific Northwest, so that fishing boats don't get into trouble. Despite problems from melting global warming, these scientists can "boldly go where no man has gone before." The ship maps the Northwest Passage, a sea corridor connecting the Atlantic and Pacific Oceans through Canada's Arctic Archipelago islands and along the north coast of North America.

Europeans spent 300 years trying to find this passage to Asia, but it wasn't discovered until the searches for the missing explorer John Franklin allowed the Amundsen expedition to cross the ice in 1904–1906. According to NASA satellite images, the Arctic's "death spiral" from global warming opened the passage's seven possible summer routes in August of 2007. Year-around travel is predicted by 2050.

Much has changed in surveying since Mark Twain's days when depth was measured by dropping a line in the water. Now side-scan sonar sends sound waves in a swath and builds images of hazardous obstacles, wrecks, etc. At 231 feet long, the *Rainier* carries five aluminum launches to scan shallow waterways. The launches also conduct diving projects and shore support.

There is life beyond the ice for the *Rainier*. In 2019, she visited the lava spills around the northwestern Hawaiian Islands to survey new waters, creating images of the lava flow. In January 2021, the *Rainier* mapped the waters around Guam and the Northern Mariana Islands.

The Crow

Where I grew up, we didn't have crows. I've learned how smart they are since I moved here and hope that they'll help us as humans seem determined to destroy the world. The cacophonous, brazen, gutsy crow that I liked to feed while my partner walked the dog on Ona Beach. They're too smart to vote for a man like Trump. As soon as we drive into the parking lot, the look-out crow recognizes the sound of our car and squawks to notify the others. They fly in and surround me, silently waiting for the peanut toss. Each one hops once toward a peanut until they stash up to four peanuts into their beak and fly away to hide them.

Over time I begin to recognize various crows. One day I walked out of my back door and was literally bombarded several times by a crow I called Speckle. Eleven miles he had followed me home for his peanuts. The next day he was back at the park.

Crows have a sense of humor, playing pranks on people as well as each other. And they never forget. Testing out smarter than most children, crows can do complicated decision-making with eight-step puzzles. In a specific order. I don't think I can do that.

Teatime

Every afternoon when the chores have mostly let us be, my partner and I end the day with what we call Teatime. God help any unsuspecting soul passing by because joining us is mandatory. Once the gathering of drinks, snacks, and other comfort needs has concluded, we ask each person to describe the best three things that happened to them during this day. I think of all the activities I have ever been a part of, Teatime has been the most effective in changing me from negative to positive.

A new study wanted to know why social conservatives are more inclined to believe 'Fake News' than liberals. It has nothing to do with intelligence. It's all about how hyper-attuned we are to a threat level. The more we feel threatened by possible dangers around us, the more we are willing to trust the threat rather than ignore it, even when it's easily proved a blatant lie.

Did you know you can "rewire" your brain to be happy by simply recalling three things you're grateful for every day for 21 days?

Green Gables Bookstore and Bed & Breakfast

Reading about interesting buildings around town—Sylvia Beach, the two lighthouses, Rogue Ale, Hilan Castle, etc.—a reader reminded me I should maybe write about what I know. Not sure exactly how to take that, I still decided she might be right.

I do know about the building at the end of Coast Street in Nye Beach called Green Gables since 1992. It was only ten years old when we bought it in 1990 from the builder, David Turner, who rented from us for the next two years until we retired. When we moved in, the house still had subflooring, and the sheetrock on the walls were only partially taped and unpainted.

We added a garage, destroying the architect facade on the back of the house which I always regretted. Later, we took the roof off the garage and extended the bookstore with a second turret bedroom on top. In the spirit of cutting costs, we made shingling the addition a new experience for us. I cut

over 1,000 diamond-shaped shingles to match the main structure.

During the early months when we worked on the property, townspeople would stop by and tell us great stories about the house. Outside of the many haunting ghosts, one local said it was an historic house removed from a hilltop up the Yaquina River and barged down to Newport. Maybe just jesting the naive newcomers. I put a waterfall pool in the front yard and stocked it with goldfish. They kept disappearing. Several replacements later I realized I was feeding the local raccoons.

When we started the outside painting, we ran several test strips to see what colors we liked. I got so many comments from people driving by such as, "You will NOT paint it that color!" I was beginning to wonder who actually owned the house.

We hired many wonderful people in those days, some who became really good friends. Hank, our wonderful house painter and carpenter who built the bookstore shelves in the basement, preferred to work at night so that he would be home with his kids during the summer days. We gave him a key so that he could come and go without getting us out of bed to let him in. We always knew when he came because he would open the front door and holler up the stairs, "Honey, I'm home."

When we were finally ready to open, we invited the Chamber of Commerce members to brunch, the tradition for new businesses. We were told to expect two or maybe three people. On a really wild, windy, rainy, stormy day, we had over twenty visitors. They were kind and welcoming, except for one who cornered me, intently quizzing me about whether I bought all my construction materials in town. He made a big deal out of supporting our townspeople but never shopped in our bookstore.

During the first busy summer when we ran Green Gables as a bookstore, people kept knocking on the door asking if we were a B&B. What the hell, why not? We'd never even been to a B&B, but it seemed a good way to make a little money.

And, along with selling books, that's what we did for the next seven years. Our first guests were there during the early morning earthquake in 1993. An early riser, I was on a ladder hanging shades when it hit, immediately bringing Nel in to remind me we had guests and what the hell was I doing, anyway? "Hanging on," I said. "It wasn't me." At breakfast the next morning Nel couldn't resist. "So," she says to our guests. "Did the earth move for you last night?" We always gave them their choice for breakfast when they came much to our occasional enjoyment and distress. One guest, a chef, asked for oatmeal. The conversation went something like this:

"Would you like something in it?

"Maybe add pieces of apple?"

"Sure."

"A few nuts?"

"Sure."

"Brown sugar?"

"Sure."

"Grapenuts?"

"Sounds fine."

"Filet mignon steak?"

By that point, Nel just stared at him.

Another asked for lox and bagels. Nel knew what they were but not me. I was from Arizona. We had no idea where to get such a thing, so we went to JC's and asked the butcher who kindly fixed us up. After he stopped laughing, reminding us we were in a town famous for fishing for salmon.

Sometimes the guest taught me how to cook. We had an elderly couple that worried me getting up and down the stairs who ended up being more agile that I was. He was a retired architect professor from Oregon State University in town to design a house built out of found wood on a small island stuck out in the middle a couple of miles up Yaquina River. While he chugged back and forth upriver, the wife, bless her, taught me how to make poached eggs.

Another guest insisted on omelets, another unknown experience. After staring at recipes from seven cookbooks and even more attempts at omelets, we were finally successful. Guests now claim I make the best omelets they've ever had. Good thing no one ever asked for souffles.

One morning we waited for an hour for a couple for breakfast and finally checked. Seems they had a fight during the night and left a note. We overate that morning, but who cares. Then there were the guests who spoke no English. Three women from the Netherlands, and a couple from Italy. We did a lot of hand waving to communicate.

Two delightfully funny ministers told us about how all their parishioners thought they were married. Later they had to drive fifty miles from their church to actually have the ceremony. When they got their marriage license, he said in his loudest preacher voice, "I didn't know you were THAT old." After they left us, they wrote us another funny story. On their way home in their rented car, they found a gun under the seat. The cops gave them a really hard time when they turned it in, almost locking them up.

Green Gables Bed & Breakfast and Bookstore at Newport, Oreg

An impressive guest was the tiny, and I mean teeny tiny, woman who taught airline pilots how to fly huge planes like the Boeing 747. Then there was the food taster. Can you image? Tasting food all day long for a living? Only thing might be better is wine taster although I probably wouldn't last through a morning break. One of our overnight guests played Ellen DeGeneres's girlfriend in one of her television shows. She and her husband were on their way to Canada for a play they were starring in.

As far as we know, our most famous guest dropped in one Christmas Eve looking for a bed, a freelance photographer who was working for Newsweek at the time he took the iconic photo of a man defying tanks in Tiananmen Square, China. The tank man was dragged away before he got run over. No one seems to know who he was or what happened to him after that. The photo got him the 1990 World Press Photo award. He took the tank picture from a balcony high up on a hotel as the bullet hole in the wall behind him reminded him he was a sitting duck. He was really a nice guy who talked freely about his experiences. This was his last trip into danger zones, he said. He was tired of being afraid. I read he died last year.

Guests loved wandering down to the bookstore after hours. We enjoyed both businesses but wanted a bit of peace and quiet, so we sold the Gables in 2000 and moved down the street.

And accidentally started another B&B for another four years.

Fourth of July Fireworks

Good morning, everyone, and a glorious morning it is. I'm watching the sun chase the night's shadows off Table Mountain as I sit here drinking my coffee, musing about the coming fireworks in three days and worrying about the vulnerability of the hill I live on.

Will the dry vegetation on the side of the hill catch fire this year from my neighbors' illegal fireworks? Even so, I enjoy the fireworks although one year the fog was so thick we only heard the explosions. After a while, though, even that got funny.

We always watch the fireworks with friends and get a hug. This year, it looks like nature is with us. The weather looks promising, warmer than usual temperatures, some light, patchy fog that shouldn't disturb, enough breeze to blow the smoke away but not enough to feel chilled although blankets are handy.

The fireworks will be fired off the end of the International Port, and I miss the fireworks barge in front of our house. I'm sad it sank.

Tsunami Dock

So much talk about ocean cleanup. So many places to cleanup. I still remember the headline on March 11, 2011, and the aftermath: 18,000 dead with waves reaching 128 feet above sea level. It was the date for the earthquake and tsunami in Japan.

In June 2012, four months and 5,000 miles after the disaster, a dock floated across the Pacific Ocean and landed on Agate Beach, Newport. With a view of the Yaquina Head Lighthouse in the background, thousands were drawn to Agate Beach where the 66-foot-long, 19-foot-wide, 7-foot-tall concrete/Polystyrene dock had arrived intact. This disastrous invader generated so much national interest that somewhere about 73,000 visitors from all over stopped at the Agate Beach Wayside during the summer.

The journey at sea ended for this dock, but a great story had just begun when a use for the cut-up parts was decided. Hatfield used one corner to mark the entrance to their tsunami evacuation trail and a memorial to the almost 20,000 people who died.

The Newport Tsunami Dock Foundation put another corner on the plaza next to Ripley's Believe It or Not on the Newport bayfront for a tsunami awareness and information center.

Along with the debris came hundreds of living passengers. The dock alone carried 100 different species, three of them posing threat to native organisms before it was scraped clean, scorched with weed torches, broken up, and recycled. I also found a very large basket on Grant's Creek Park filled with hundreds of living species. All things considered, our beaches have had little invasive debris.

Japan and Oregon have almost mirror-image earthquake subduction zones off their coasts, and the county has made extensive preparations to get us ready. The last 9.0 earthquake/tsunami we had here was in 1700, and the next one can occur at any time. How big or just when we can't know. All I can tell you is to head for high land as fast as you can.

August 2019

Unidentified Aerial Phenomena

When I was a kid in my teens, I stumbled across an older friend who looked somewhat zombie-like from fear. "Whatsup?" I asked.

"It fell." His voice was quiet and hesitant. "From there." He looked up. "Just next to my house. Tore up old man Webber's corn patch but good."

"What fell?"

"This thing." For the first time he was almost angry. "Don't you listen?"

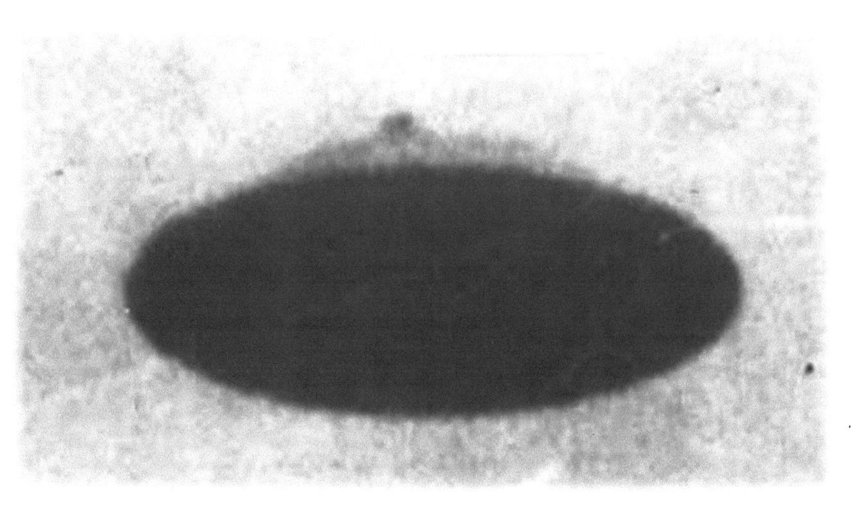

"Sorry." He stared at me, waiting for something. "They were everywhere. Small like a baby with funny clothes on. One of them moved."

"What!"

"Just an arm, it was reaching ouuut . . . to me." He shook his head. "Then a helicopter came and made me go home."

I waited for him to start laughing with a "gotcha" grin. It didn't come. He returned to his almost-zombie mien and wandered away. He never spoke of it again. Neither did anyone else. Until now.

I always believed something alive was out there. How could it not? This earth is only a speck in an ever-expanding universe. Among the billions of existing planets, chances are many teem with life. Seems *X-Files* are real, and our government has decided to release just a few of the "not in the interest of national security" photos so we don't panic. Remember Orson Well's famous 1938 radio show, *War of the Worlds,* when Martians were killing us off with "Heat Rays"?

Mass hysteria captured thou-sands as people panicked, running from a Mars attack. One man came home to find his wife with a bottle of poison; she said she would rather kill herself than be killed by Martians. Maybe twenty people lost their lives from the panic, but no one knows for sure.

I don't blame the government for hiding UFO's (renamed UAP,

"unidentified aerial phenomena") from us all these years. One description has a UAP doing 700 g-force, flying at 13,000 mph. I would think if a human flew at that speed, they would end up a smear on the wall. Or the one where the *USS Nimitz* tracked an object that traveled 60 miles in 3 seconds. The government admits these flying objects outstrip us by 100 to 1,000 years at the moment and we're like 'meh...

The McMinnville (OR) UFO photographs were taken by a farming couple, Paul and Evelyn Trent, in May 1950. The photos reprinted in *Life* magazine and in newspapers across the nation are often considered to be among the most famous ones taken of a UFO.

Then I remembered where the information came from. Trump. As if Trump's reign wasn't odd enough already, on August 4, 2020, he established the Unidentified Aerial Phenomena (UAP) Task Force (UAPTF).

Years earlier, on June 25, 2013, our government declassified the history and purpose of Area 51, a US Air Force base in Nevada. Because the base had been declared a secret base and was so intensely guarded, conspiracy theories popped up every-where, especially as the nearby area along the "Extraterrestrial Highway" was already a popular tourist destination.

Seems like this upsurge in dangerous conspiracies during Trump's time brought back a new interest in Area 51 and UFO's. Naturally, Hollywood and mass media took up the cry, creating the "Storm Area 51" meme that went crazy viral. Over a million people signed up to join the exodus to the Nevada desert one dawn morning searching for aliens. On September 19, 2019, thirty years after the first mention of UFO's and the aliens supposedly sighted in Area 51, 2,000+ showed up, rocking and rolling, ready to hunt down little green men from outer space. Wonder how many had guns?

Politics:

Trump Owns Our Justice System

Wow! Did you see that? Trump has taken ownership of our justice system. You don't like jail? Buy your way out. Starting in 2017, Trump pardoned his rich friends and political allies. We all know that Trump's business buddies, the oligarchs run our government and have been since Reagan gave them a running start, first by killing PATCO and the labor unions along with it, then by killing the Fairness Doctrine that required honesty in broadcasting which opened our airwaves to lies and fake news, and last, initiating "trickle-down" economics where the rich got richer off the backs of the middle-class by lowering wages and raising prices.

He effectively removed most rules, regulations, and laws governing big business, which, as any owner/CEO can tell you, is ruthless. Customer competition is ruthless. Push to pay the lowest wage, fewest benefits and charge the highest prices is ruthless. As the eye is always on the profit margin, everyone, especially the stockholders, are ruthless. Eisenhower's Republican programs aiding and protecting the working class were systematically destroyed, making way for the new regime—Greed.

As we watch Trump get away with changing our constitution, especially now that he owns our justice department, Supreme Court, and Congress, Trump could delete our 2020 election while hiding behind the cross, singing, "Um ba ya oh, I am the anointed king of the universe." Before you laugh, voters, think about it. We might as well take our constitution and shred it.

Politics:

Loss of Democracies

It is a sad fact that, historically, democracies never survive. According to the 2021 Freedom of the World Report, the last fifteen years have seen global freedom for 75 percent of the world's democratic countries on the decline. Even in our own time, we have witnessed loss of democracy as dictators took over Libya, Syria, Iraq, Afghanistan, Yemen, Congo, Colombia, and Vietnam. Major safeguards protecting our democracy have been whittled away by corporate greed removing public service and protection against polluting, one after the other. We don't think the world owes us anything because it was here first, and we are here to take care of it. We don't want to hurt others, we want to help because the giving, not the taking, makes us feel good. We don't think we have the answers for anyone else and are pleased as all get out to find satisfying answers for ourselves.

We think all of us should be free to find our own way in this world as long as we don't hurt or diminish others. Let me repeat that. AS LONG AS WE DON'T HURT OR DIMINISH ANYONE ELSE. We think everyone has value and should be helped to reach whatever reasonable positive goals they set for themselves. We believe in our constitutional rights for all in "Life, Liberty and the pursuit of Happiness." No one should be denied these rights. I repeat. No one. Yet here we bleeding-heart liberals sit, unwilling to fight as we watch our friends and loved ones vote away our freedoms. And that, my dear friends, is how easily democracies are lost.

Place Your Bets

Having grown up on them, I do love horses. Especially fast horses. Presently the Guinness World Record winner for fastest horse is a Thoroughbred named **Winning Brew**, clocking in at 43.97 mph in the 2018 Kentucky Derby. In 2019 the Kentucky Derby was won by **Rich Strike**, an underdog with the second longest odds (80-1) in racing history.

My favorite racing story is the ostrich against the horse, the ostrich usually winning. My grandmother loved to tell me stories of the ostrich farms she passed on her way into town from the farm. She said they were brought into Arizona to work the cattle. After all, they were easy to saddle, had a comfortable running walk for traveling, ate anything in sight and not so much at that, laid an egg as big as a dozen chicken eggs, and had a leg hock as big as a turkey. And they tasted like chicken. Don't forget the feathers, a rage even today. And the skin, a favorite for beautiful leather bags. The farms were gone by the time I came along. Seems the sight of an ostrich scared the cattle so bad they scattered to the four winds.

But I digress. When it comes to racing, I even love the losers. I read about **Zippy Chippy**, the horse who never won a race even after 100 tries and was barred at several racetracks because he often refused to even leave the gate. Yet he won the hearts of people like me. Not a bone of competition in us. I bet he didn't have ulcers. Or anxiety attacks.

[**Update**: Zippy died at the ripe-old age of 31 on April 15, 2022, having made a success of his life.]

Fruit Fly

Gaaa . . . they're back! I've got this neighbor, a lovely woman otherwise, who refuses to pick up fallen fruit from her many trees or allow anyone else to clean it up. Or pick it. Or...Oh, hell! I am inundated with fruit flies. It's not fun to fan them out of my face or pluck them out of my fruit juice glass. Some things I really don't want to share.

The only saving grace about these tiny insects? Like fruit season, they are short-lived. But not short enough. So I've been looking for ways to get rid of these pests.

What I discovered, however, is, like our matches to the hagfish and lamprey, we are even more closely related to the fruit fly, and, because of this matching DNA sequencing, we use them to research all kinds of ways to repair our many health issues.

Like our ancestors, the fruit fly originated in sub-Saharan Africa and left over 15,000 years ago to migrate on to the Eurasian continent. They managed to reach America a few hundred years ago to happily find a way to my juice glass.

Most important, the fruit fly is the first multi-cellular organism to have their total genetic makeup deciphered. In fact, the fruit fly shares around sixty percent of its DNA with us, along with around 75 percent of our human disease genes which could aid in finding breakthrough cures. Because they only have four pairs of chromosomes to our twenty-three pairs, traits are much easier to identify and manipulate. Much of what we learn about heart failure, autism, memory, learning, sleeping, and extending human life began with the study of fruit flies.

The heart of the fruit fly, like that of the human, has an epigenetic marker and two genes causing heart failure that can be passed on to their children. When the level of the epigenetic mark was lowered in the fruit fly, two subsequent generations had no heart problems. In another study, because 90 percent of autism sufferers experience some form of sensory difficulty, scientists have been measuring fruit fly brain responses to sensory disturbances to help us understand and, hopefully, relieve the causes of autism. Another study discovered nine genes shared in both fruit flies and humans that confirmed a difference between high and low learning abilities. Research is also looking at Sirtuin 6 (the aging and DNA repair gene) and discovered that the stronger Sirtuin 6 is, the longer we live.

Accepting our close relation to lampreys, hagfish, and fruit flies, I had to wonder about other of our brethren and found chickens match our DNA by 65 percent although other birds are much lower. Dogs match us by 84 percent; cats by 90 percent; mice by 90 percent; and pigs by 98 percent. But the most fun one is that we are 60 percent matched to the banana; there was a time we matched 100 percent. Ain't science grand!

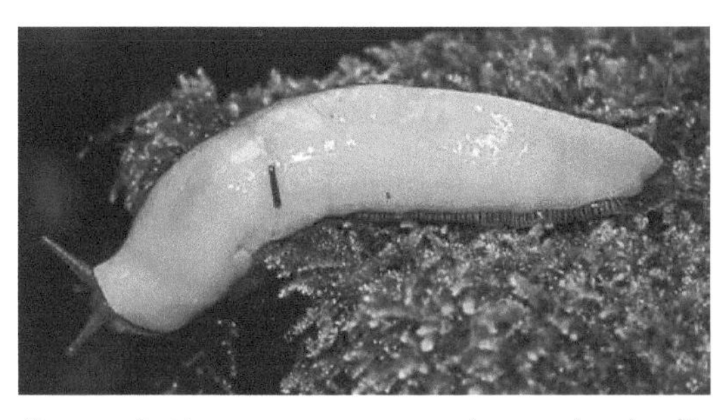

Slimy Slugs

Euuu—slimy slugs! The banana slug beats our DNA with bananas with a 70 percent match. Our relatives are everywhere, including where we step. Do be careful out there. You might step on your . . . ooops! I read where some people keep slugs as pets.

Someone described the slug as a mouth with large foot. Scarier yet, they can have as many as 27,000 replaceable teeth. They are built to deconstruct anything fresh or dead such as plants, kitchen scraps, pet food, insects, worms, and dung. They even eat each other, another reason for so many teeth. Some die at the end of a season; others live up to seven years. The slime of a banana slug contains an anesthetic that causes the mouth of the predator grabbing the slug to go numb, forcing them to drop the slug without harming it.

Oregon has ten species of pest slugs. Except for the marsh slug, the rest are exotic imports. Slugs use slime for self-defense, moving, keeping wet, and mating. Like the slimy hagfish, researchers look into the slimy slug for ways to help humans with areas of research such as robotics, investigating how slug slime and muscles control movement. Or how slime changes its consistency as it moves. Or what makes the adhesive for moving over different textures. Or whether slime can create a new type of surgical adhesive.

Unlike their relative the snail, slugs have lungs and don't need calcium to build shells. It's easier for them to travel in dirt, but the downside is no shell. They are egg-laying, transgender animals that start out as male and develop female organs as adults. Because only 5 percent of slugs eat above ground, damage to plants' root systems can be devastating. And fast. Banana slugs, second largest in the world growing up to ten inches, can travel six and a half inches a minute; the milky slug can travel as much as forty feet a night. Did I mention this was underground? This charming banana slug was found on the Oregon Coast slogging along on the Cape Falcon trail. Enjoy the action-packed video found in the source section!

One thing, if you're gonna make a pet out of a slug, remember slug slime stickiness expands with water and is hard to remove. Let the stuff dry and rub it off.

Seriously? A pet?

Here Is the First All-Female Hurricane Reconnaissance Mission!

The NOAA crew features Capt. Kristie Twining, Cmdr. Rebecca Waddington, and Lt. Lindsey Norman.

"It might be easier to find your way home on a lighted path, but life is so much grander when you can light that way for someone else."

– Robert Clancy

September 2019

Moles

I once read eating live lampreys killed England's King Henry I. What did he expect! I also read William III was killed when his horse stepped in a mole hole, flipped, and broke his neck. I'm hoping for a better result from the humps of dirt surrounding me whenever I go outside, as I watch them multiplying at an alarming rate. So, I looked up moles and found more trivia than you want to know.

The word "mole" comes from the Old English word "mouldywarp," which means dirt thrower. They got that right. I also found out they are the world's best tunneler; like miners following a paystreak, moles dig a tube-like labyrinth of highways, byways, freeways, hallways, and subways to make a home, often covering the size of a football field. They have grocery stores, bedrooms, bathrooms, dining rooms, pantries, storerooms, and even, according to scientists, fortresses. Unless they have been told by a cranky parent that they are now grown and it's time to dig a new hole to the surface to find their own place to tunnel a home, they never see the sun. Or any light. And although they do have small beady eyes, they are nearly blind. They live underground mostly alone their whole lives with no doors, windows, and no fresh air. They require little oxygen. The mole never gets too hot or cold. Imagine never paying a utility bill. With no opening to the top, the mole can't be caught or even smelled by predators, and nobody comes knocking.

So what are those mounds of dirt? Never an entrance or exit, they are dump holes through which the mole pushes the dirt up and out of the tunnel being built. The mole can dig 65 feet a day, move 400 times its weight in dirt, and push 30 times its weight uphill. Comparing this would be like Hercules weightlifting eight bulls above his head.

Cylindrical in shape for easy access through tube tunnels, the mole looks like a digging potato, showing no legs, necks, or ears. Whenever a mole needs to turn around, it folds in half and somersaults. Blows my mind to realize this potato can dig miles of elaborate tunnels using hands with huge claws. The bumps covering the snout bumps and known as Eimer's organs act like our index finger. It touches to identify slugs, bugs, and worms to eat. The mole also has incredible whiskers which can pick up the teeniest vibration, especially from crawling worms overhead, the mole's favorite food. Its snout has 44 teeth, all needed to eat over 100 worms a day to equal 70 percent of its body weight.

So why do they need pantries? They gather and store extra worms by biting off their heads and shoving them into the dirt walls in their pantries. A worm can regrow a head in eight days, but the paralysis from the mole's toxic bite lasts a few months. That gives the mole plenty of time to set the table and pour a glass of wine.

I've been studying ways to get rid of my mole. Trouble is, I've built up such an admiration, I'm thinking of keeping it around just to count the mounds. Or I could wait four years (average mole lifespan) for the mole to die.

(Thanks to Rachel Poliquin for *Moles*, her hilarious and informative book for young readers.)

"And into the forest I go to lose my mind and find my soul." – John Muir

Whenever Serendipity catches up with me, the roller coaster ride is worth it. That happened to me when a friend sent me a link to the Yakona Nature Preserve. Coincidentally, I was boarding the *Discovery* the same day for a trip up the Yaquina River cruising along that same preserve.

Located where the Yaquina Bay narrows to become Yaquina River, this 250-acre peninsula was bought by Bill and JoAnn Barton in 2012 and turned into a forest sanctuary as a living laboratory on coastal ecosystems. I am reminded of Albert Einstein's view on nature. "Our task must be to free ourselves by widening our circle of compassion to embrace all living creatures and the whole of nature and its beauty." The Bartons envisioned a nature preserve, day-use public park, and education center. They hope to introduce the public to the area's flora and fauna and its rich history, including the lost Yakona tribe and the glory days of the development of the Yaquina River settlements.

This peninsula was home to the Yakona tribe as early as 1,000 BC, when they foraged for water and the rich food between Beaver Creek and Cape Foulweather. This tribe deliberately flattened their foreheads with wooden blocks, earning the name "Flathead" so that they would be easily identified to gain a higher seat at the table in the hereafter. Unfortunately, the European settlers brought so many diseases that 80 percent of the defenseless Yakona were quickly wiped out. In addition, the Hudson Bay Company mistakenly blamed the Yakona for the death of two trappers and slaughtered even more of them. By the end of the 1890s, only eighty remained.

Four decades earlier, the government created the Siletz Reservation, 102 miles of coastline between the Siuslaw and Umpqua rivers and going inland twenty miles. The treaty was never ratified, and the unified tribes, including the Yakona, met at Yaquina Bay and signed away their rights and the homes of their children.

Many other native treasures were also destroyed and/or lost over the years in the march for civilization such as small, delicious oysters and the Sitka spruce tree used for the manufacture of airplanes during World War I. Only six Sitka spruce still stand, each over ten feet in diameter.

Back to my serendipitous moment. I found myself on this amazing cruise boat among delightful people eating delicious catered food and watching the beautiful scenery. Absolute heaven as I watched sea lions sunning on the rocks and green, green pine trees spreading out forever. I was on a fundraiser for children at the Samaritan House Homeless Shelter. How is it possible, I asked myself, for the richest nation on the earth to have over eleven million of its children going to bed hungry with two and a half million of those homeless. That was my serendipitous moment. I ask you to help wherever you can.

Losing Weight

Last week my good, long-time friends from Arizona visited me and turned me onto a watch-like counting toy (no name I can find). I was impressed with all it can do—count steps, miles, and calories; record temperature, heart rate, and blood pressure; measure how long you sleep; tell time; and more. Wow! Who wouldn't want it. Now that I have replaced both knees and both hips plus surviving two back operations, I'll be on an exercise regime to overcome five years of not walking so that I can get back to my beloved beaches. Amazon woman, here I come!

This device arrived in two days, and I immediately fastened it on my arm, walked a few circles, checked how many steps, checked my blood pressure and heart rate, and thought, wow, what a bargain. All this for fifty bucks, although I was a little put off that I had to swing my arm as I walked to count my steps, rather inconvenient when I'm pushing a walker.

Wait...there's more. You know when you try to cook something you have never cooked before, and you can't find the recipe and maybe half of the ingredients are missing? Along with your mind? I'm one of those people who gets lost and refuses to stop and ask directions or I ignore the written directions and jump right in having no idea what I'm doing.

I'm sure you have a relative somewhere like me when the more we're told how wrong we are, the more determined we're right. Wondering how to set the time and stopwatch along with tracking my steps day by day, I pick up the teeny manual with its teeny unreadable words and read, "Search Google Play, Ying Yong Bao." What the...really? Then it tells me I need to operate this item through a cellphone. Not my computer or Kindle reader. A cellphone.

I have lost track of the hours I have spent charging my rarely used phone, attempting to find the app and download it only to read, "Your phone is a piece of crap." Maybe not those exact words but you get the drift. Back to Amazon.

Admiring the new Samsung 10, I move on and order a used refurbished Samsung 6 for a hundred bucks (because I'm cheap), to replace my Samsung 3, really heartbreaking because I love my old phone. Mainly because I know how to use it. So now I'm beginning to wonder how far I could have walked, and money saved if I'd kept to manual counting. I guess this is another one of those "Suck it up" moments that life so kindly delivers with a gentle warning ---- PAY ATTENTION!

P.S. I still love my friends.

"Turns out, the most beautiful things in my life were never on my to-do list." - Rachel Hollis

October 2019

Rosh Hashanah

I do love "feel good moments"; here's one of them. I'm not Jewish although I admire many of their traditions. This one part of Rosh Hashanah called Tashlikh means "cast away." The tradition began in the thirteenth century to the consternation of religious leaders who worried such rituals were not up to snuff. They especially opposed throwing bread or sending "sin-filled" baskets into water. Or jumping in and swimming to be cleansed of sins. Even shaking away any evil clinging to one's clothes. They finally gave in and accepted the "tossing of bread on the waters" ritual.

Here's how it works. Before sunset on the first day of Rosh Hashanah (check a calendar), find a body of running water, preferably one containing fish, and throw pieces of bread into the water. Throw your sins and guilts with the bread. If you don't have a running stream, use a hose in a bucket or bowl. And if you can't find bread to toss, you can use cake.

I like to bake a loaf of challah bread for the ceremony because I like to braid it. And nothing smells or tastes better than fresh baked bread. Leave your dog at home. Last year mine ate the pieces before they could hit the water.

Some people see Tashlikh as a bonding time for women to gather and open to truths about our lives, our community, and how we have grown and supported each other.

November 2019

Undersea Gardens

As sad as I am that the Undersea Gardens had to go, watching her waddle up the river like a pregnant elephant was an entertaining sight. She had two tugboats, one pulling and the other occasionally pushing her back into the channel. As she jostled about, she seemed to have a life of her own like she really didn't want to go. After forty-six years of battering by storms, leaks, mildew, and old age wear and tear, she was still beautiful. According to rumor, the empty hole left by the Undersea Garden will be a parking lot. And her carcass will be decommissioned (aka destroyed).

The tourist attraction opened in 1966 as a "people-quarium"—the bay's marine life outside and visitors inside. At least the over 1,000 living creatures in her bubble found good homes. Some spiny dog sharks and invertebrates went to the Oregon Coast Aquarium, other animals to the Hatfield Marine Center, and still more back home to the sea.

The first time I visited Undersea Gardens I needed a second tour. The octopus had just emitted a great black cloud, obscuring everything. The spewing ink is its defense, blinding the threat while the octopus swims away. It contains a compound called tyrosinase which, along with being harmful to a predator, causes temporary blindness and loss of smell and taste. The effects of the potent ink can kill the octopus if it doesn't get out of the way.

An egg layer leaves thousands of tiny white floating dots. Laying eggs begins the female's slow march toward death. They stop eating, dedicating themselves entirely to guarding their clutch, and eventually waste away. The males don't get off any easier—they die shortly after mating.

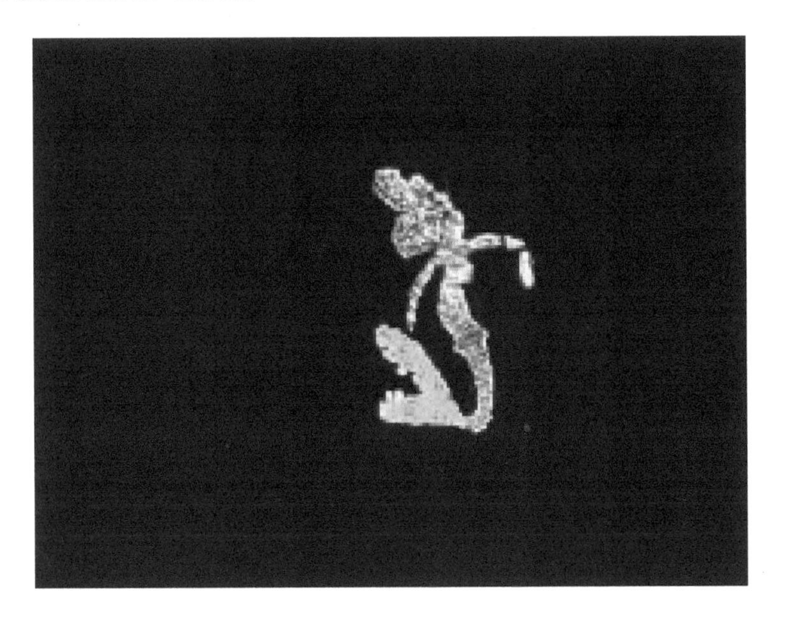

Christmas Lights

Once again, the whimsical lighted boats parade their Christmas lights. I spent the evening with dear friends who have collected the most gorgeous display of Christmas lights. Unfortunately, they live the hell and gone up Beaver Creek and down a country lane called S-Low Road, aptly called Slow Road because it is very slow. My photo can't do the lights even close to justice, but I will always have my memories.

"**The Importance of Being Held** ~The average length of a hug between two people is three seconds. But researchers have discovered something fantastic. When a hug lasts twenty seconds, there is a therapeutic effect on the body and mind. The reason is that a sincere embrace produces a hormone called 'oxytocin,' also known as the love hormone. This substance has many benefits in our physical and mental health. It helps us, among other things, to relax, feel safe, and calm our fears and anxiety. This wonderful tranquilizer is offered free of charge every time the closer we get to someone, have a person in our arms, cradle a child, cherish a dog or a cat, dance with our partner, or simply hold the shoulders of a friend."

– Lorraine Cannistra, *Sacred Dreams*

Current Day Yaquina Bay
Fishing Fleet

Yaquina Bay Fishing Fleet
August 21, 1931

Part III – 2020 – The Pandemic

No one knew a world-wide devastating disaster would consume the year 2020.

"Gonna ask my momma if that offer to slap me into next year is still on the table."

– Tiisha Simms

"We are at our best when we serve others. Be civilized."

– Ira Byock

Oregon Coastal Forests Are the Best:

We are lucky that our coastal range and our beaches have little to seriously hurt you as long as you have no life-threatening allergies. We don't have rattlesnakes or any other poisonous snakes. We don't have the dangerous grizzly bear. We do have black bears, cougars, raccoons, skunks, elk, deer, and a few other animals such as rabbits and squirrels. Do remember not to get between a mama bear and her cub or a mama anything no matter how cute they are. Mother love is a strong protective emotion in most living creatures.

Have a good time and don't get lost. If you do, head north or south to find a stream to follow to the sea. Remember moss always grows on the north side of the tree. Take plenty of food and water. A special warning—keep your kids off the logs on the beach, especially after a storm. You never know when a sneaker wave will roll a log over in only four-inch water, pinning them underneath, drowning them. Go prepared and have a way to notify people.

Animals

Black bears are the only bear living in Oregon, and not one has killed a person in the state's history. They can become aggressive with a lot of menacing hopping toward you and back again when threatened or scenting food. Keep your food and garbage locked away. If you're in the wilderness, make noise to let them know you are there so they will avoid you.

Cougars usually stay hidden. If you come upon one, stand your ground, maintain eye contact, speak loudly, and use your arms to make yourself appear larger. If the big cat attacks, the ODFW recommends you "fight back with rocks, sticks, garden tools or any other items available." Cougar attacks occur much less frequently than fatal lightning strikes or fatal bee stings. Such an attack has never occurred on the Oregon coastal range or beaches.

Skunks, typically docile creatures, will leave you alone if you give them the same courtesy. Just in case, here is a remedy for de-skunking. Pour a bottle of hydrogen peroxide in a large bowl; add one-fourth cup of baking soda or vinegar and 1 teaspoon of dish soap. Mix with your hands, hop in shower, and scrub away. **This solution is safe for skin and hair for a few minutes only.** Keep out of eyes because it will sting really bad.

Spiders

Oregon has no reported deaths from spider bites. A few species in the state can hurt, but these are more likely to be in a basement, and behind rubbish rather than the forest. Spiders are rarely seen because they prefer dark, dry, quiet places. Be mindful while exploring old and abandoned buildings.

Yellow sac and hobo spider bites can be painful, but the black widow spider may require medical attention, leading to "abdominal muscle cramps, nausea, profuse perspiration, tremors, fever, labored breathing, and restlessness." The coast has no brown recluse spiders. Or, FYI, cockroaches.

Poisonous Plants:

Stinging nettle may not be toxic but contact can cause short-lived severe burning sensation. Watch for jagged leaves with tiny hairs' remove needles with tape.

The death cap mushroom looks very much like our common white button or cremini mushroom. The most feared of all toxic mushrooms, it causes gastrointestinal chaos, liver shutdown, and kidney failure before death. It's best identified by its yellowish cap and white gills, but don't try identification yourself without a lot of training.

Western poison ivy, unlike its Eastern counterpart, grows as a shrub that can reach three feet tall. If you touch one, change clothes as soon as possible, and rinse or shower with large amounts of cool water, no soap, to get rid of the poison. Keep the clothes in a plastic bag to wash separately. You can treat the rash with calamine lotion or a solution of baking soda and water. These provide comfort but do not actually cure the rash. To avoid painful rashes, heed that old adage: leaves of three, let it be . . .

Deadly nightshade, a lovely but lethal small black fruit, grows within star-shaped leaves. It's especially dangerous for kids and pets. Do not force vomiting, but drink plenty of water, wash hands thoroughly with soap, and seek treatment for poisoning.

Poison Hemlock can cause rashes, rapid heartbeat, nausea, paralysis of the central nervous system, and death if you eat it. The poison has no antidote. Wild carrot, also known as Queen Anne's Lace, can be mistaken for poison hemlock. It isn't as dangerous, but leaves can cause rashes and blisters.

Food in the Forest

Before you leave home, charge your phone and download a GPS. On your walk, mark your path and notice such landmarks as broken trees. If you plan on hiking far, take an axe, knife, plastic bags, and a large trash bag to carry your bounty. Don't forget your water. And it won't hurt to take along a compass, matches, cheap plastic raincoat, good hiking boots, short length of duct tape, and energy bar or nuts.

Bark: Highly nutritional, people can also easily store the bark. Don't kill the tree; just cut narrow vertical two-inch strips. Find firs and pines—trees with needles. The outer bark is not edible. Scrap off the tender white meat between the outer bark and the inner trunk and boil it. Eating raw bark can give you stomach cramps.

Pine Needles: You can make tea by dicing them into the smallest possible pieces and dropping them into a cup of boiling water. Let steep for several minutes until the water turns a yellow-green color, like green tea. Strain out the needles and drink up.

Pine and Fir Cone Nuts: These are available from late August through October. Scour the ground for open, round pinecones and then dig out the seeds to eat.

Edible Ferns, Or Fiddleheads: The two edible varieties in the Pacific Northwest, the bracken fern and the lady fern, taste like a cross between asparagus and young spinach.

Edible Weeds: A few safe ones are dandelion, cattail, lamb's quarter, miner's lettuce, chicory, and sorrel. Dandelions are actually flowers, not weeds, and a highly nutritious plant loaded with vitamins and minerals. Every part of the dandelion is edible. I tried cattail once and spent a couple of hours trying to make flour for flat bread. This became one of those times when you had to be hungry enough to eat anything, but I had a good time anyway.

Wild Berries: The color red is nature's symbol for "Stop right there!" If you're not an expert, do follow it. Edible berries usually grow in clusters: blackberry, huckleberry, and blueberry.

Food to Store

Maybe it's time for each of us to prepare for the next "Stay in Place" edict and hope for the best. Do avoid the "Stand Your Ground" Syndrome and don't get shot at. Or avoid the "Alice in Wonderland Syndrome." Or just jump in the rabbit hole with Alice before the world distorts into a place we don't recognize.

In gathering the best food to last, I learned that "expiration date" means nothing. It only indicates what the manufacturer decided is when it's generally past the peak. So, I developed a set of general rules.

Vinegars, vanilla, sugar, salt, molasses, corn syrup, and honey will last forever.

If I go with packaged foods, I do instant oats or grits, refined white flour, and white rice. Dry beans, lentils, and pastas will also hold up with time. Unrefined foods still have fat content which turns rancid. Breads and nuts should be frozen to last a long time.

Glass lasts for a year. Check the top of glass containers for the telling bulge or rusting.

Plastics are the worst because they are gas-permeable and should only be kept a few months.

Eggs, amazingly so, are quite long lasting, up to three months when refrigerated.

Milk, one of my main staples, has always been a toughie so look for the "UHT" (ultrahigh Temperature) on the carton. Usually on most organic brands, this milk is pasteurized at a higher temperature than other milk, 275 degrees Fahrenheit, which destroys all viruses and bacteria. The milk is then aseptically pumped and sealed into cartons.

If you meet Alice before I do, say Hey.

Hatfield Tsunami/Earthquake Building

Named the Gladys Valley Marine Studies Building, this new science center from Oregon State University is almost done. OSU is one of only two universities working on current environmental problems, making this new building even more essential. Gladys Valley was a famous alumnus of Oregon State University where she met

her husband, Wayne Valley. She graduated in 1931 and was a secretary in the science department for eight years. Late in the 1940s, the Valleys moved to the California bay area and became one of the largest home builders in California. She never forgot her school. For over seventy years Gladys left her legacy as student, staff member, and benefactor.

Expected to handle over five hundred new students in the classrooms and labs for continuing research, this uniquely designed building will also save the lives of the hundreds of people working on that flat piece of sandy land. Everyone working at Hatfield, NOAA, and the Oregon Aquarium have only 15 minutes to get to safety. The last major tsunami/earthquake was in January 1700, and the next one is expected 300 years after that date. Designed to withstand a 9.0 earthquake and subsequent tsunami, the building will

handle 900 people on its roof. An access ramp joins stairs and elevators, leading everyone to the top.

[Update: The building was finished in 2020.]

Gladys Valley Marine Studies Building at night

March 2020

Toilet Paper, a New Worry in the "Supply Chain"

When stores run out of toilet paper, try smiling with the comments below!

> "Success is like toilet paper - it only seems important when you don't have it." – Richard Jeni
>
> "I've learned that life is like a roll of toilet paper. The closer it gets to the end, the faster it goes." – Andy Rooney
>
> "Problems are like toilet paper. You pull on one and ten more come." – Woody Allen
>
> "My aunt in Knoxville would bring newspapers up, which we used for toilet paper. Before we used it, we'd look at the pictures." – Dolly Parton

This one's not so funny. Just interesting. "Before you rip off three feet of toilet paper, consider that each year 500,000 acres of virgin boreal forest in northern Alberta and Ontario are being clear-cut to make the stuff. These forests are home to some 500 First Nation communities, as well as caribou and bears, moose and wolves, and, in the summertime, billions of songbirds." – Alex Shoumatoff

April 2020

Food Lines

Oh my God! How long can we depend on the kindness of others for food? What happens when they run out? Many people in the lines waiting to get to food pantries say this was the first time they were ever in a food line They never ever expected to be there.

Mass Graves

I cannot explain the powerful effect this mass grave photo had on me—reminiscent of the Holocaust. It was taken on Hart Island, New York, after the city became overwhelmed by the huge number of "unclaimed" deaths from COVID, meaning that no one hired a private funeral director for a burial. The number of people buried during the pandemic may be ten percent of the people who died of the coronavirus.

I am a changed person because of the photograph. I will always be very grateful for the "stay in place" edict from our governor. Thank you, Kate Brown, for trying to take care of us. You have saved hundreds, if not thousands, of lives.

Post office - Newport, Oregon

Politics:

Save Our Post Office:

I grew up in the middle of the southern Arizona desert in a town of 1,500, depending on the next birth or death. I still recall the thrill when I was twelve years old and was allowed to go the post office for the first time by myself.

Once I even rode along with my Uncle Harold who had the second longest mail route in the United States. It was exciting until the afternoon summer sun heated our refrigeration-less car to 114 degrees on the outside while we traveled over 150 miles from one cactus to another. He made this drive six days a week for forty years. He was my hero, a keystone sentinel supporting the human truth that "neither snow nor rain nor heat nor gloom of night stays these couriers from the swift completion of their appointed rounds."

Ever accommodating, Arizona mail still has delivery by mule train into the Grand Canyon. The post office in Peach Springs, Arizona, had a walk-in freezer for food deliveries. Even though street delivery started in 1863, I still enjoy my trips to the post office.

Although social media, email, and texting have made an incredible difference in communication, the postal services remain our major system to connect, one we can always depend on, one that provides a major stabilizing force in all our lives. Considering the tragic events around us, God knows we could use a stable force.

A bit of history explains how easy it is to lose one of our treasured foundations, i.e., even an actual Cabinet department. The USPS was born in 1792, with Article 1, section 8, Clause 7, "to establish post offices and post roads." Benjamin Franklin was appointed the first Postmaster General of the United States Postal Service and got a whopping $1,000 a year to build the post office services from Massachusetts to Georgia. Originally, senders didn't pay for mailing items; the recipient had to pay. The first postal stamps issued on July 1, 1847, cost five and ten cents, and by 1855, this revenue supported the USPS. The Postmaster General joined the President's Cabinet in 1829, but that position disappeared under Richard Nixon in 1971. A law moved the postal service to the Executive Branch, and that, ladies and gentlemen, is how easily a public service can be set up for sell-off and bring about the death of a presidential Cabinet department.

So, what happens to the money you and I spend for postal services? According to the 2010 OIG report, the agency paid out $12 billion to private businesses: FedEx got the most ($1.37 billion) to provide air transport and delivery overseas; tech supplier Northrop Grumman got $494 million; and UPS, $95 million. The rest of the $12 billion went to outside rental payments, purchases, outsourcing, and contracts to private corporations such as consolidators, pre-sort companies, and mailers like Amazon—all losses to the post office and to you and me as we watch money leaking by the billions to our new "business partners." And the rich got richer.

Big business, however, needed one more push to drive the USPS into bankruptcy so that what was left could be sold. Lo and behold, George W. Bush rode the elephant into the room when he signed the Postal Accountability and Enhancement Act (PAEA), requiring USPS to save an annual $5.5 billion up front covering future health care cost for retired workers until 2056—that's 50 years into the future. According to a report from the Institute for Policy Studies: "This extraordinary mandate, which applies to no other federal agency or private corporation, created a financial 'crisis' that has been used to justify harmful service cuts and even calls for postal privatization." Without Bush's law, the USPS would be solvent in spite of the selloffs. Even during Bush's recession, the worst in 80 years, the post office revenue was $611 million in the black.

Roy Ulrich from AlterNet had a clear explanation why this business model doesn't work for operating governments: "The idea that a businessman would make the best president—or governor or other political leaders—is bogus. Some of the biggest presidential failures—Warren Harding, Herbert Hoover, and Andrew Johnson—were successful businessmen. The entire focus of business is making a profit while government provides the foundation for businesses—building infrastructure, educating, and defending people, and supporting industry. Business leaders have no 'separation of powers' or 'checks and balances' while these are the bases for democracy. Business leaders worry only about profit advantages for their own companies, but presidents are responsible to the entire world, not a finite group of shareholders, investors, and employees. The wrong words by a president can drive down the stock market or cause military conflicts—even wars."

I wonder which Cabinet department will be next. Interior? Education? Either one could be hugely profitable to big business. Or what major service? Social Security? Medicare? Police? Fire? My bet is on Social Security. For the sake of us all, the next time you vote, Republican or Democrat, make sure your vote doesn't go to just another business shill.

Do you remember before the internet it was thought the cause of collective stupidity was the lack of access to information? Well...it wasn't that.

May 2020

Politics:

The Republican Platform

I wrote this to a teenage boyfriend who found me seventy years later. He's now a born-again Christian obsessed with Donald Trump. He wrote me often attempting to convert me until I sent him this reply. I did not hear from him again. I kind of miss our discussions.

Beyond children forever lost to their parents, climate deniers, and judicial incompetence, or rampant pollution from deregulations, and the destruction of marine life from ocean warming and pollution, I am pissed about big business partnering with far-right religious zealots legitimizing tax cuts for the rich, starting wars to get conservatives reelected, and refusing money needed for social programs.

I cannot figure out the conservative platform beyond their strange self-identified far-right morality such as denying women free choice in most everything and promoting bigotry among some white men against anything. They syphon off our taxes by privatizing and profiteering such as the housing of border immigrants in tents at the outrageous cost of $755 per person per day, the same as the cost of one night in a Trump hotel. Republicans promise fiscal responsibility and smaller government while, at the same time, every time, expanded the government and spending.

I'm nostalgic when remembering the Republican party from the past, that party I was part of. I'm talking about Eisenhower's Republicans who "supported workers for equal pay for equal work, worker safety, higher wages, union expansion, trust-busting, and anti-monopoly laws." The 1956 GOP platform came out in favor of the United Nations, school desegregation, stronger Social Security, and national health care. The 1956 GOP platform wanted "an immigration policy in keeping with the traditions of America by providing a haven for oppressed peoples based on equality of treatment; freedom from implications of discrimination among racial, nationality and religious groups; and flexible enough to conform to changing needs and conditions." Other parts of the GOP platform stated, "America does not prosper unless all Americans prosper" and "we recommend to Congress the submission of a constitutional amendment providing equal rights for men and women."

As far as I can figure, I have nothing in common with the new Republicans who have nothing in common with any party ever formed. I was a Republican until the early 1960s when the two parties swapped sides and Eisenhower's Republican platform became Kennedy's Democratic plat-form. I grew up with the old-time Republicans, and I surely do miss them. And that's why I'm pissed!

Sea Lions

I have often seen our sea lions rest in large groups with a flipper up the air. I looked it up and found a process called thermoregulation. Their capillaries are close to the surface of the skin and catch sunbeams to warm the body. To cool down, they put their flippers into the water before raising them back up into the air, using evaporation to cool them off. Called "sailing," this behavior often leads people to believe the animal has been injured or ill. The sea lions get reported to authorities as an injured orca or whale.

M/V *Bluefin* Buoy Repair/Replace Ship

A recent visitor to the NOAA dock is the *Bluefin,* privately owned by a company called North Wind Inc. The company operates sports, recreation, and amusement services and rents out to anyone with the money. Presently, she's dropping and repairing NOAA tsunami, hurricane, and weather buoys. The *Bluefin* goes from buoy to buoy, generally 300 to 500 miles apart, that will hopefully giving forty-five minutes after the shake to get out of the tsunami's way, a lifesaver longer than the usual fifteen minutes. The *Bluefin* had just repaired Dutch Harbor's buoy when the warning activated, giving the whole town time to get to the hills. The tsunami never materialized, but the warning worked!

According to Captain Mark, the trip starts in Seattle. "We go up the coast of Canada, round Gulf of Alaska; will generally stop in Kodiak, Dutch, or Adak—we've stopped in all three in the last three years. We will be servicing all the buoys along the way. Once we depart the Alaska Port we follow the coast over to Russia, The Philippines, on down to Guam, it's generally our next stop. Then we will usually hit American Samoa after that, and service all buoys down there. We have stopped in Tahiti on occasion and the Galapagos on occasion; it sounds like we will stop in this year. Then we will shoot over to Hawaii and handle all buoys around the Hawaiian Islands. Next we will head down off the coast of the South end of Central America, we will then proceed North stopping in to San Diego next heading north to cover buoys off the California, Oregon, Washington Coast. On the last leg we end up back in Seattle, this route generally takes four to five months."

"My wife purchased a world map, gave me a dart, and said, 'Throw this, and wherever it lands, I'm taking you for a holiday when this pandemic is over.' Turns out we're spending two weeks behind the fridge."

First Auto Trip up the Coast from Newport

Once upon a time in the early 1900s, Newport's Commercial Club, mama to today's Chamber of Commerce, was fed up with the way the world ignored Newport and decided to drive a car from Newport to the Siletz River and back as a publicity stunt to attract traffic to Newport. They overlooked the fact that Newport wasn't much accessible with a car. Highway 20 was passable just a few months a year, and the only car going north and south had to travel along a treacherous beach with soft sand spots left by ocean waves that would suck up a car in minutes. People got to Newport by boat down the Yaquina River.

Yet the Commercial Club talked a Studebaker dealer from Portland into handing them a fine Flanders 20 touring car for the first-ever car trip from Newport to the Siletz River. With a winch on the bumper, the car was loaded with picks, axes, saws, shovels, gas, oil, food, and, luckily, blackberry brandy, and beer. Nothing but the best. On a Saturday morning, July 20, 1912, the Commercial Club "pathfinders" left Newport on a trip where no car had been before and apparently scared the crap out of watchers along its path. Reminds me of when my dad talked about the first car he ever saw. It scared his older brother so bad he grabbed his sister and youngest brother, ran into the house, and shoved them under the bed. Dad said he stood his ground, mainly because he was too scared to run.

First Auto Trip up the Coast from Newport, Continued

After I mentioned the trip between Newport and the Siletz River, a friend kindly sent me a booklet about this trip called "Pathfinder." According to records of the trip, "the start was made at 7:35 Saturday morning from the Abbey Hotel, and the car proceeded up the beach to Otter Creek, 10 miles, where the real work began." They climbed Bald Knob at 550 feet with 1½ miles of axle deep mud filled with stumps. With all brakes set, it was a wild ride to the bottom at Rock Creek, across its rickety bridge and finally onto the beach to a road from nowhere to nowhere. They traveled at forty miles an hour for three miles on a road made from Indian shell mounds, finally stopped by Fogarty Creek."

The photos in the book alone are awesome. The tour from Newport to Siletz River and back took twenty-three hours;

they dug, sawed, pushed, pulled, and swore almost every yard of the way.

According to Jack Fogarty, the first car to arrive in Newport from Toledo came on the foredeck of his steamer *Truant.* The Commercial Club had to wait another fifteen years before the trail they blazed was traveled again. A touring car owned by Pacific Telephone and Telegraph did appear in April 1911 with both vehicle and passengers covered in mud from driving the now Highway 20. Not until the opening of the Yaquina Bridge on September 6, 1936, however, was Newport really discovered by cars. That and the imaginary trip from Newport to Boston on Highway 20 made me ponder all things car.

> **Nobody is angrier than an old white guy in a blue suit who gets treated the way that the system treats everyone else. – Ken White**

Highway 20

Every time I turn the corner onto Highway 20 from Highway 101 on my way home, I read on a little green sign that Boston is 3,365 miles. Why in the world would I care how far Boston is? So I looked up Highway 20 and found out that it's really, really famous. Here in my own little town, who knew?

I've heard driving Highway 20 is on some people's bucket list, although even if I had one, it wouldn't be on mine mainly because I'm not a very good traveler. I did beat out my father who never got out of the state of Arizona where he was born except for a trip to San Diego to get my sick mother out of the heat, and a ride he caught with a friend delivering a load of cattle to Lordsberg, New Mexico, just to say he had. But if I did have a bucket list, Route 66 would be on mine.

What's so great about Highway 20? For starters, I would cross a dozen states—Oregon, Idaho, Montana, Wyoming, Nebraska, Iowa, Illinois, Indiana, Ohio, Pennsylvania, New York, and Massachusetts. A bit of history told me Route 20 coming from the East Coast became a U.S. highway in 1926, terminating at Yellowstone Park. In 1940, it continued westward, often paralleling I-90 until it reached the Pacific Ocean in 1960. Today Highway 20 travels through famous cities, sweet towns, and a whole lot of beautiful scenery.

Starting from the Pacific Ocean at Newport, Oregon, a traveler can visit both lighthouses, walk fabulous wide beaches, and wander tide pools teeming with sea life. Plus trips to the aquarium, Hatfield Marine Science Center, and beer-tasting at our world-famous brewery Rogue Ale. Over the coastal range, Willamette Valley has 250 wineries. Do spend the night somewhere.

From there I crossed the Cascade Mountain Range through Santiam Pass to Bend where I stayed a few days and got spit on by a llama. The trip after that turns desolate mile after mile reminiscent of Shelley's poem "Ozymandias," "where the lone and level sands stretch far away." I left Highway 20 where Highway 20 joins U.S. 26 in Vale to the Idaho border and headed south for a tour around Oregon.

If I had stayed on Highway 20, my next stop would be Idaho with massive ocean-like lava flows in a place called the Craters of the Moon National Monument. At Hagerman Fossil Beds I might have found a mastodon bone or eaten one of their famous potatoes, my favorite food. The Idaho Potato Museum has a huge array of potato peelers.

Montana doesn't take long. Ten miles later on U.S. 20 is Wyoming with Yellowstone National Park's energy exploding in the hot springs, bubbling mud-pots, and geothermal weirdness of the geysers. The Historic Trails Interpretive Center describes the history of settling the prairie before the road passes through Wind River Canyon where the shifting of tectonic plates formed amazing landscapes. I like canyons, especially the time I rafted down the Grand Canyon, overwhelmed by the way the river had carved out a mile deep crevice.

Ashfall Fossil Beds State Historic Parks in Nebraska with its active research and dig sites goes back twelve million years with bones of strange creatures.

Highway 20 enters Iowa at Sioux City and the Lewis and Clark Interpretive Center. Next on the potential places to visit is where the kicky movie *Field of Dreams* was filmed. You're supposed to drive until you find the cornfields, maybe staring into the corn stalks waiting, hoping "They will come."

Illinois, watch out, woman driver on the bridge. I've been on the Mississippi River in a riverboat at New Orleans but not crossed it on a bridge. When I think of Illinois, I remember architect Frank Lloyd Wright, the most famous person I ever met. When he was in his eighties, I went to his architect school at Taliesin West to pick up a friend. I sat at a table with Mr. Wright and thought he was a kind man. I will not mention the behavior of his young blond wife. The drive through Chicago would remind me of the icy few days I spent there, facing the winds off the lake.

On to Indiana where I would stop in Gary where Michael Jackson lived for his first ten years. I admired his talent even when he turned stupid. Next, the RV and Motorhome Hall of Fame displays new inventions for better living on the road. In Newport we call them land whales. Built in the middle of Amish land, I find the juxtaposition between fancy motor homes and horse-drawn buggies to be strange bedfellows. Nothing, however, was more striking than watching ten horses tied together plowing a field.

Just west of Columbia, Ohio, Highway 20 heads east to Cleveland and the Rock 'n' Roll Hall of Fame, taking me back to my teenage years when every Saturday night found us rocking and rolling in a big barn known as River Bottom. It was a dry river bottom. Except when it rained.

The trip through Pennsylvania, like Montana, is pretty short, a 45-mile trip beside a bunch of Great Lakes. Highway 20 also goes parallel to a well-traveled CSX railway line also serving Amtrak. Reminds me of all the fun I've had racing trains.

Most of my visits in New York have been along the Hudson River and in New York City. I would enjoy visiting Harriet Tubman's home and the Baseball Hall of Fame. A stop in Seneca Falls to see where the home of the first convention to advance women's rights is a must. In Massachusetts, Highway 20 is called the Boston Post Road because it carried mail between New York and Boston in the seventeenth century. The road treks through Old Sturbridge Village, a living history of New England from the 1790s through the 1830s where volunteers dress in period clothing and re-enact historical times. In Boston, I would like to rest at the Old North Church, famous for one of the few Revolutionary War sites still with us. Reminds me of Paul Revere's "one if by land, two if by sea."

And there it is—that funny green sign that reads Newport, Oregon 3,365 miles. It was an informative trip, but I'll stick with my usual trek around Newport and call it a day.

Today (May 27) My Twin Brother Died

He was the last of my beautiful, wonderful, loving three brothers. The photo with my twin reflects our different personalities.

Nicknamed Sunny, he was always good-natured, happy, and I was always objecting and questioning something.

My Brothers

Left to right: Rusty, Sunny, me, and Poop. I'm not repeating my nickname. Known as the Hardesty brothers in their farming and dairy days, they were listed in the phone book by their legal names. I would often get phone calls asking which one was Poop, or Rusty, or Sunny. They were the best brothers anyone could have, loving to laugh and tease. Sometimes too much, but now I'm glad they did. So many wonderful heartwarming memories. I always knew they were there and had my back. Knowing they aren't there anymore has left a huge hole.

Poop liked to play hard, sometimes giggling like a little girl. It took him five years to graduate high school at the same time as Rusty, his brother one year younger who graduated with honors and was the school's outstanding athlete. (Rusty and Sunny never did anything wrong.)

Sunny Rusty Poop Me

Poop's last year was spent mostly in shop, building, he claimed, a farm roust-a-bout.

On the last day he sneaked in a jalopy body, dropped it on the four wheels and sped away with the shop teaching running after him hollering, "That's not supposed to be a car."

On their graduation day in a small school auditorium, Rusty was giving a speech on stage, and Poop got giggly drunk with a friend, the bottle hidden under their gowns.

He broke out of the procession line, left the ceremony, and climbed over seats to get to my mother. "Here," he said, handing his diploma to her. "You earned it." Climbing over more seats, he disappeared out the back door, still giggling.

My Mom and Dad

They went through the same school in a small southern Arizona town where all of us kids attended school. Marrying soon after high school graduation, they are sitting in an old and yellow Ford later restored by a friend.

My Mother

I saw my mother angry only once—when my oldest brother didn't come home all night. She packed a suitcase and sat it out on the porch. When he hit the door, she said, "See that suitcase? If you ever do this to me again, you can pick that up and go!" She grabbed the suitcase, dragged it back in the house and unpacked it. He never did that again. My mom was an amazing woman, always kind and soft-spoken, always reasonable, and smart. She was the one everyone went to for advice or just to listen, who held the family together like moms do.

She escaped into the desert, prospecting, maybe because her father was a prospector and miner. With her pickaxe, she would wander in and out of old abandoned mines and over hills, pecking at anything, picking up anything she found interesting. Her set of chemicals told her what minerals she had. One smelled so rotten egg strong it would run us out of the house for hours. She never found much of value, but she could tell you about every rock and plant that grew on the desert along with all their uses.

My mother went to an old Catholic Church in a mesquite flat a few blocks from us that was built with adobe brick. Miserable hot during the summer and leaky during the rainy monsoon storms in August. My older brothers would no longer go to church with my mother, but she still dragged me and my twin with her.

One day following a monsoon dust storm, or haboob as it's called now, the wicked wind and drenching rain slammed the old church. It fell apart, bell and all. After that, we met under the only tamarack tree in the area, where the church smokers once gathered before mass. In 117 degrees, hot sweat all over us, salty silt silky and puffy like flour finding every crevice, the taste of dripping salt from the pine-like tree leaves adding that special burning sensation in every pore.

I can never forget. No chairs, kneeling and standing, kneeling again, standing, kneeling again . . . One day in mid-July, my mother who never EVER swore said, "What the hell am I doing here?" She got up, grabbed our hands, and we went home to never return.

I was deaf until I was ten and escaped a great deal of the church's indoctrination. Any time I was caught doing anything wrong, I used that as my excuse for years, but it never worked. My mom died when I was in my early twenties. I still miss her.

My Dad

Soon after my mom died, my dad moved to the cotton farm that he and my brothers owned. He had the farm to his back and the desert for his front yard. What I admired most about my dad was his generosity of heart, love for others, and his need to help, especially the down-trodden, many of whom became his good friends.

Everybody was his friend—Willie, the Pima Indian he rode the desert with; Harold Williams, the one-armed Black painter he sponsored; and the Mexican immigrants he befriended year after year when they returned to work the farms for my family.

I remember stopping to eat with many of his friends. The Basque sheepherders even their dessert made from mutton, two cotton-picking migrants who used a broom handle to make delicious tacos, the Cocopah hunting party who fed us menudo. Later he told me they made it from dogs. I refused to believe him although I knew he never lied. We took Harold the painter out to dinner one evening. Dad ordered pinto beans and Harold started laughing. "I've been living on pinto beans for days now," he said. "I'm a bit sick of them." My dad handed me the plate and reordered.

Because of his experiences roaming Arizona, he was recommended to a film crew as a guide for filming shoots. He

even became an actor, just sitting of course. He's the one with the white shirt sitting in the wagon at the top left corner of the photo.

My dad knew Arizona like the back of his hand. He left the state only twice in his life, once to take a load of cattle to Lordsburg, New Mexico, and the other time to take my ill mother to his sister in San Diego for the summer because the Arizona heat was killing her. This was before the days of even the swamp cooler.

So she could stay home through the summers, my dad's friend Roland helped him build an early evaporative cooler. Roland loved his airplanes, and they took a propeller and cut it down to fit on a ¼ horse electric motor. They set it in a box mounted in a window and draped wet gunny sacks over the box. The fan pulled the air through the wet burlap into the room. My mom was the hit of the town with visitors that first summer. Before long gunny sack coolers stuck out windows all over town. In 1939, the Goettl Brothers from Phoenix saw one of these coolers and made a fortune. Because of their swamp coolers, people were able to move to the Southwest in droves.

When I went off to teach school, Dad's letters included drawings and great descriptions. The top two drawings (above) were about his cowboy days. The third drawing of the windmill and tank was out at Lost Well. He covered the tank with drawings and drew on every tank he found in the desert, starting in the late 1930s. He was born a couple of miles down Palo Verde Road from old Highway 80 and wrote about going to school with the fourth drawing:

"We got to school and other doens the best way we could. Some of us had to start a little sooner to get there on time. A donkey was always hard to ketch. So you had to start early. Most anyone could have a burro if you could ketch him out in the wilds as there were plenty. You better get a young one as the older the harder to jentle. Later years I've been envited on Wild Jackass cookouts or cookins. I never went. Ain't that they were good enuff to eat but we weren't good enuff to eat them."

My Dad's Mother

She was a whirlwind unto herself. I was always told she was half Choctaw Indian from eastern Texas: my dad described his grandmother as "Black as the ace of spades." Not according to my DNA. I'm half German, partly English and partly from the Moor civilization of Spain and North Africa. I wonder if his grandmother claimed to be Native American to hide from the danger of a possible slave history. According to family history, she sold her daughter, my grandmother, to a Dallas merchant at the age of fourteen for $400.

One afternoon when our house was full and loud as usual with people milling about, my grandmother burst in the door, waving a shotgun. Those were the days when nobody locked doors, mostly because nobody had anything worth stealing. A faithful Southern Baptist against everything, she cornered my dad, shouting she would not let a son live who made bootleg liquor. She waved the gun in his face, got on her knees, and prayed for him, stood again, and cussed at him, repeating all this for what seemed for hours.

At this time I was deaf, although I could read lips fairly well. Scared for my father, I watched people leave the room and in a few minutes, slip back in, quietly sitting. I finally followed one of my uncles out the back door and watched him fall in the grass, laughing his head off. When he was back in control, he went back for more of the show. It seemed like hours before my dad finally convinced his mother he wasn't guilty.

Seems he had followed our sheriff who turned onto a small road leading into the salt flats and found him at a still. Before my dad could accuse him of anything, the sheriff told my grandmother it belonged to my dad.

Even funnier was that my uncle, my grandmother's favorite son, was collecting the bootlegged liquor from the sheriff's sons and selling it out the back of his store. He owned a conglomerate of service station, grocery store, and cabins on the banks of the Hassayampa River, once a stop for weary travelers trying to cross the desert.

My grandad, an alfalfa farmer at the time, bought the business for him saying, "Well, he's too small to pull the plow, and too big to ride it. Might as well do something he can do."

Portrait of Me

I unknowingly modeled for this painting by Maud Frances, a family friend.

Neither one of us was religious so I'm not sure why she painted a baby in my arms and a covering on my head.

She said the expression came from when I finally won a card game of Canfield.

I would take a break from studying for college and drop in to relax, visit, and play a few hands.

Maud Frances

One of my fondest memories was when Maud would stop by to visit with my dad at his service station downtown during World War II. He would take a couple of chalk pieces in his pocket from fixing tires, and they sat on the sidewalk drawing for each other while a crowd gathered to watch. I did love this woman as my second mother and considered her one of my best friends.

Moved

Our neighbors moved early yesterday back home to be with their children. Our dog, a standard poodle, fell in love with their small dog, partly miniature doxie named Lacy. Coco is one of those shy dogs that hides behind you when she's scared—and she's scared of almost everything she doesn't know. Especially other dogs.

Except for Bunny who was a giant English Mastiff weighing over 150 pounds. Coco had no idea it was a dog until Bunny was in the house, and then it was too late to react without considerable embarrassment. She avoids other dogs except for Lacy who was in and out of Coco's legs until Coco joined the play. She knew when Lacy left for the last time. Heart-broken, she wouldn't eat, stayed in her bed, and wouldn't play as usual with the cat. Or go with Nel to get the mail and visit with our neighbor.

June 2020

On the Road Again

If I were to pick one thing that changed my life the most, it would be my car.

Back to its history. In 1862, Etienne Lenoir, a Paris engineer, built a combustion engine, attached it to a horse buggy, and drove 12 miles, but the first car anybody could buy was built in 1885 by Karl Benz. The Mercedes-Benz has been around a long, long time.

Women weren't allowed to drive before the car's improvements, like the electric starter (1896) by a British electrical engineer. I watched films showing the hand-turned crankshaft, fitting the term "cranky" describing people who did the turning, especially when the crank snapped back, sometimes breaking a wrist. In America, the owner of Cadillac added the starter because a friend was killed by a crank.

Joseph Jones invented the first speedometer in 1899 because his wife wanted to know how fast he was going. Maybe the beginning of back seat drivers? Bet he was sorry.

Nesselsdorfer Wagenbau-Fabriksgesellschaft, a Czech auto-maker, added bumpers to its "Prasident" model in 1897. Problem was they fell off after a short trip.

The first heater in 1907 used the exhaust through pipes under the seat. Sad to say they usually stank, often leaked, and even caused a few asphyxiation deaths.

And a Chicago teenager added the first car radio to a Model T in 1922. No surprise there.

Helene Rother was the first woman car designer, finding a job with Nash Motors in 1947, she added class and comfort to driving with her own brand synonymous with luxury. She was a god-awful driver, involved in considerable fender-benders and often picked up for speeding. When she got the job with Nash Motors, she bought a Nash and promptly totaled it. Born in Germany, the single mother moved to Paris but fled to a North African refugee camp when the Nazis came. She sailed for New York after four months in the camp and got a job as an illustrator for Marvel Comics before Nash hired her in 1943.

One famous car, owned by Sean Kierman and hidden by his family for decades, was the green Ford Mustang "Bullitt" Steve McQueen drove in the 1968 movie. I remember the scenes of his flight for freedom in Mexico, a bad guy who won. The car ended up at the Detroit Auto Show with a new 2018 Ford Mustang.

[**Update**: After hiding for another two years, the car was sold for $3.4 million.]

I have a few more road trips I like reading about. The first one across America started in 1903 with a $50 bar bet by retired doctor H. Nelson Jackson who took on the journey from California to New York with bicycle-racer mechanic Sewall Crocker. They picked up Bud, a bulldog wearing driving goggles, in Idaho. Despite primitive or non-existent roads and no road signs or gas stations, they made the trip in 63 days, 12 hours, and 30 minutes and won his $50 wager. The trip cost him $8,000.

Alice Huyler Ramsey was the first woman to drive across America on a road trip. On June 9, 1909, Alice began her trip from Hell Gate in Manhattan to San Francisco. She took along a friend, Hermine Jahns, and two sisters-in-law. When they started, Alice was the only one who knew how to drive, but the other three soon learned. In the 3,600 miles they traveled, all but 152 miles had terrible roads. Ramsey and her crew learned fast, changing eleven tires, cleaning spark plugs, and repairing broken parts. They followed telephone poles from town to town, slept in the car, passed through a manhunt for a killer, and got surrounded by a Native American hunting party with bows drawn. At one time, waiting on a repair, a passerby shouted, "Get a horse!"

Another trip, the one from hell, was when Army Lieutenant Colonel Dwight Eisenhower joined the 1919 Transcontinental Convoy and traveled 3,200 miles across the U.S. with a load of trucks, motorcycles, and 300 solders. The slow "walk" over washed-out, rutted, often non-existing roads was plagued with accidents and broken equipment, and Ike never forgot the experience. He got his 1956 Congress to fund the Interstate Highway System for which I am highly thankful.

Less than six months after Harry Truman and his wife Bess walked out of the White House for the last time, they drove a Chrysler New Yorker from their home in Independence, Missouri, to New York and back again. With no Secret Service protection and just his small Army pension, the two pumped their own gas for the 19-day trip, stopping at road-side diners for eats, and sometimes staying overnight with friends. Once a Pennsylvania State Trooper pulled them over for driving too slow.

In 1960, one captivating author took his 10-year-old standard poodle named Charley for a 10,000 trip in a GMC pickup and camper shell he named Rocinante (Don Quixote's horse). John Steinbeck's book *Travels with Charley* came from their journey from New York to California across Texas and back home. Much of the book was about the death of local cultures and the trashing of America. One time, he got into trouble in the South because his "blue" (meaning faded-black) poodle was mistaken for a Black man.

Other firsts for traveling women were Amelia Earhart's flight across the Atlantic, Valentina Tereshkov, the first woman in space, and Janet Guthrie, first woman driver in the Indy 500.

Gaggle of Geese

On a fine day, I waved at a gaggle of geese flying over the house. I love to listen to the honking as they wing north. Evidently what I watched was really a "wedge" or "skein." Geese are called a gaggle only when they land. The wedge I watched were Aleutian cackling geese with distinctive white collars at the base of their black necks. Thirty years ago, they were on the endangered species list before Fish and Wildlife removed the invasive species killing them, the Arctic fox, from their summer nesting grounds in the Aleutian Islands. These foxes were introduced on the islands to promote trapping and found, of course, bountiful food.

Using the recognizable V shape, the flapping of the wings gives lift to the followers. It also makes visual communication easier, and honking helps co-ordinate position shifts. Geese first mate around two years old and remain monogamous to the end, an average life span of 24 years. Any space left between the geese means one of them lost a mate.

Fewer and fewer geese seem to fly over each year. Many of them prefer their winter-feeding grounds in Oregon and California and decided to stay. We have also created their favorite feeding grounds; short grass and nearby water with unobstructed views to watch for danger in places such as lawns, golf courses, parks, farming fields, and airports, all perfect for them.

At times, birds are usually considered just a messy nuisance, bird strikes, especially around airports, can be dangerous. Geese are also known to attack and protect their territory. All in all, I find them mesmerizing creatures.

July 2020

Birthday month – I did not claim this year.

Today is my birthday. Also stay at home day. Also take out the trash day. Just another pandemic day for a classic pandemic joke, "The garbage man stuck a pamphlet for AA on my recycling bin. Judgmental prick, mind your own business."

Irony: Using a device that transmits inordinate amounts of complex information tens of thousands of miles through thin air – via antennas and satellites – to convey to others that "you don't trust science."

We Even Got the Horoscope Wrong!

I am (or was) a Cancer, and this is my horoscope for today, July 17, 2020: "Emotional issues rooted in the past could leave you feeling inhibited today. You might also be a bit more touchy than usual, and see insults where none were intended. Curb the impulse to take offense. Try to confront and release the old issues. By day's end you should be feeling more positive."

All these years I religiously read my horoscope every day hoping the good news was real.

I thought I was born a Cancer, but I'm really a Gemini. My horoscope should be reading: "Acquaintances you make now could be with you for a long time, so it would be in your best interest to be completely genuine from the moment you meet. It can be tempting to hide behind standard social roles and nonthreatening small talk, but it's not the right move for you now. Unless you make an effort to really know who they are, why would they make an effort to really know who you are?" So one tells me to cool it and be careful dealing with others while the other says to let it all hang out there.

According to NASA, the ancient Babylonians created the zodiac over 3,000 years ago by matching a twelve-month calendar with star constellations.

There were, however, thirteen constellations so the constellation Ophiuchus was ignored. Further-more, the axis on which our earth turns today has drastically changed from Babylonian times. Everything shifted.

Astrology not only tells us how to treat each other but also what job to look for, or who to love, or how to deal with ...

Now we have to replace thousands of items with zodiac signs such as jewelry, cups, plates, books, journals, candles, totes, hats, other clothing, etc.—even tattoos.

NASA says all the chaos it caused isn't their problem. They study astronomy, not astrology. The brand-new astrological dates and signs. Maybe.

Capricorn: January 20 to February 16
Aquarius: February 16 to March 11
Pisces: March 11 to April 18
Aries: April 18 to May 13
Taurus: May 13 to June 21
Gemini: June 21 to July 20
Cancer: July 20 to August 10
Leo: August 10 to September 16
Virgo: September 16 to October 30
Libra: October 30 to November 23
Scorpio: November 23 to November 29
Ophiuchus: November 29 to December 17
Sagittarius: December 17 to January 20

> *"Nothing in life is to be feared; it is only to be understood. Now is the time to understand more so that we can fear less."*
>
> *— Marie Curie*

001 Cabled Array across the Cascadia Subduction Zone

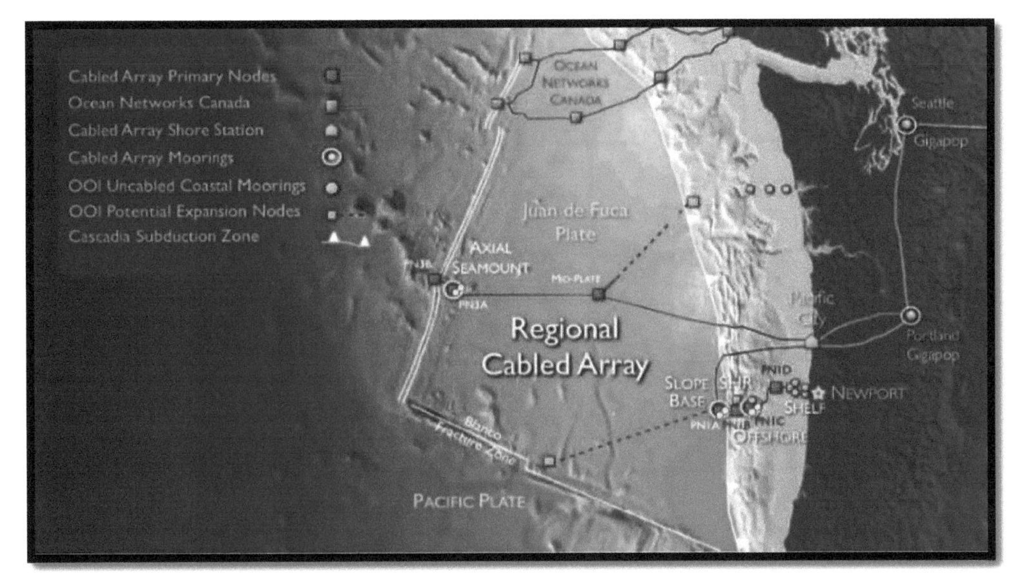

A friend reminded me research ships don't just come and go in the bay for my entertainment. Some of them are part of an ongoing $239-million project installing and protecting a 200-mile horse-shaped cable network. Called the 001 Cabled Array, it brings a constant stream of near-real time data directly from an alien world 9,850 feet deep in the sea. The system is the first ocean observatory to span a tectonic plate.

Starting from Newport, the cable drops down the continental slope via Pacific City across the Juan de Fuca tectonic plate near the Cascadia Subduction Zone to Axial Base and Seamount. The most advanced underwater volcanic observatory in the world, Seamount, is covered with geophysical, chemical, and biological sensors. Their cameras send real-time information on relationships between seismic activity, fluid flow, and biological activity as they monitor the Juan de Fuca plate where it dives under the continental plate, causing our number-one earthquake threat.

Connected to the cables is an extensive mass of equipment such as sensors, 3-D Velocity Meters, broadband and low frequency receivers, sonar, meteorology instruments, 3-D temperature array, cameras, water samplers, particulate DNA samplers, seawater PH, seismometers, spectrophotometers, etc. Some are self-explanatory. The rest?

Some instruments track currents that bring nutrients up to the continental shelf, important to fisheries; some track and analyze dead zones caused by low oxygen; some measure earthquake impact and changes on life in hydrothermal vents; others study microbes that, void of sunlight and vegetable-base foods, have used carbon dioxide, hydrogen sulfide, methane, and metals to form their food source; others plot ecosystem shifts through changes in sounds from marine mammals such as whales and dolphins; some collect data streams that aid in weather forecasting; some monitor changes in health and number of sea creatures; others study reasons why major marine ecosystem food sources shift; some determine the effects of global warming on marine life in the different water columns; many measure the 'breath-ability key' critical to ocean survival.

Among the research discoveries was a ridge seeps methane hydrates, a potential energy source. Above all, this research reminds us that the ocean is the ultimate life-support system for the entire planet. Our health depends upon its health.

Ships scheduled to repair the Coastal Endurance cables usually stay in Newport during April and return in October. Ones repairing the Axial Seamount and continental slope stay here during July and August.

The R/V *Thomas G. Thompson*

When two buoys appeared on the NOAA dock, I waited to see who would pick them up. Here came *Tommy*, back to help repair the 001 Cabled Array.

A frequent visitor a few years ago, she hadn't been to Newport for a while. Turns out she spent eighteen months getting a mid-life facelift and refit at the tune of $52 million.

New diesel engines, navigation and ship-positioning systems, and sophisticated sonar, allow her to map the ocean floor in sharper detail and even differentiate between species of fish and other marine life. The ship's laboratories were updated and critical sensor systems replaced.

Belonging to the University of Washington marine science studies, she carries twenty-one officers and crew, two marine technicians, and up to thirty-six scientists, many of them students.

After the refit, *Tommy* left Seattle and headed for New Zealand to join Woods Hole Oceanographic ships for a three-year expedition. The trip took them around the world, clocking more than 100,000 nautical miles. They even passed Indonesia's Krakatoa's volcano in mid-eruption.

The *Thomas G. Thompson* is one of four "global class" research ships, all built to the same basic design. The three sister ships are *Ronald H. Brown* (NOAA), R/V *Roger Revelle* (Scripps), and R/V *Atlantis* (Woods Hole Oceanographic Institution).

Jason and *Medea*

A long way from home, *Jason* and *Medea* have boarded *Thomas Thompson* to join the research and repair ships working on the 001 Cabled Array. *Jason* and *Medea* are the two parts of a remotely operated vehicle (ROV) system.

While *Jason* dives to the seafloor, *Medea* acts as a go-between, delivering power and commands from the ship and returning video images and data. She also provides a buffer for *Jason* from the ship's movement.

The ROV can drop 6 miles deep on a fiberoptic cable to film, collect rocks, sediment, and even lift heavy loads. Equipped with still and video photography, sonars, lights, and various systems for sampling, the duo is mostly used to study hydrothermal vents. They were named after the ocean explorer of Greek mythology and his wife.

The R/V *Marcus Langseth* Research Ship

It's May 6, 2020, and the *Langseth* just came in. Like the *Atlantis* research ship with *Alvin*, the only peopled submersible, the *Langseth* is the only marine seismic profiler ship mapping miles below the seafloor with 2D and 3D imaging. Operated by the Lamont-Doherty Earth Observatory (LDEO) of Columbia University along with other institutions, the *Langseth* generates views of the interior of the earth's faults, including tsunami-producing earthquakes, and magma chambers, in details unmatched by any other source.

Accommodating about fifty-five people, the *Langseth* can observe a variety of happenings with nearby marine life to content of salt in sea water. She travels only about 150 days a year, searching for high priority projects requiring 3D imaging. At the cost of $70,000 a day, she ain't cheap.

Not all is wine and roses with her, however. In 2015, the National Research Council published a report named "Sea Change: 2015-2025," mapping the next ten years in marine science and recommending the *Marcus Langseth* be deactivated with these resources used elsewhere. The assistant director of NSF's geosciences wrote the agency will no longer support the ship by the summer of 2020. In a case like this, scientists would ask the White House science adviser for help, but Donald Trump never filled the job.

I guess all I have to say at this point is that you better get down to the Hatfield dock and take a look. It is a sight you may never see again.

[Update: Since the change of presidential administrations, the *Langseth* is still working. On a journey up north last summer, she recorded the biggest earthquake off the coast of southern Alaska, the 8.2 magnitude quake 20 miles under the ocean floor.]

School Openings

Since the day Trump insisted schools will open this fall, I have been fighting this serious fear. He's not talking via home computers. Of course not. It's the physical building that will open, and students will get in their car or buses, on bikes, or walk, trot, and run to get to school any way they can. He cited countries that were opening their schools this fall as his standard. During a twenty-four-hour period at the time Trump made this announcement, the rate of COVID-19 cases in the countries opening their schools were Germany, 224; Denmark, 0; Norway, 3; Sweden, 0; and United States, 61,719.

In July [2020] with openings, cases in these countries were on the rise: Germany, 509; Denmark, 49; Norway, 10; and Sweden, 152. Without reopening schools in the U.S., new cases are now near 80,000 daily.

The Centers for Disease Control and Prevention (CDC) does have guidance for opening schools during pandemics such as distancing, physical barriers, smaller classes, staggered scheduling, and much more. But Trump found these too expensive and ordered CDC to change their guidelines citing COVID-19 illness in children is highly unlikely. Beyond opening the schools, he has no plans. He had no plans when this pandemic began and still doesn't. He also had no plans when he separated children from their parents at the border either. So many are still lost.

As a thirty-year veteran of the school system, I know children will stick their masks in their pockets more times than they will wear them. Social distancing? What's that? Most children are not afraid of contact; they feel indestructible and indifferent to the possibilities of harm. They also socialize by gathering, whispering, and pounding on each other. We create activities and sports to provide that—dancing, boxing, wrestling, basketball, football, soccer, the list goes on. If you do send your children back to school, keep in mind schools don't have enough teachers or space in the classrooms to keep students at a social distance and wearing masks. And there never will be.

Regarding school openings, I am not willing to give up the life of a child, not one, to schools opening. It is a price too high. The loss of a few months of education is nothing compared to the chance to use that education.

August 2020

Working to avoid the virus reminds me of the story of the two friends chased by a bear. "You don't have to outrun the bear; you just have to outrun the guy next to you."

NOAA Ship R/V *Oscar Dyson*

A frequent visitor to Newport, during the month of May of 2020, *Oscar* came in and out for several weeks. I was greatly pleased to learn that she has a woman commander.

Sarah Duncan became intrigued with the sea from the tales her grandfather told her while they played cribbage. He had been a tugboat captain who worked the British Columbia's inside passage. She said, "During my senior year of college, a classmate showed me the website for the NOAA Commissioned Officer Corps, and I instantly became fascinated with the idea of working on a research ship. Looking back on it, I really just jumped into this epic adventure headfirst without knowing what to expect."

Five Cs Yacht

This beaut came into the South Beach marina and docked at the Marina gas station. I am intrigued by these huge yachts traveling in and out of our bay. Along with a diving deck and selection of water toys including a full out tender lowered by a hoist, the *Five Cs* is ready for water fun. She sleeps eight people and crew. With a jacuzzi, formal dining, cocktails, and lots of sunbathing, what's not to love. And for only $271,000 a week.

NOAA *Ka'imimoana* Research Ship

In August of 2014, the NOAA ship *Ka'imimoana* (Hawaiian for Ocean Seeker) was towed into Yaquina Bay and sat. And sat. This ship is the only NOAA ship dedicated to the research of climate change. I waited for months to see this ship leave port and return to duty. Finally, I got excited about the activity surrounding the ship but realized the ship had been stripped of all identification. Like the ship behind it, *McArthur II,* this majestic ship was decommissioned on June 18, 2014. Who watches out for us now?

Arizona Summers

I am so glad to be out of Arizona where summers are hot, hotter, and then even hotter more than Hades. Having so many friends and family still there, though, I feel sympathetic. It's too hot to stay outside to visit, which blows the hell out of social distancing. It is so hot, in fact, nobody remembers or even cares about the nice winters to come. I am reminded of the rancher, when asked how long he had lived in Arizona, answered "27 summers."

Then there's:

1. Satan called. He wants his weather back.
2. The heat index is somewhere between OMG and WTF!
3. God, whatever you're baking, it's done.
4. I'm realizing I need to change my ways. As hot as it is here, no way do I want to go to hell now.
5. Heat makes everything expand. Kinda like I'm not really fat. I'm just hot.

R/V *Oscar Dyson*

One of my favorite ship stories is the *Oscar Dyson*. As the first of five in NOAA's advanced fishery research class of ships, the *Oscar Dyson's* main duty is to restore, protect, and manage ocean and coastal resources. Homeported in Kodiak, Alaska, the *Dyson* has a welded-steel hull extra-strengthened for the icy Alaskan waters. She's rigged for longlining, and trap fishing and can trawl in depths of over a mile. She can run so quiet the fish she surveys won't be disturbed. She has a scientific sonar system, Acoustic Doppler Current Profiler, and a multibeam sonar system. I have no idea what any of that means. It just sounds important.

Actually, this story is not really about Oscar. It's about his wife, Peggy. Back when email and cell phones were a glimmer in an inventor's eye, mariners across the North Pacific would stop and listen when they heard their radio station boom, "Hello all mariners, hello all mariners, this is WBH-Two-Nine Kodiak." In fact, they did more than stop to listen. They depended on it, often with their lives. Twice a day, every day for twenty-five years, Peggy Dyson broadcast the marine weather and personal messages, everything from birth announcements to World Series scores, to mariners at sea, eager to get word from home. All sitting at a mic on her single sideband radio from in the back bedroom of her home on Kodiak Island.

"I'd get calls from fishermen, 'Pay my electric bill or I'll be cut-off,' or 'It's my wife's birthday and I need you to send flowers,' Peggy says. 'In all the years I've been advancing them money, no one has ever reneged.'"

Dyson began her volunteer career in the sixties by radioing her husband, the late commercial fishing pioneer Oscar Dyson, on Channel WBH-29 while he was at sea. The fleet soon caught on to her schedule and tuned into WBH-29 to hear the weather and news from Kodiak. Her broadcasts became a mainstay for mariners and the Coast Guard, especially search and rescue operations such as the rescue of the fishing vessel *Mary Lou*, caught in a storm in 1984. Many skippers made life-saving decisions based on Dyson's weather broadcasts, such as the crabbing vessel that heard Dyson broadcast a severe weather update and turned back to Dutch Harbor. "When you're out on the water you're just glad she's there. She became so central to the lives of those on the water that in 1975, the Weather Service made Peggy the official weather girl of the North Pacific with a small stipend.

Am I the only one wondering why this NOAA ship wasn't named after her?

"President Donald Trump is burning the harvest and salting the fields. He seems determined to leave behind a broken nation."

– Eugene Robinson

Biker's Convention

Although health officials have been warning of a major coronavirus virus spike, thousands of bikers descended on the small South Dakota city of Sturgis for an annual ten-day motorcycle rally. They expressed defiance of measures meant to guard against the virus. I really do hate to believe in survival of the fittest especially when dealing with stupid.

"The fault lies not with the mob who demands nonsense, but with our leaders who do not know how to produce anything else."

- Miguel de Cervantes

September 2020

Mr. Munk

Sometimes even lazy photographers like me get lucky. I was sitting in my chair photographing out my window when I caught this guy on my rope fence.

"Lost in his daydreaming,
Cute little chipmunk,
Dancing in the smoke of clouds,
Swirling round and round."

- Richu Karan Garg

Forest Fire Smoke

The smoke is so bad we cannot see out our windows. Many of us wear our masks inside. The air won't clear for several days on the coast, and it could return. Inland, many towns have been burned out, and many north of us are being evacuated to Newport's Rec Center.

Forest Fire Smoke, Continued

It's still bad out there, and I am still in a mask. Luckily, the wind has died down from gusts up to 60 mph. Two guesses what that does to a blaze. The Lincoln City fire closest to us has been stopped, and people can return to their homes. And the shifting winds bring rain although the offshore wind returned. If you are anywhere near a fire, please be careful. Smoke is filled with volatile organic compounds, carbon monoxide, dioxide, and nitrogen oxides ash, much of which is particulate matter 50 times smaller than a grain of sand. If you must be in any kind of smoke, use at least an N95 mask carefully fitted because cloth masks will not capture small wood smoke particles. Also, if you have a N95 mask with an exhalation valve protecting yourself from COVID-19, cover the exhalation valve with another facemask.

Wildfire smoke can be particularly deadly, especially when it "ages." Smoke changes with chemicals and sun action as it travels, often across continents. The damage is caused when this smoke is inhaled deep into the lungs.

Although we do have a good deal of natural defenses against both large and small particles, there is a limit before serious lung damage develops. Even more, recent research indicates just small exposures to any smoke can cause COVID-19 virus to be deadlier. This also includes anything that stirs particles about such as burning candles, lighting gas stoves, vacuuming, and smoking.

Forest Fire Smoke, Continued Again

The smoke came back. We're using this suggestion from Coastal Cleaning Services: Clear smoke in the house by filling a crockpot with water, adding one-half box of baking soda, and leaving it on low without a lid.

I swear it's working: the bottom of my crockpot is brown from air particles and the air smells much cleaner. **Don't sniff the steam from the crockpot**. Baking soda is not a healthy vapor for the body.

Who Is Jesus Christ?

Everywhere I look, especially around churches, Jesus Christ is portrayed as White, speaking English just like us. Even politicians such as Ma Barker (governor of Texas in the early twentieth century who objected to teaching Spanish in public schools) was heard to say, "If the King's English was good enough for Jesus Christ, it's good enough for Texas public schools."

Sixth oldest known image of Jesus Christ

Jesus was an Arab Jew who spoke Aramaic, an ancient Syrian language. He was a protester working to reform Judaism, not destroy it, and he did it through teaching compassion and good works. As did Leo Tolstoy. And Mahatma Gandhi. And Henry David Thoreau. And Albert Einstein. And Martin Luther King Jr. And the Dalai Lama. And how about you?

"Obviously, you don't have to vote for Joe Biden. But you can't use our Jesus and the Bible to defend your support of Donald Trump."

– Jennifer Abel

If you are an American, your heritage is either Native American, slave, refugee, or immigrant. There is nothing else.

Politics:

NOAA Deputy Assistant Secretary

NOAA's new deputy assistant secretary, David Legates, is a climate denier and a flat-earther. He blames the sun and not people for global warming. To him, global warming is not a problem. He claims it's actually good for "many species such as lobsters and blue crabs who will actually thrive on the addition of carbonate and bicarbonate ions and its slightly lowered Ph content" caused by increasing ocean acidification. In 2007, he co-authored a paper, partly funded by the Koch Industries, American Petroleum Institute lobbying group, and ExxonMobil, that question findings about climate change destroying polar bear habitat. In 2014, he testified before the Senate debunking the science that humans cause global warming. Legates is tied to Heartland Institute that funds information about climate denial and discounts the scientific evidence from NOAA. Jane Lubchenco, Oregon State University professor of marine biology and former NOAA head, said, "He's not just in left field—he's not even near the ballpark." And he's second in charge for NOAA's "observation and prediction."

The United States Army Field Band

On September 14, 1814, 35-year-old lawyer Francis Scott Key wrote the poem, the "Defense of Fort McHenry," after witnessing the bombardment of the fort. The poem became our national anthem.

October 2020

Politics:

Political Stockholm Syndrome

A friend found out her beloved sister voted for Donald Trump. When she asked why, her sister said, "Well . . ." Then dead silence. I think a rock-hard head best defines how we hang on to our conceptions. Or misconceptions. Nobody can talk me out of my convictions.

Except we can change, but only over long periods and an inch at a time. I am not who I was at 21, 40, 65, and so on. Although the change was so slow, I'm still looking for it.

Whether I agree or not, family and people I have known changed me. Education changed me. Working changed me. Radio changed me. Television changed me. Internet changed me. I, too, have been caught up by PSS (Political Stockholm Syndrome). The Urban Dictionary explains that PSS is when we know politicians who we support are corrupt, that they lie and cheat, but something they say or do "called to us" and we bonded. That bonding stops us from listening to any criticism about them.

Coming from a mixed family (Dad a Republican, Mom a Democrat), I grew up with interesting/ confusing opinions in a house always filled with friends and family. In my twenties, I became a passionate Republican because I found a home. I worked for the GOP as a precinct worker, attending state conventions and spending months census-taking on farms, ranches, and Indian reservations throughout much of southern Arizona.

Although I wasn't entirely sure what all a Republican stood for beyond fiscal austerity, it must have been PSS that made me follow Dwight Eisenhower anywhere. Didn't matter that people said he had a violent temper, or that he was a segregationist, or he had a long-term affair with one of his drivers, or people said his wife had a drinking problem. (She actually had Ménière's disease, a problem with her inner ear affecting her balance.) I didn't even care what his politics were. The Nuremberg laws would have ruled his overthrow of the Guatemala government a hanging offence by many. I didn't care what he did. He protected me, he won me a war, and he was my hero.

Jimmy Carter was the next president who brought out my PSS. I was in a chaotic place in my life, with a new job and moving, and Carter had a goodness about him like a favored granddad I could trust. I could relate to his human rights platform.

So I became a Democrat. I didn't care what anyone said about him, and people around me had a lot to say, especially when long lines formed around gas stations, prices skyrocketed, and hostages weren't released—until minutes after Ronald Reagan was inaugurated. It made me realize how easy it is to destroy a good man. I saw conspiracies everywhere and registered Independent.

Then came Donald Trump who implements his new "Herd Immunity" program which opposes masks and social distancing. Without vaccinations and other protections, millions more people would die. And did.

A "Herd Immunity" program, which normalizes even mass death, scares the crap out of me. This attack against vaccinations is confusing. Telling conservatives not to get the shot kills off conservatives. Why would anyone choose to kill their own? That's like Angelfish eating their own spawn. Same goes for telling conservatives that elections are rigged, so why bother to vote?

Apart from being exhausted, financially unstable, nearing a mental breakdown, and being fat, everything is great. Thanks.

Controlling Stress Levels

Living through increasing COVID count, election divisiveness, and an approaching cold winter preventing connections to loved ones puts us in a world of hurt. Looking for stress-relieving actions, I read an article about the connection between our eyes and breathing and how the two control our brain, and therefore, our stress levels.

Stress follows a continuum: at one end we are catatonic, and at the other we are in a full-out panic attack, racing heartbeat, dilating pupils, hyper-ventilating, all symptoms needed to get the body to move. We have millions of tiny sacs of air in our lungs that collapse under stress. Because physiological sighs will inflate the sacs, we can control stress by managing the only organ in the body we can control, the diaphragm. When we breath out, our diaphragm moves down, our heart enlarges because of the added space causing blood to flow slower. If we want to speed up the heart, we breathe in more than we breathe out.

So, an effective way to control stress is through "physiological sighs," meaning deep inhales through your nose twice and exhales slowly through your mouth once. Continuing this will control your heart rate as well as levels of alertness, stress, and calmness.

Good Science News

We could definitely use these:

1) Transparent solar cells could be imbedded into panes of window glass (especially in those all-glass high rises) absorb the sun rays that turn into electricity to power the building.

2) Scientists are changing photosynthesis to produce bigger crops on much less water.

3) In another experiment, solar panels suck water out of the air to help water arid land.

4) A type of blindness affecting about one in 4,000 children might be cured with a revolutionary gene-editing treatment.

5) A universal flu (influenza virus) vaccine has passed one of the significant clinical trials.

6) Patients have been declared "cured" of HIV.

7) In one of the more promising zero-emissions experiments, a clean method has been developed, 25 times more efficient, for hydrogen fuel production.

8) Methane traps 84 times more heat than carbon dioxide. A seaweed food has been developed to help slow climate change by reducing cow burping and farting, which reduces cow methane emissions by eighty percent. An image I shall always cherish.

"I'm all in favor of keeping dangerous weapons out of the hands of fools. Let's start with typewriters."

– Frank Lloyd Wright

> "Those who can make you believe absurdities can make you commit atrocities." – Voltaire

Politics:
Fake News

I have a story about one of the world's most powerful leaders who won by promising he would make the county great again. He warned against fake news and said regulations thwarted personal free-dom. Although many voters found him reprehensible and even feared him, he appealed to emotions rather than science-based facts. He defamed anyone who disagreed with him and surrounded himself with his corporate buddies who had no idea how to govern. He found a scapegoat by claiming certain groups were responsible for his people's miserable lives and that it was time to get rid of them. It was time for change.

Bet you think I'm badmouthing Trump, but I'm not. I'm talking about Adolf Hitler.

After the elections in 1933, Hitler, a skillful propagandist, emerged as the new chancellor of Germany, named himself the dictator, denied elections, and ruled absolutely until he lost World War II and committed suicide in April of 1945. We will never forget the destruction he left behind.

Remember the groups he blamed for the country's woes? Those responsible for his people's unbearable lives? He killed between 15 million and 32 million people, burying one on top of another in dirt pits, with another 70 million to 85 million dead in a war called the most destructive war on earth. And if he had won, he would have continued to the U.S.

I call this a successful result of Political Stockholm Syndrome that was ever perpetrated on the masses, a Machiavellian masterpiece.

Politics:
Loss of Democracy

In 2006, the Democracy Index rated 167 countries on a scale of 0 to 10 from full democracy to authoritarian regime. Ratings in 2020 reflect a steady decline in democratic countries around the world with the lowest since 2006. "The top and bottom indicate little change with Norway at number one where it has traditionally been, followed by Iceland, Sweden, New Zealand, and Finland. Canada is tied with Denmark for seventh spot. North Korea remains in its traditional last place at the bottom of the list."

Money-wise we tend to be at the top for corporations, millionaires, billionaires, etc. Yet in 2006, we rated seventeenth among democratic countries. In 2020, we rated thirty-sixth and considered a flawed, declining democracy. We are not alone. There are countless failed democratic governments reminiscent of ancient Greece and Rome that crumbled into dictatorships, leaving behind mass graves filled with lives of the innocent and patriots. Among some of our modern-day democratic failures are Libya, North Korea, Iraq, Ghana, Venezuela, Uganda, Indonesia, Bangladesh, Pakistan, Syria, Egypt, Russia, Turkey, Hungary, Poland, Philippines, India, and Brazil.

After democracy stood all these years on the shoulders of our great founders, admitting its fragility and vulnerability is hard to accept. Yet Plato worried about the survival of a democratic state. "When people govern themselves, the majority will always eventually support the tyrant." If that doesn't scare the crap out of you, I don't know what will.

Politics:

Payroll Tax Pays for Our Social Security and Medicare

Payroll tax. That's what the government takes from every paycheck. That's the thing Trump keeps talking about getting rid of. Payroll tax. Since 1937, we working people have paid into the Payroll Tax Trust for every working day of our lives, and our employers match every penny we put into the Payroll Tax Trust.

Although it's called Social Security on a Social Security card and W-2 form, any monies collected from the worker and boss does not go into a special Social Security fund; they go into the Payroll Tax Trust which was our safety net for old age. That is, until 1983 when Ronald Reagan dumped the money into the general coffers from which politicians could "borrow" at will. With just cause, objectors called it "legalized embezzlement." By the time Trump took office, $2.85 trillion was removed from that fund.

Our politicians have depleted the fund so fast, no wonder it could be gone by 2023. Our Social Security fund has not gone broke; it was robbed. What's even worse? Payroll taxes collect funding not only for our Social Security but also for our Medicare, Medicaid, Survivors and Disability needs. In other words, anyone who has a problem from medical to hunger will soon be out of luck.

"People who wonder whether their glass is half empty or half full miss the point. The glass is refillable."

– Simon Sinek

Crows

I keep talking about crows and wish I could have had one as a pet. Not just because they are the smartest animal next to humans. I admire crows because they think like me. Because they know what they know, they are the most humanlike of all the animals. They can mull over topics in analytical thought, a measure of higher intelligence.

This cognitive ability to know gives them the abilities to solve problems and make discoveries. Children can't match their capacity to complete an eight-step puzzle in order without training until they are seven.

This kind of brain power, this kind of awareness, makes me question the way they should be treated. If you are a doubter, watch this Caledonia crow at play sliding down a snowy roof.

https://www.youtube.com/watch?v=3dWw9GLcOeA

The Crow That Saved the World

I have images of crows all around me—wall hangings, photos, paintings, statues. Everything but a real one. I couldn't bear to keep one in captivity no matter how much they fascinate me. I love reading about them, seeing how they play, and knowing how smart they are. And fables about them, like this Lenape myth, "Rainbow Crow Saves the World."

A terrible winter descended upon the earth; deep snow and water turned to ice everywhere. The animals, never experiencing snow before, thought it was great fun. But the storm continued, burying smaller animals as larger animals struggled to move. The chance they might not survive the cold became a real fear.

The wise owl suggested they send a messenger to the Great Creator. Maybe He can warm up the world again. The animals agreed and debated who to send. The wise owl was blind during the day and couldn't travel. Coyote couldn't stay on track because he was easily led astray. Sure and steady, the turtle was much too slow. Finally the animals chose the Rainbow Crow, the most beautiful of all the birds with rainbow feathers and enchanted singing.

The Rainbow Crow flew up into the clouds, past the sun and moon, even the stars. No rest, beat up by the wind, the Crow had an arduous journey before he reached the Great Creator's home. Rainbow Crow knocked on the door, but no one answered until he started to sing. Unable to resist, the Great Creator graciously invited Rainbow Crow into His home, asking what He could offer for the concert. Rainbow Crow asked the Great Creator to melt the snow so the animals on earth could survive.

The Great Creator apologized to him but explained snow and ice have their own spirits. Rainbow Crow worried about

what to do until the Great Creator said he would think about fire. He lit a fire on a stick from the sun and handed it the Rainbow Crow, telling him to fly back to Earth as fast as he could. The Rainbow Crow thanked the Great Creator and plunged down the Milky Way toward Earth. The stick grew heavy, and the fire grew hot. The Crow's feathers caught on fire, turning black, and the smoke strangled his lovely song.

On Earth, the Crow gave everyone fire. The Earth thawed, and the animals danced in rejoice. But Rainbow Crow mourned the loss of his brightly-colored feathers. He was an ugly black bird with a raspy voice; no one admired him anymore. A voice called out to him. It was the Great Creator.

"Don't cry," He said. "You will be much honored by your sacrifice. Even better, when humans come to earth, they won't want to put you in a cage for your rainbow feathers and beautiful voice, and they will not eat you because you taste like smoke. You will always be free."

Continuing Work on Coronavirus Prevention

The 2020 Nobel prize winners in chemistry are working on a way to stop coronavirus. Both Dr. Emmanuelle Charpentier from the Berlin Max Planck Unit for the Science of Pathogens and Dr. Jennifer A. Doudna from the University of California, Berkeley received the prize for developing CRISPR-Cas9, a technique that modifies DNA in plants and corrects genetic disorders to prevent or treat diseases.

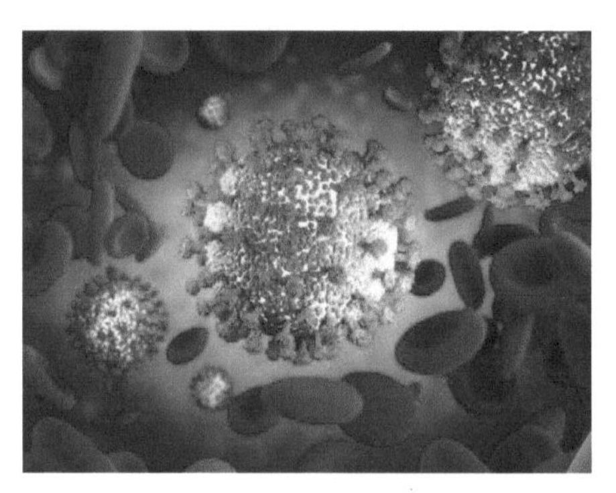

Although scientists are not sure how quickly they can rid us of coronavirus, they do think that the possibility of avoiding any new virus yet to come begins to look real as the research turns its focus on coronavirus and other dangerous microorganisms to animals. CRISPR works by using pairs of molecular scissors to cut strands of DNA at specified places, remove genes, and replace them with new genes.

A new technique called PAC-MAN will be combined with gene-altering methods used on animals in an attempt to change our DNA to inoculate us, not only against COVID and other new viruses coming, but also against influenzas and the common cold.

Dr. Francis Collins, director of the National Institutes of Health and one of the first people to decode the human genome, expressed great satisfaction at Charpentier's and Doudna's recognition. "This technology has utterly transformed the way we do research in basic science," Collins told *The New York Times*. "I am thrilled to see CRISPR-Cas getting the recognition we have all been waiting for and seeing two women being recognized as Nobel Laureates."

Lemur

Have you heard about the kidnapped lemur in Portland? Well, I picked up on it in this strange conversation. Some-one mentioned an apparently sweet lemur named Maki, but I heard the word lemming (don't ask!), and the conversation continued like this:

"Isn't that the one that jumps off a cliff?"

"No, no, no. That's a lemming."

"Isn't that what you said?"

"Do you ever listen? I said lemur."

"Oh. That's not a lemming?" Oh god. Why me? "Well," I huffed, "what the hell is a lemur?"

Immediately my email filled up with photos and articles to emphasize my ignorance. Apparently some 30-year-old fool stole a 21-year-old lemur named Maki from the San Francisco Zoo. A call went out from the police department to help find Maki. He's not only an endangered animal but also very old and requires special care. Maki was found when a five-year-old in his school's playground yelled, "There's a lemur!" All's well that ends well. Maki is back home suffering only from a bit of hunger. The zoo said Maki was easy to catch because of his advanced age, but I think he was looking for love when he let James Trinh, one of the cutest kids ever, pick him up and hug him.

Coast Guard House for Sale

A friend sent me an ad about a property for sale in Newport. Did you ever dream of living in a lighthouse? Or a cabin in the woods? Or how about owning a radio station? Or a high-rise office building? Maybe a school campus good for a small college? Or would you like to own a factory building complete with marine animals painted all around the top third? Or a bridge? You can even buy a village with gobs of houses. My favorite? In our very own town, our government auctioned off the historic Coast Guard house. Right here. On the corner of SW Naterlin and SW Bay Street. I hope whoever buys it will stay long enough to call it home.

Halloween

Every Halloween I remember in Arizona was freezing cold, too cold to even beg for candy. Except one. On that one warm evening, my brothers and friends got my grandparent's old outhouse, no longer in use of course, and hauled it to town where they sat it in the middle of old Highway 80 in front of the movie theater. Mr. Jandas, the theater owner, was gone at the time. He had driven to Phoenix to pick up his mail-order bride. When he returned, he was so excited to have a new wife he wasn't paying attention to the road. He was also half-blind. He ran into and over the outhouse, scattering wood everywhere. The new Mrs. Jandas got out of the car, grabbed her suitcase, and hiked to the Pharmacy/bus stop. She took the next bus back to Phoenix.

November 2020

I just read a handsome hand-drawn yard sign that said:

**"I love you."
You're probably thinking, "You don't even know me." But if people can hate for no reason, I can love.**

Politics:

Van Jones

This had me sobbing along with CNN commentator Jones, who had expressed concerns about Donald Trump for four years. When his network called the presidential election for Joe Biden, Jones broke down in tears. "It's easier to be a dad, it's easier to tell your kids character matters—it matters."

The R/V Marcus Langseth at Night

System Overhaul Tax

According to the IRS government statistics bureau analysis comparing individual incomes of 2016 to Trump's new Radical Republican tax system, the 2017 overhaul generally dropped income for the lower class, left middle class the same, and vastly increased income for the upper class that made out like a bandit.

Trump's successful economic program cut taxes and interest rates for the rich who bought more stocks and increased stock value, thereby profiting themselves. This "Trump tax law, the most significant tax policy change since 1986, was passed without a single public hearing or a single Democratic vote."

Moon Reflecting on Yaquina Bay

"As ancients seen, so do I
A throbbing light, a painted globe
Upon a pinpricked sparkled sky
Suspended in the nothingness of black
Always there, poetic universal rhyme
Dangling upon an invisible track."
- Mayiia

My Favorite Tchotchkes

Does anyone else use inanimate objects to get you through the day? I collect things, old and new, that make me smile and put them where I spend much of my time. Some have a fond memory tied to them; others are just cute.

Mouse: My favorite is this one with the "I'm in love" face as he holds on to his bouquet of flowers. I keep him beside my computer because his expression cracks me up.

Chicken: Another tchotchke that makes me smile. Obviously made from a metal can and lids, I picked this up for $5. Nel offered $3 but walked away when the owner didn't lower the price. I bought it anyway. I think it's priceless from all the smiles this rooster gives me.

Nel gave me the elephant for our anniversary. When the elephant's trunk goes up, it means good luck. Must be successful. Together since 1969, we are still healthy and happy. Lucky me!

Serenaders: Even with the name I gave them, I'm sure they are both complaining about something. I just don't want to hear it.

Apache Well Wheel: Early in our years together, Nel and I would explore the Verde River area on the McDowell Indian Reservation with my dad. Passing by a home one day we spotted this wheel hanging over an old abandoned well.

We stopped and my dad got out and knocked on the door. He talked to the elderly Apache Native American who owned this relic and bought it for $25.

It now hangs in a window, reminding me of all the days I spent with him, roaming the Arizona desert.

Why I Don't Go on Vacation

My view looking out my window upriver, across the river, and downriver out beyond the Yaquina Bridge to the ocean. The photos show how the Yaquina River constantly changes her moods, providing endless river watching. Even in the wild winter storms, our weather stays temperate from the ocean. Totally fed up with the Arizona heat, I wanted to live near the ocean where it mostly stays between 45 and 70 degrees all year around, but I didn't expect such overwhelming beauty.

Across the river from my window – Marine Hatfield Science Center and NOAA

Yaquina River upstream

My view to the west of our famous Yaquina Bridge and the ocean beyond with the lights from the crab boats coming home.

Fences for Fido

Jiggs was a happy dog with his present. He got a free secure fence and home built by Fences for Fido, a group of volunteers dedicated to getting dogs off chains.

Adopting a Pet

When you adopt a pet, take time to meet the scared ones, the shy ones, the ones that don't stick out to you. The ones that hide under their bed or blanket. The one that hiss, the ones that bark, the ones that cower, shake, and cry, looking at you with confusion. The ones with boring colors or missing

limbs. The older ones, the frail ones. The ones who seem beyond repair, the ones who seem to have given up. Because they aren't...and they haven't. They just need you. And sometimes you just really need them too.

Mocha, Our Rescue Cat

She was so ugly she was cute. She lost her whiskers to our other cat who chewed them off. I didn't care how she looked.

She was the most loving cat we ever had.

I was told once that a water squirt gun would train a cat to stay off the tables and counters. They were so wrong. My loving cat enjoyed every squirt.

The spots in her eyes came from the time that a guest accidentally stepped on her tail, and she slammed her face into the door jam. Her face swelled up, and the vet said to put ice on it—if we could. We got out a package of frozen peas, and she stayed in our arms, sinking her face into the cold. The spots never went away, and she kept her eyesight—and personality.

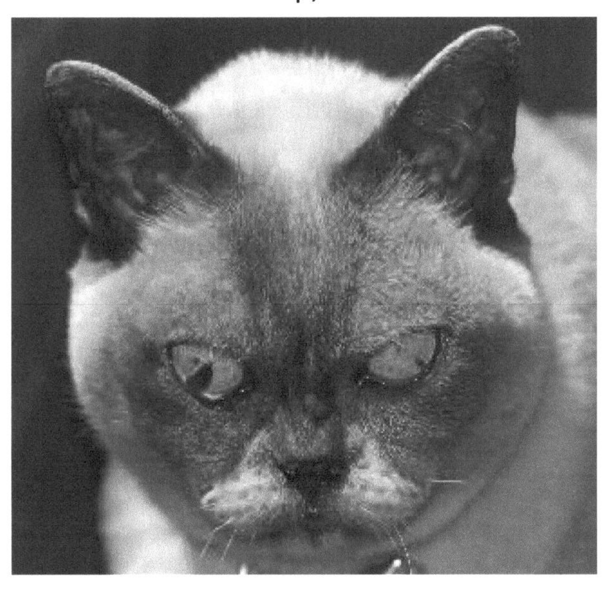

Kahlua, the Whisker Chewer

I loved this cat dearly, but I felt she didn't love me back. She was feral to the day she died at seventeen years old. Although she would occasionally get in my lap and allow me to pet her for a short time, I was never allowed to pick her up. She ruled the house and everything in it.

"Do not be dismayed by the brokenness of the world. All things break. And all things can be mended. Not with time, as they say, but with intention. So, go. Love intentionally, extravagantly, unconditionally. The broken world waits in darkness for the light that is you." - L.R. Knost

Coco

She shares Loni's life, the protagonist in my mystery novels.

My Sophomore Yearbook

Art Francis from Buckeye Old Timers posted this page on my social media. It's out of a yearbook for my sophomore year, 1950.

Top right is Miss Audrey Chapman, English teacher. She was the reason I became an English teacher. I figured that if she could keep a job anybody could, even me. Second down in the center was my biology teacher. Can't remember his name, but I do remember all the little messy things we had to dissect.

Third down in the center was Vera McCormick, typewriting/business. I don't remember why but she kicked me out of class. I sat in on Miss Brittenham's class (second down on the left) during study hall and learned to type for no credit. I didn't care; it's a useful skill. When I got a teaching job in the Phoenix high school district, I had McCormick for a principal. That was uncomfortable.

Third down on the right was Margaret Salmon, my home ec teacher. She and our art teacher, not pictured on this page, traveled the desert looking for rattlesnakes. I took the art teacher to Palo Verde Butte, a known rattlesnake den, and found her a snake crossing the road. She took a .22 rifle and emptied it. Missed every time. Made the snake mad enough to come after her, and she nearly left me behind. I did not go with her again. Bet that's more than you wanted to know about my education.

The Elakha Sea Otter

The cutest sea otter ever, called the Elakha (a Chinook trading language word for sea otter), sadly became almost extinct in the wilds along the coast of Oregon centuries ago. The fur trade, of course. By the mid-1800s, only a few were left in captivity; their descendants can be seen at the Oregon Zoo and the Oregon Coast Aquarium.

Fortunately, an organization, the Elahka Alliance, is working to replace this sea otter. Not just because they are adorable, which they are, but because they eat lots of sea urchins. Sea urchins who busily strip and deforest kelp beds through California and half-way up the Oregon coast. Kelp

forests that provide critical shelter and food for thousands of sea species including the fish and shrimp we eat.

The other key species eating sea urchins, the sea star, now faces extinction in a massive die-off that started in 2013. According to Marine Multi-Agency Rocky Intertidal Network, October 28, 2020, a disease called "sea star wasting syndrome" is just one more symptom of our out-of-whack marine ecosystem caused by global warming. No matter how small or insignificant things may seem, everything relates to the other for preserving the balance and ultimately, our survival. The term keystone species refers to organisms critical to the survival of other plant and animal life around them. Without them, ecosystems collapse.

Seeing how some people wear their masks, I understand how contraceptives fail.

Species Survival

A "well, duh" moment and new twist to Darwin's evolutionary theory that should have been obvious. Many scientists now believe the most successful strategy for species survival is not survival of the fittest with winners and losers, but cooperation and friendliness. Our "best friend," the dog, is a prime example. Joining humans evolved the dog fiefdom into a massive population explosion compared to the wolves who stayed in the wild, too often near extinction. Looking around, it does appear that competitive "beat 'em up, kill 'em quick" has proved a terrible survival stratagem.

Consider the number of hominins that started on this earth and only the homo sapiens survived. So far. Some say nine hominins once lived on earth; others, such as the Smithsonian National Museum of Natural History, list twenty-one. And they have funny names too, like homo habilis (handy man), homo erectus (upright man), homo neanderthalensis (the neanderthal), homo floresiensis (the hobbit), homo naledi (star man), and homo sapiens (wise man). Although I question how wise we are now.

In the beginning, most of the human species had the same abilities, big brains, and artifacts as homo sapiens do. It seems that friendship is the real evolutionary winner. We should never forget the Holocaust. Or 9/11. I want to remember that day when the New York twin towers came down by those who came to help those looking for safety. Together. It fast became the biggest boat rescue ever, even bigger than World War II Dunkirk boat rescue of 350,000 French and English soldiers. Friendliness and cooperation.

First Sign of Civilization

A student once asked Margaret Mead what she considered the first sign of civilization. He expected her to talk about artifacts found such as arrowheads, pot shards, petroglyphs, etc., but she surprised him by discussing her find of a once-broken healed femur, a break once meaning sure death. She said, "A broken femur that has healed is evidence that someone has taken time to stay with the one who fell, has bound up the wound, has carried the person to safety and has tended the person through recovery. Helping someone else through difficulty is where civilization starts."

Cecilia Payne

The person who discovered that our universe (the stars including our sun) is primarily made of hydrogen and helium, lost the honor of her find to Henry Norris Russell, a preeminent astronomist at the time. He believed that predominant elements on both the earth and the sun were almost identical and persuaded her to change her 1925 thesis. Four years later, he came out with research proving her thesis and received all the credit for her discovery.

Most people study how Newton discovered gravity, Charles Darwin discovered evolution, and Albert Einstein discovered relativity, but Payne's discovery about the universe? Not a peep.

Payne always had to fight sexist discrimination. Her father died when she was four, so she had to earn her education at Cambridge while her mother paid for her brother's tuition.

Cambridge refused degrees for women until 1948 so Payne moved to the U.S. She was the first person to obtain a

Ph.D. in astronomy from the all-female Radcliffe College, a "coordinate" to Harvard. Yet, as a woman, she couldn't attend the all-male Harvard. Astronomy experts called Payne "brilliant," but her thesis adviser, Harlow Shapley, hired her at a pittance and advised against her being hired to an important position at another institution.

She taught several astronomy courses, but the catalog didn't print her name. Harvard didn't hire women as professors for decades, and Payne didn't get a decent salary until Shapley retired in 1954. She finally became the first woman at Harvard to be promoted to full professor in 1956 and the first woman to be a department chair at the university. In 1976, the American Astronomical Society awarded her their highest honor, the Henry Norris Russell Prize for her lifetime in excellence in astronomical research. The award is named after the man who blocked Payne's groundbreaking find regarding astrophysics.

Free Water from the Sea

Researchers at the Massachusetts Institute of Technology have invented a desalination unit weighing 22 pounds. At the push of a button anyone can have instant clean drinking water from the sea. And from most anywhere else. This unit is even powered by the sun. And no filters!

"I think women are foolish to pretend they are equal to men. They are far superior and always have been. Whatever you give a woman, she will make greater. If you give her sperm, she will give you a baby. If you give her a house, she will give you a home. If you give her groceries, she will give you a meal. If you give her a smile, she will give you her heart. She multiplies and enlarges what is given to her. So, if you give her any crap, be ready to receive a ton of shit."

- William Golding

Painted Hills in Central Oregon

Thanksgiving

Some people think the state lockdown mandate will make this holiday a lonely time. Without the presence of our usual loved ones, we decided to fix Eggs Benedict. I read that two million people still traveled through the Portland Airport. Somebody's not staying in their bubble.

December 2020

A word is dead when it is said, some say.
I say it just begins to live that day.
– Emily Dickinson

Words

I love words. Obviously. I was an English major, and I like to write. But I'm not a wordsmith. I just love that one special word where nothing else fits. Like rush-hour-traffic, serendipity, epiphany, sonder, wanderlust, ethereal, cromulent, hinky, wowser, despicable, fester, mooch, or "pee-yew!" Or "He didn't say one word as he masticated his way through the meal."

Some writers take a clump of words when one will do. Like ineffable, meaning some things can't be expressed by words. Or *tacenda*, which you could maybe apply to this post, meaning some things not to be spoken. Speaking of clumps, I like, "Your freedom ends where my nose begins." So wear your damn mask!

Then there are those swear words that say what nothing else can. How effective is telling someone to urinate off. Or when you hit your finger with a hammer, how helpful is shouting "defecate!"

Other words can make some people cringe. For example, the word bitch. One of my fondest memories of my grandmother is when she would come to door and holler, "You bitches, get in here." And always followed that with a big grin and a big hug, followed by food. Call me a bitch any time. But you better smile.

Politics:

More Political Stockholm Syndrome

It's alive and well! This guy's desperate heartbroken cry, "I will die for my president," scared the holy crap out of me. This comes from Rush Limbaugh's talk show caller who had Rush nearly speechless. I place some of the blame of this guy's syndrome along with millions of others like him on (Presidential Medal of Freedom) Rush.

Upcoming Inauguration Day

I understand Trump may be moving to Mar-a-Lago over the holidays and not return. I'll be glad to help him.

Christmas Lighted Boat Parade

The First Vaccination for Covid

In Britain, the first person to receive a "jab," as it's called across the pond, was Margaret Keenan, the week before she turned 91. William Shakespeare, an 81-year-old who hails from Warwickshire where the bard was born, was the second. The program was called "V-Day."

Why Salmon Die

Anyone who says to you they don't believe in the scientific method to solve our problems, please don't listen. It's our knowledge of science that got us here and science that will save us. A small example. For years, coho salmon have been mysteriously dying. No one knows why. Beaucoup money spent on reclaiming waterways for returning salmon only to arrive and die. It took twenty years of extensive research and manpower in several research centers to find the cause.

Tires. Every time someone drives on a road, flakes of rubber chuck off into the rainwater, into the streams, into the rivers, the ocean. According to Ed Kolodziej, an environmental engineer and chemist at the University of Washington: "This chemical is just one of a vast number of contaminants that washes off roads whenever it rains.

This giant soup of pollutants, which includes trillions of microplastics, rush down drains and into creeks and ultimately into the sea." The "smoking gun" turned out to be a chemical named 6PPD. In a tire, it keeps the rubber together longer. Knowing how much corporations hate to cut into profits, however, fixing this might be a long fight. We live in a pond where everything we do creates a ripple, affecting everything else.

Happiness

One thing I know—you can't be happy unless you know how to be grateful. It's not always easy. That's when I remind myself of the little times. Like the time we were rolling down the Colorado River through the Grand Canyon in a river raft, and Georgie (the woman who owned the raft) pulled up a bag of oranges out of the water and tossed them to the passengers. At ninety degrees and wearing a Mae West, I was more than grateful. I was ecstatic!

Sometimes I think about what it would be like to have lived in a different place and time. Settlers 150 years ago would think a great Christmas present would be a pair of shoes. Or an orange. Or about people hearing whistling bombs and running through the streets of London during World War II who would find, at the last second, a hidey hole. I don't have it so bad.

The Blue Heron

My third favorite bird. Not because it is the largest heron in North America standing an unbelievable four feet tall or because this ungainly, huge blue bird is easy, even for me, to identify. I admire the way they fish, standing in the water knee-deep ever so quietly, waiting, long neck drawn back in a curve, waiting, watching for a shimmer in the water, waiting, moving so very slowly forward, waiting, then ... strike! So fast its mohawk feathers fluff out, high in the air as it proudly displays the catch of a fish in a dagger-like pointed bill. And they also eat snakes, frogs, mice, and dragonflies.

For entertainment, I watch them lift off to fly. With a "whoop-whoop," they spread their six-foot wingspan, hop a few long ungainly slow steps, and leap in awkward elegance into the air, flapping in desperate determination to stay aloft.

After that it's a ballet in grace as they swoop and arc over the water, huge feet trailing the tail as they head back to their nest.

I need a pet and had many, including a fox, skunk, house-broken rabbits, horses, donkeys, the usual dogs and cats, etc. No birds. As special as they are, I'll leave them to the wild.

During these trying days, I am blessed. A pair of blue herons fly by my window as they circle from their nest in a pine tree nearby on their way to their river estuary feeding ground. They live in colonies, and females lay three to seven green/blue eggs, usually in nest in a tree.

Year after year they have raised their babies in that tree; last year three of the cutest little ones survived. They purportedly live up to twenty years—if they make it through the stupid adolescent years. These birds are protected by the Migratory Bird Treaty Act of 1918.

Not Everything Is Cancelled

Sunshine is not cancelled.
Spring is not cancelled.
Love is not cancelled.
Relationships are not cancelled.
Reading is not cancelled.
Naps are not cancelled.
Devotion is not cancelled.
Music is not cancelled.
Dancing is not cancelled.
Imagination is not cancelled.
Kindness is not cancelled.
Conversations are not cancelled.
Hope is not cancelled.

Politics:

Bigotry

A bigot—someone who makes up stupid-ass reasons to belittle someone else for being different and, therefore, to feel superior and, for some stupid-ass reason, to feel better. Why do we need hurt others to feel superior? Is it ego? Superego? Id? Sub-conscious? Entitlement? Or are we born that way? Or are we just plain stupid?

I'd like to vote for stupid, but I really think that we are born that way. Maybe a left-over behavior from our "fight or flight" Neanderthal days when we needed to instantly recognize danger by the differences in the world around us. Some people don't care what kind of snake is at their feet; they're killing it. All snakes are bad. Before we crawled out of the swamp and slime and threw our animal instincts into the fire to burn our way into civilization, back when we still had to fight and defend our place in the world, back when we had to recognize differences and, therefore, the enemy to survive in the world of survival of the fittest, we might have to be bigots to live.

How many racists we thought we had

How many racists the 2020 election revealed

Then came civilization when cooperating and helping each other brought an explosion in progress and successful enterprise. The aggressive bigoted part of the animal survival from cave days that we carry with us from childhood is no longer useful or needed.

So to all of us bigots, the next time we have a bad day and we need a lift, reach out a hand and help someone different from you. The good feelings you get will be a much greater high and will last much longer than your hate. Just try it.

> "I've learned that people will forget what you said, people will forget what you did, but people will never forget how you made them feel." -Maya Angelou

Politics:

Trump's Worst Offense

In a recent *Bloomberg* poll, people were asked what bothers them most about Donald Trump. The one listed above all others was when Trump mocked reporter, Serge Kovaleski, who had arthrogryposis, a congenital condition that affected his joints. Made me wonder who could possibly vote for him after watching that.

My choice for the worst thing he did, however, was separating kids from parents and tossing them in cages. Then ordering workers not to coddle or comfort crying children. The movie *Sophie's Choice* should be on everyone's watching list. I don't believe anything is worse than cruelty to children. And animals.

May you never know the fear of having your human rights challenged every time there is an election, and may you never know the pain of watching loved ones vote against your right to exist fully, equally, and authentically.

Children in Need

One person can make a difference. Here's one example how. Nel read an article about someone who paid for school lunches for all the kids who were in arrears. The school refused to give them a full lunch until the bill was settled. She went to a local middle school and did the same thing. The school principal wrote a letter of thanks for the newspaper. Our state Rep. David Gomberg read the letter and got legislation passed to make school lunches free in Oregon for all children whose family cannot afford them. Who knew? Just another act of random kindness.

In my rural county, people have appalling and desperate living conditions: 60 percent of the children live in suspect poverty level with one-third of them under the poverty line. Of the 17 percent of homeless students in the county, 209 students are unsheltered, making Lincoln County #1 in the state in this category. How can children living in these conditions grow up to be mentally and physically healthy? Or have access to learn skills to improve their conditions?

Thinking back, I remember times when the acts of kindness from others made all the difference in my life. I count my stars every day for the fortunate life I have been given.

"For the rest of my life, I don't ever want to hear another Republican lecture anyone about law and order, family values, or morality. The party of Trump has lost all credibility on those matters."

- Keith Boykin

Tasmanian Devils

There's always good news somewhere. According to the *National Geographic*, the Tasmanian devils have returned to the mainland of Australia for the first time in 3,000 years. These animals are another of the keystone species, and scientists hope the predator will rebalance ecosystems in the areas decimated by invasive species.

Scientists are overcoming the contagious facial cancer which almost wiped out the "devils" and found new food for the animals after hunters destroyed their diet, megafauna. Tasmanian "devils" can now start to thrive on the island with no dingoes, the devils' predator.

Politics:

Trickle-Down Economy

In the throes of a devastating pandemic with unemployment soaring, manufacturing down, sales down, GDP a disaster, poverty rampant, and the middle-class stability all shot to hell, the stock market continues to maintain all-time highs and the rich get richer. Before the pandemic, the major change was Trump's 2017 tax cuts for the wealthiest and for corporations by 41 percent. The conservative trickle-down economic theory has never worked.

According to the London School of Economics at King's College's analysis of eighteen countries over the last fifty years, tax cuts only increase inequality. Only the super-rich benefit. Trump's tax cut led to a record one-trillion dollars in stock buying, inflating the value of businesses, and making the rich richer, after lying that the cuts would trickle down in expanding businesses, increased numbers of jobs, and higher wages. During the first year of the pandemic, the richest people in the U.S. increased their wealth by 20 percent, burying $584 billion in the stock market while 45.5 million people lost their jobs and the economy tanked.

> **"I don't know what word in the English language—I can't find one—applies to people who are willing to sacrifice the literal existence of organized human life so that they can put a few more dollars into highly stuffed pockets. The word evil doesn't even begin to approach it."**
>
> **- Noam Chomsky**

Donald's Wall of Lies

Donald Trump finally has his wall. Installation art in Soho fashioned 20,000 of his false and misleading statements into a 100-foot-long mural of his quotes.

Lies included were all documented and fact-checked by the *Washington Post*.

Yaquina River Sentinel

Language

Language has always fascinated me. Maybe because I was deaf until I was 10. Corrective surgery generated one big roar until I could separate one tone from another. Like learning a musical instrument. I always wanted to learn different languages but didn't have the retentive memory for it. So I take my stand with English. If it would only stand still. Like everything else around us, language is ever fluid. The Bible, the most universally known and read book, was originally written in Ancient Hebrew, Ancient Greek, and Ancient Aramaic. In the following years, it was translated into other languages, including ancient, better known as old English.

Following is the beginning of the famous Old English poem, *Beowulf*. I had a class on this poem, and it was like learning another language. Translating into modern English was crazy: the word GIRL meant BOY and the word for girl was *mæġden*.

Hwæt! We Gardena in geardagum,
Þeodcyninga, þrym gefrunon,
Hu ða æþelingas ellen fremedon.
Oft Scyld Scefing sceaþena þreatum,

Monegum mægþum, meodosetla ofteah,
Egsode eorlas. Syððan ærest wearð
Feasceaft funden, he þæs frofre gebad.

Translation:
How we have heard of the might of the kings.
How those noblemen brave things they did.
Often Scyld, son of Scef, from enemy hosts
From many people mead-benches took.

Terrorized warriors. After first he was
helpless found, he knew the recompense for that.

Then there's confusion from related words in different languages like PAIN which, in French, means BREAD. And the Urban Dictionary adds new words every day such as MOMALA (a mom in extended families), and DOG SHOT (to get hit when you aren't looking). Translating, especially from ancient languages and one language to another, is a turkey shoot. Like Ashleigh Brilliant said, "To be sure of hitting the target, shoot first, and call whatever you hit the target."

"Limbaugh getting the Medal of Freedom is like Jeffrey Dahmer receiving the International Culinary Award."

Christmas

Today is the 25th, but this is a year without holidays. This fall has strung the days out, one into the other, one much like the last. We get our paper by mail now, no longer a trip to the paper box out front in the morning when we stood around a few minutes watching the dog run around smelling her "news-paper" to see if maybe a deer had passed by. Maybe a word with a neighbor from across the street. Then a bit of breakfast followed by an early supper.

Today we have mashed potatoes and gravy from a package, a bit of dressing from a box, and cranberry sauce from a can for our supper. We're not much on meat anymore. Yet we are still alive and healthy, food on the table, roof overhead, and I am forever hopeful that we can add the holidays back in 2021. I think about a glass half full or half empty. I decided I'm going to fill the damn thing to the top with a good red wine and cry, "Salud!" to all the people I love.

"Socialism is a scare word they have hurled at every advance the people have made in the last 20 years. Socialism is what they called public power. Socialism is what they called Social Security. Socialism is what they called farm price supports. Socialism is what they called bank deposit insurance. Socialism is what they called the growth of free and independent labor organizations. Socialism is their name for almost anything that helps all the people."

– Harry S. Truman, 1952

The R/V *Sikuliaq*

It's the end of the year 2020, and the *Sikuliaq* is back. She sailed in from her home port of Seward (AK) in 6 days and 23 hours. Since May, the *Sikuliaq* was exempt from the National Science Foundation ban on sailing during the COVID crisis to continue her ecological survey project, collecting water and plankton samples in the Alaskan gulf. For the first time since the pandemic began, an NSF ship was allowed to leave port after the ship's COVID lockdown. Requirements for the exemption: the ship returns to the departure port; the three scientists live in the home port; the ship goes no more than one day from port; she has a plan to protect the people aboard from the coronavirus. But she ended up here in Newport.

Commercial Crabbing, 2020

It's the tail end of 2020 and the exodus has begun. The 424 commercial crab boats from six major ports will be setting crab pots for 400 miles from Brookings to Astoria following the tradition beginning with the establishment of the crab season in 1948. This year's opening was delayed by sixteen days because crabs tested for too little meat. Washington crab season will be even later. The commercial boats will be out until August 15, the end of the season.

Sand on the coast glows during the summer. That's because bio-luminescent, tiny bits of phytoplankton called dinoflagellates are washing ashore.

"We must all hang together,
or we shall all hang separately."
- Benjamin Franklin

“Before you speak, let your words pass through three gates: Is it true? Is it necessary? Is it kind?”

- Rumi

Good Old Days

One of my friends reacts to my nostalgia with a more direct approach: “So much of ‘back in the day’ is now overlaid with the reality of what a horrible time it was for women, Black people did not exist for white people except as domestic servants (and could not sit at the Woolworth’s counter), Latinx were also invisible (except in the fields), and don’t even think about LGBTQ people.

Nostalgia has lost much of its appeal since the civil rebellions of the 60s and 70s, and especially this past year. “

“Live your life in such a way that the entire planet doesn’t dance in the streets when you lose your job.”

– Jason Longwall

Cold Moon, December 31

If you’re looking for another way to wish 2020 farewell, look up. This year, December’s “Cold Moon” ends a year of thirteen full moons. October had two full moons, sometimes known as “blue moons” used for two moons in one month.

It’s 11:59 on December 31, 2020, and the fog is finally lifting! Let us all lift a glass and never ever speak of this year again.

Part IV – Building Bridges –Year of 2021

"Greatness is not measured by the walls we build but by the bridges." – DaShanne Stokes

When Joe Biden became president in 2021, the relief was felt around the world. Certainly, through my little knothole. There were still many problems to solve, many left over from the previous administration. But at least now we can begin, and that start will be the repair of the Yaquina Bridge.

January 2021

Yaquina Bay Bridge

Of all the extraordinary sights to experience around Newport, the one that hits you in the chest and makes you sit up and pay attention the most is our Yaquina Bay Bridge.

Although our new tsunami/earthquake marine studies building ain't bad. Or NOAA. Or Hilan Castle on a hill. Maybe even a lighthouse or two. I also like that it doesn't take long to get to Cape Foulweather, the first place Captain Cook landed in the Americas. Or stand on the side of the road and look down. The Yaquina Bay Bridge is not only on the historical registry but also a famous and photographed architectural structure on the West Coast, decorating travel media and logos on all sorts of objects such as the sleeves of our Newport police. The bridge's fame is just a step behind the Golden Gate, and our builder, Conde McCullough, is the second most noted American bridge builder, even more famous than Golden Gate's Joseph Strass.

Conde McCullough (1887-1946) was a bridge engineer who built a dozen bridges on Oregon's Highway 101, the last half with Franklin D. Roosevelt's WPA program during the 1930s. When Yaquina Bridge was completed in 1936, Highway 101 was finally opened from Mexico to Canada. McCullough became so famous he was required reading for any student of structural engineering, his design always recognizable as a McCullough bridge.

One person compared the bridge to watching a ballet dancer leaping and dancing across the river. The Art Deco pylons and spires, Gothic piers, and arched railing panels all blend into a striking silhouette wrapped in a red sky of the setting sun. Grand staircases at the south end lead down to the bottom of Safe Haven Hill, a tsunami refuge.

For the past year, the bridge has worn a white coat accompanied by colossal amounts of scaffolding. I have watched the coat creep along the bridge piers, like scaffolding the Eiffel Tower on its side. The bridge is getting a three-year facelift, filling in wrinkles and flaws with a bit of green makeup. Fifteen years ago, I first watched a paint job on the bridge, a valiant and massive job to save her from a watery grave. Concrete is porous and rebar rusts, causing catastrophic bridge failures such as the one at the bridge in Waldport that had to be replaced.

The paint color? ODOT green, of course. Actually it's Verde Green, the color McCullough chose to paint all his bridges. I can't even imagine the $30 million needed to scrub and paint a bridge that took 30,000 cubic yards of concrete and 3,100 tons of rebar to build, including pilings buried 70 feet into the bay.

In this "Save Our Bridge" project, the actual painting process is called "Cathodic Protection." Underneath that coat, protecting workers and the surrounding area, sandblasting removes loose and damaged concrete. It also cleans the bridge's steel floor beams and stringers along with any exposed rebar before patching everything with fresh concrete. A special zinc paint sprayed on the surface acts as an anode to provide free electrons to the metal. The process finishes with an electrical charge sent through the metal to attract free electrons from the zinc in the paint into the metal. The zinc, not the metal, corrodes, protecting the less active electrons in the metal. The workers are also retrofitting the bridge with seismic upgrades, but I have no idea how that works.

Oscar Dyson Research Ship

Oscar is back. A NOAA fishery research ship, she is homeported in Kodiak, Alaska, but comes to Newport for repairs. *Oscar* quietly shimmied in behind *Bell Shimada*, her sister ship. Like the Yaquina Bridge, *Oscar* has a white coat for repairs.

World Is Healing

While we quarantine ourselves day after day, the world around us is returning to the wild. Along with the ozone healing, our earth's water and air are visibly cleaner.

Attracted by empty streets, wild animals are leaving their home environment and wandering freely around ours. Goats roam Llandudno, Wales. In Delhi, India, barrels of monkeys hop fences; in Mumbai, India, peacocks perch on parked cars; in Nairobi, Kenya, a pride of lions sleep in the streets; in Tay Ninh, Vietnam, thousands of ducks stop traffic; in Chachoengsao, Thailand, a parade of elephants force the road to close; deer wander Paris—and my back yard. And so it goes. Maybe we can find space in our space for these creatures. Maybe, while we and our earth heal, we can create green space and learn to live with our wildlife. At the least, we could slow our lives down to share with the goats, lions, deer, elephants, and waddling duck collisions. And save the deer.

This hiatus also gives me a chance to watch birds flocking and migrating. Stellar jays circling, landing, stuffing their beaks with peanuts. The older ones manage up to three at a time, much to the aggravation of the younger ones who quit in frustration with only one.

Hummingbirds squabble at my feeders. Crows chase bald eagles and buzzards four times their size away from their nests. A skein of geese flies over while sparrows hang around and swallows flit by. An occasional European starling, a newcomer ignored by birders.

Not sure I want the raccoon to return, however. A young pair found our dog door and came in for supper every night. I wandered in on the sweet couple happily washing and eating until I took the broom after them. I got them outside, but they were most reluctant to leave, arching and hissing like cats. Had me nervous so I opened a window and chucked canned goods at them, hoping to convince them to find a free meal elsewhere.

I made so much noise at 4:00 in the morning that Nel got out of bed and suggested a different strategy. Swiping them with a broom moved them over the fence into the neighbor's yard. I had wondered why the dog water dish looked so dirty all the time. Did you know wet dog food looks a lot like mud?

Wow. Me on Wikipedia. My amazing publisher, Lori L. Lake, put me on Wikipedia, an honor I never expected or even deserve. I would like to thank her for her support.

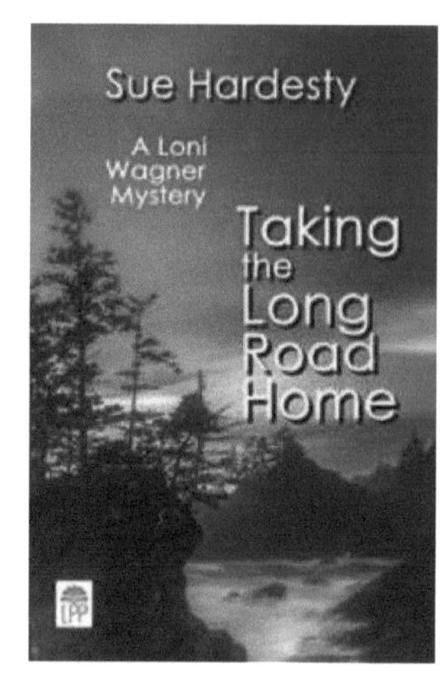

Fibonacci Sequence

Matthew Rozsa wrote, "Nature is fond of patterns, on both the small scale and the large." For an example, he uses the Fibonacci sequence, which is the repeating pattern of numbers in which each subsequent number totals the sum of the previous two.

The so-called golden ratio of 1.618 can be seen in nautilus' spiral shells and the planets and seeds and much more of nature. Scientists find it "from daisies to databases." The Italian mathematician was born in 1170. The mathematician can tell you EVERYTHING, including everything about you is numbered. Every seed, every leaf of grass, every finger, every computer, every rock—every object is alive with the language of the universe. Numbers, symbols, equations are the mechanized force that, without it, nothing will work.

Even though I love language, I still have a problem with the concept of math as language. For example, I keep hearing about a "silo." Not that tall round, filled-with-bulk-feed thingy. This new silo is "a system, process, department, etc. that operates in isolation from others" such as the time Sony had two separate departments working on the same electrical plug and nobody knew it. There's also a term, "siloed Trumpers," meaning Donald Trump's followers isolated by his lies.

The one universal language that never changes and that everyone understands is numbers. Numbers are like words: pluses and minuses are the punctuation, and equations are the sentences. I have never been fond of numbers. Sometimes my 2 + 2 doesn't equal 4. In a black and white world, however, there's always a correct answer.

Ancient discoveries reveal numbers were probably our first language, used for trade in the early days. Building pyramids and temples exploded into remarkable mathematical discoveries and ensuing math equations changed the world: Chaos Theory, Law of Gravity, Fourier Transformation, The Square Root of -1, Logarithms, Maxwell Equations, Black-Scholes Equation, Navier-Stokes Equation, Normal Distribution, and Euler's Polyhedra Formula.

Some math puzzles even have a $1 million reward for their solutions.

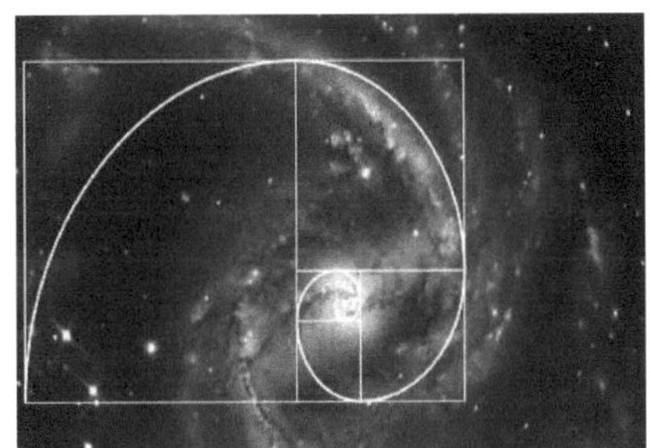

"Let's set the record straight: I don't want free health care. I want my taxes to pay for health care, not war or violence. I don't want money for nothing. I want the opportunity for a good job that pays for at least my basic needs. I don't expect every election to bring the results I want. I just want my vote to count. I don't want businesses to be unprofitable. I want them to stay out of the regulatory and political process. I don't want the wealthy to pay for everything. I want them to pay their fair share. I don't want open borders. I want a path to citizenship for Dreamers and realistic immigration laws that are dignified, humane, and fair."

– Michael Okuda

Isolation

I'm still waiting to be rescued from the pandemic. Even so, I think I should be the last to save. Educators and parents should be first because they raise the children. If I can help one more parent to stay around by getting the shot before me, I can hang out in isolation a few more months. I got a roof, food, Kindle, cable, flushing toilet, and money to pay my taxes. Hey, I'm good!

Massive Sea Star Die-off Now Worldwide

Climate warming is still happening, and sea stars are still suffering from "Wasting Disease." More than 20 species of sea stars are now considered critically near extinction.

"They don't call the trillion-dollar Wall Street Bailouts 'Socialism.'

"They don't call nearly $1 trillion in oil and gas subsidies 'socialism.'

"They don't call the billions in farmer bailouts 'socialism.'

"But health care, wages, food for poor people?

'Socialism.'"

"The whole aim of practical politics is to keep the populace alarmed (and hence clamorous to be led to safety) by menacing it with an endless series of hobgoblins, all of them imaginary." – H. L. Mencken

Table Mountain, from the Knothole, with her first coat of winter snow.

February 2021

We haven't seen much sun for a while now. Just the occasional sunray here and there. Still, I am grateful for the rain.

What Is Freedom?

Recently I saw a poster of a young girl with a cigarette and a glass of wine along with the quote, "I Am Me. I Am Free..." I doubt a glass of wine and cigarette will make her free. It's more like an act of rebellion, the "I'm the boss of me" syndrome typical of the young. Smoking and drinking are not freedom. Those two trapped me in years of hell.

The poster also declared, "I'm not NORMAL. I don't want to be." What is normal anyway? In psychology and psychiatry, the word means typical, or average, or standard non-destructive behavior. It's how we are expected to behave. Conforming socially to an agreed upon set of patterned behavior might be an obsession which is not normal. "Normal" changes over time.

The concept of normal came from the Latin word, "Normalis," a carpenter's square.

Does that mean acceptable social behavior was once considered square? In past centuries, schools educating teachers were called "normal schools" from the French "école normale" for school intended to establish a pattern or "norm" for all other schools to model.

So back to what is freedom? My pick for definition of freedom is from Janis Joplin singing "Me and Bobby McGee."

"Freedom's just another word for nothin' left to lose.
"Nothin', it ain't nothin' honey, if it ain't free."

Or my second choice, "Your freedom ends where my nose begins." And, of course, likewise, my freedom ends where your nose begins.

Take your pick or add your own.

Plants As Fuel

Learning more from science has changed our world view. Now a plant can produce fuel for planes and ships. And it's not ethanol. The new fuel comes from the last free commodities left, sunlight and air. Making enough to provide sufficient amounts to be useful and profitable is the next trick. According to the Institute for Advanced Sustainability Studies (IASS), the plant uses a procedure producing syngas (a mixture of carbon monoxide and hydrogen) and processes it into methanol, kerosene, and other hydrocarbons.

Sea Star Wasting Disease

Sea stars continue to die off, reminding people of the damage created by climate change warming the oceans. In the past, die-offs in the environment recovered. Not anymore. In the largest marine disease event known, the "Wasting Disease" is killing sea stars by the millions. Highly contagious, this disease started on the U. S. West Coast and moved all over the world. Sea stars breathe by waving their feet to create moving water, passing oxygen through outer tissues of small gill-like structures and through their feet. Not only does warming water in itself "deoxygenate," but blooming organic matter and bacteria also use oxygen, causing sea stars to suffocate and drown. More than twenty species of them are considered critically near extinction. Lack of oxygen also causes the death of other sea creatures such as shrimp and crab, as well as a real danger to the general fish population. On top of all this, the increase in storm frequency delivering large algal blooms to coastal areas depletes more oxygen. Sick sea stars can be identified by puffiness in the center, twisting arms, and color change.

Bird Bills/Beaks

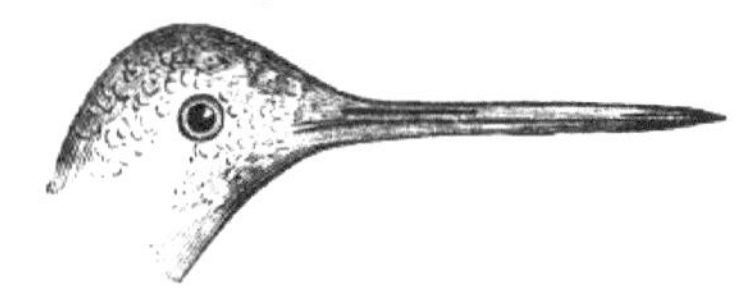

One day when I was watching birds at my feeder, I wondered why bird bills and beaks have so many different shapes. The only bird I had for a pet was the duck I raised from an Easter duckling who followed me everywhere. Maybe that's why I have an affinity for their well-being.

My family hunted white-wing and quail for food when I was a kid. We also killed lots of chickens. This was at the end of the Great Depression, and food was scarce. One day the fence was gone from our back yard, and a common shape appeared on a plate for supper that night. Everyone was very quiet as they passed plates and listened to me worry about my beloved missing duck. I had been looking for him all day. Then it hit me, and I broke out sobbing. My dad picked up the platter and threw the duck out the back door. We all ate meatless that night. Maybe that's why I turned vegetarian.

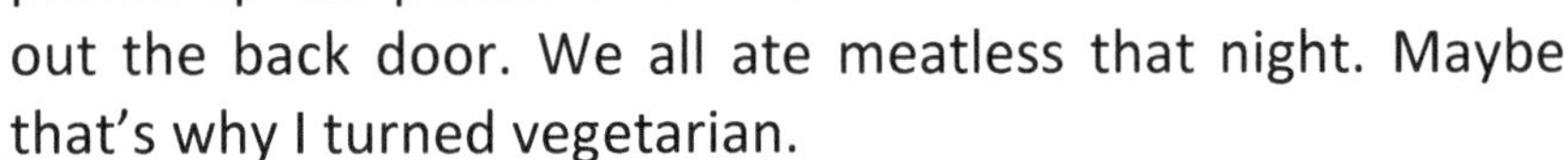

I loved watching the duck use his bill to feed and drink. Like a goat, he would eat anything. Grab, nibble, shake, and gobble. Worms, slugs, grass, leaves, grain, and fruit. He was crazy about fruit, especially watermelon. Occasionally I would find him eating gravel and worried he was hungry until someone told me it was a natural part of a duck's diet. Something about their gizzard grinding food for digestion. The best part of the duck's flat bill is it can strain muddy bottoms to find critters to eat.

An even stranger assistance to finding food, the kiwi's nostril at the end of a long beak can sniff out worms underground. With a beak built for flipping, the cormorant dives in the water and comes up with the day's meal, tosses it in the air, catches it, and swallows. The stork's bill crushes. The flamingo filters. The spoonbill snaps. The tailorbird stitches. The great blue heron stabs. The eagle rips. The ibis probes. The macaw climbs. The woodpecker drills. The pelican scoops. The puffin clutches. A vulture shreds. An endless use for beaks and bills.

March 2021

Feeding the Hungry

AT LAST! Hang in there everybody—help is coming.

AT LAST! Someone is finally doing something about our hungry children.

AT LAST! A legislative bill where people are more important than money.

AT LAST! Monthly payments per child for most of the rest of the year.

AT LAST! My tax money is going for what I believe in, taking care of each other.

Over 10 million children go to bed hungry every night. We all know, of course, some of the money may be wasted, but when measured against a child with a full stomach, such waste becomes irrelevant. Someday, because that child had a full stomach that could develop a healthy body and mind that can contribute to mitigating any loss the naysayers scream about. Which is more important, feeding a child or feeding a weapon?

"I hate that when the discussion turns to helping people, there's always someone who takes the most ungenerous, contemptible stand toward others. If by helping legitimately needy people, I accidently help some lazy people, so what? How is that worse than helping no one?"

– Jason Bradley

Immortality

Half a million dead from the coronavirus in the United States and the rest of us wondering how long we'll last makes me think about other species. The common thought is that every living thing dies. It's the rule of nature. The oldest living thing is the bristlecone pine tree located in the American West. The oldest one lived a comfortable 4,800 years.

Several species have an essence of immortality. The sea anemone, for example, never naturally dies and has no predators. Instead of growing older, it just grows bigger. It also never moves very far, usually just swaying back and forth with the surf through eternity, swallowing whatever passes by. Only a major environment change like global warming kills it.

According to some believers, I am to be reincarnated. If I could choose, I would pick the *Turritopsis dohrnii*, commonly called the immortal jellyfish. No brain to worry, no heart to care, no bones to break. Just 95 percent water surrounding a batch of neurons. This reverts to a younger self when the jellyfish is threatened, and it starts the life cycle all over again. Incredibly graceful, it glides through ocean waters catching the currents wherever it may, living forever. Unless a sea slug eats it.

If you're looking for an inspiration to help you survive until you and your loved ones get vaccinated, channel the jellyfish. Avoid sea slugs, stay eternally young, never stop gliding.

Who came first, the chicken or the egg?

Even before chickens, dinosaurs laid eggs. Microbes were the first signs of life, embedded in 3.7-billion-year-old rocks. The first egg-layer was the armored fish, living in the oceans over half a billion years ago and likely the ancestor of all egg layers, water, land, and air.

Our egg-laying ancestor was known as *synapsids*, who laid eggs for millions of years, as did the earliest mammals for billions of years. Even today some mammals still lay eggs.

The first live birth was found in a marine reptile from China, 245 million years old. The first humanoid who gave live birth was the homo erectus appearing in Africa between five to seven million years ago.

Over time, humanoids moved out of Africa and the hot sun, causing the amount of melanin in their skin to diminish. Melanin filters the sun's deadly ultraviolet rays while making vitamin D from the sun. As humanoids moved north and the earth had longer dark hours, they produced less melanin to lighten our skin so that more UV light could pass through for sufficient vitamin D. Critically important to our bodies, vitamin D gives us strong bones and teeth, a healthy immune system to fight off illnesses, a feeling of wellbeing, delayed aging process, and much more.

So we all have surface color variations in our skin formed by the environments of our ancestors, but we are all pretty much the same underneath.

Women and the Glass Ceiling

In the past, I believed men were better at running businesses (demanding profit) and women were better at leading government (protect and serve), maybe the reason for the glass ceiling. I researched the issue in reliable sources such as *Scientific American* and *Forbes* trying to prove my point. Do I ever get tired of being wrong?

The most common style of leadership, Transactional, is being replaced by the new Transformational style, meaning Emotional Intelligence, in both business and government. This system emphasizes team management, motivation, engagement, and shared vision; promotes high ethical behavior; and encourages respect and trust. Women are significantly better at Transformational style because they have a higher regard for people and the tasks they ask them to do. It's all about team-building and communication. Women are also more visionary.

Harvard Business Review found that women are better leaders. A study of over 60,000 leaders, twice as many men as women, concluded both men and women worked harder with a woman boss because greater importance was placed on inspiring, motivating, and communicating. Women are better at taking initiative for change, providing teamwork and relationship building, dealing with stress, frustration, and anxiety, all leading to a feeling of wellbeing and confidence in the workplace. Women like to create change and talk it out much more than men.

In business, women on boards and in leadership usually take the initiative to make changes, bringing about 42 percent higher sales, for a 66 percent higher return on invested capital and 53 percent higher return on equity compared to businesses with no women leaders. In London, businesses with no women in leadership had a net profit margin of 1.5 percent compared with those with the 15.2 percent net profit margin in businesses with at least one to three women in leadership. In the public sector, women leaders of countries around the world outperform men, especially in this COVID crisis.

A frequent complaint women have about men is that they don't listen. The biggest complaint men have against women is that they are always trying to change them. Something to think about.

> "I'm not upset that you lied to me; I'm upset that from now on I can't believe you."
>
> – Friedrich Nietzsche

Politics:

Lying in Politics

Curious about all the acceptability of rampant lying in advertising and politics, I read about the Fairness Doctrine of the United States that the Federal Communications Commission (FCC) once insisted upon. The policy, from 1949, required truth in advertising and both sides of controversial issues to be honestly presented in balanced and equitable fashion.

Ronald Reagan had the FCC abolish this policy in 1987. Could we reinstate it? I am fed up with all the lies, especially those dangerous ones that do serious damage. Like killing people when we are told to drink bleach to cure illnesses.

Birds Visiting Yaquina Bay

The ring-necked duck (above, right) migrates inland for winter, usually in small flocks at night. They can fly from the Pacific, Gulf, and southern Atlantic states as far as central Mexico and the Caribbean.

The surf scoter (above, left) is a "molt" migrant. Once they nest, they fly where they can molt their flight feathers. For a brief time, they cannot fly before they leave for wintering areas on the east and west coasts where they hang out along harbors and fishing piers. They breed on freshwater lakes.

"I wish I could show you when
you are lonely or in darkness
the astonishing light of your
own being." - Hafiz

"He who from zone to zone
Glides through the boundless sky thy certain flight
In the long way that I must tread alone
Will lead my steps aright."
- William Cullen Bryant

My Funny Jays

My jays still steal my chipmunk's peanuts and make a fuss while declaring their territory. I hid the peanuts in a bush, but the jays figured that out. Now I watch the birds disappearing in and out of the bushes, hoping to get there before the chipmunk.

A Story of Great Bravery

Being called a birdbrain shouldn't be called an insult. Humans have been outsmarted again; we are no longer in that exclusive club of having the only cerebral cortex awareness of space and time with high-level, abstract decision-making. Meaning we not only know what we know, but we also take the next step into knowing or figuring out what to do with what we know. No surprise that the macaque monkey perceives subjectively. But so do the crow, barn owl, dove, and the pigeon.

This bird story started on October 2, 1918, in the Meuse-Argonne Offensive which ultimately won World War I against Germany. The unit of about 550 men had pushed in much further than anyone expected and ended up not only surrounded by the Germans but also lost to the rest of their battalion. Out of food and ammunition, they had no way to get help.

Even more disaster hit when their own people started shelling and killing them at the same time the Germans closed in, killing more U.S. soldiers. Out of radio range, they could communicate their location and stop the shelling only by carrier pigeon. Unfortunately, Germans knew pigeons carried these messages and trained solders to shoot them down. In this battle, only one pigeon was left. Named Cher Ami (dear friend), the pigeon, already with a high rate of 12 successful missions, flew into the air with this message attached to his leg.

"WE ARE ALONG THE ROAD PARALELL 276.4. OUR ARTILLERY IS DROPPING A BARRAGE DIRECTLY ON US. FOR HEAVENS SAKE STOP IT."

The pigeon was quickly shot in the chest and fell to the ground. In spite of the severe wound, he flew back into the sky and traveled twenty-five miles to the base in record time. Medics saved him although he was blind and had lost one leg. He saved 194 men that day and was awarded the French award, Croix de Guerre with Palm, the only animal to ever receive such a high honor. Gen. John Pershing sent him home, and Cher Ami returned to the U.S. a hero. He managed to get around on a peg leg until he died on June 13, 1919.

But Cher Ami has not been forgotten. His stuffed body sits beside his award in the National Museum of American History within the Smithsonian Institution, and he has been immortalized by a novel, children's books, short stories, poetry, essays, and even films.

The debates about whether Cher Ami was male or female were settled in 2021, honoring the 100th anniversary of Cher Ami's display at the Smithsonian. A DNA test determined Cher Ami was a biological male.

"When people govern themselves, the majority will always eventually support the tyrant." – Plato

Newport Activities

Land Activities

Newport Recreation Center

Biking Trails

Bird Watching

Canoeing

Brian Booth State Park

Golfing

Salishan: Salishan Golf Links

Newport: Agate Beach

Waldport: Crestview Hills

Hiking

Mike Miller Park

Brian Booth State Park

South Beach State Park

Kayaking

Skateboarding

Shopping

Sea Activities

Crabbing

Clamming

Sailing

Surfing

Whale Watching

Deep Sea Fishing

Tide Pools

Oyster City

As much as we care and how hard we try, greed somehow creeps in and too often destroys our resources. This story began with a shipwreck.

When the schooner *Juliet* ran aground in storms, Run aground by storms, the crew spent two months along the Yaquina River until they finally reached the Willamette Valley, reporting on the abundance of oysters, clams, and various fish.

It was the small and delicate oyster, species *Ostrea lurida*, that brought about three new settlements along both sides of the Yaquina River: Oysterville, Oyster City, and Winant, all on the Grand Ronde Reservation.

An Indian agent by the name of Ben Simpson attempted to protect the area until 1866, when our Department of the Interior moved the reservation to Cape Foulweather, freeing the Yaquina River for harvesting.

These oysters are now extinct, another loss because there were no restrictions or laws in place to stop the over-harvesting.

Wave Energy

Another OSU Hatfield Marine Science Center wave-energy experiment has begun south of Newport. If we can successfully use the ocean for energy, 64 percent of U.S. kilowatt needs can be produced in the waves. The past years have seen many failed starts, but the government has approved PacWave South for the Hatfield Science Center, the first grid-connected wave energy test site to be developed. It costs $84 million, and the two-square-mile site on the ocean floor can test as many as twenty wave experiments at one time. Any approved developer can test their designs by attaching to the "testing berths" on the ocean floor.

The ocean is a harsh mistress when dealing with mechanical stuff. In October 2003, I watched a Hatfield experiment, the AquaBuOY, a very large, very yellow squarish platform, be towed under the Yaquina Bridge and out to sea to generate energy. It survived huge storms, but the day before it was due to be hauled back to shore, it sank 115 feet to the ocean floor.

One experiment used a series of anchored floats that generated power by bobbing up and down with the waves. Aside from the costs outweighing benefits, powerful storms often ripped a buoy or two from their moorings and left them rolling around on the beach.

In another Hatfield-sponsored project, the *Pacific Storm* towed a buoy named SeaBeav 1 and anchored it. Alas, another failure. One company, attempting to build turbines on a barrage, couldn't get funding because windmills would produce the same power at one-third the cost.

In another failure, a company used a hose-pump on the ocean floor.

Other countries are searching for wave-energy success. Scotland developed the Pelamis Wave Machine in 2008 that looked like a merger of a snake and train. It was finally decommissioned in 2016.

Scotland also developed a huge oyster-like machine that opened and closed with the waves. It lasted longer, but its installation and noise interfered with marine life. Denmark went for a Wave Dragon, a floating wall directing waves up and over the top. That was scrapped in 2011.

"If a political party does not have its foundation in the determination to advance a cause that is right and that is moral, then it is not a political party; it is merely a conspiracy to seize power." – Dwight Eisenhower

Oregon State Aquarium Birds

Sometimes people in Newport forget how lucky we are to have the Oregon State Aquarium. Covering 23 acres along the Yaquina Bay, it is among the top ten of its kind in the United States and home to the largest outdoor seabird aviary in North America. Some of the birds are really ugly, like the turkey buzzards. The puffins are among the cutest birds. I've been told that the only way to determine their sex is to catch them mating, and so that's what some of the aquarium workers do: grab them and slap colored bands on them to distinguish the males from the females.

Along with the birds are exhibits, indoors and out, of a huge number of marine mammal species and a nature trail with native plants and free-roaming wildlife that overlooks the Yaquina Bay estuary.

Bird Brains

This guy has been hopping around in my yard for a few days. I thought it was a young robin until I noticed its white belly and the spots on its wings. It's in the sparrow family—a spotted towhee, pronounced "tu-hee."

All birds are human smart. Once we thought birds' intelligence was limited because they had no neocortex, but no longer. Birds also have the part of the neocortex brain called the pallium, that complex cognition and creativity part of mammals. It's a different shape but still there.

Can you imagine migration? The bar-tailed godwit flew 7,500 miles from Alaska to New Zealand—the longest non-stop flight ever recorded. The Arctic tern travels from one pole to the other. The tiny, teeny ruby-throated hummingbird flies 1,243 nonstop miles from Mexico to North America. Along with strong flight muscles and innate knowledge where they head, migrating birds can also modify their flexible digestive system to cope with long flight demands.

"When you talk, you are only repeating what you already know. But if you listen, you may learn something new." – Dalai Lama

Genes

Scientists have identified a set of human genes that fight SARS-CoV-2 infection, the virus causing COVID-19. Knowing which genes help control viral infection will help the understanding of factors affecting disease severity and suggest therapeutic options. The genes in question are related to interferons, the body's frontline virus fighters.

Types of Diseases

So much has been discussed about COVID. What is it? How do we cure it?

Virus: The simplest form of germs, viruses may not be alive because they are only genetic material enclosed in protein and must go into a living being—even bacteria or fungi—for survival. Viruses invade a cell, insert its DNA string, and glue themselves to the cell DNA string. They create thousands of clones until they burst through the cell membrane, killing the cell. These viral strands invade new cells, and the process is replicated over and over until enough cells in our body are dead and so are we. There are more viruses on earth than there are stars in the universe, and they cannot be killed although they can be stopped from reproducing. They infect nearly every organism on earth. Widespread viruses are the common cold, flu, and warts. More serious viruses include measles, rubella, chickenpox, shingles, roseola, smallpox, HIV/AIDs, encephalitis, meningitis, herpes, gastroenteritis, hepatitis C, polio, Dengue fever, West Nile virus, swine flu, yellow fever, and COVID-19.

Stopping Viruses: Because all viruses are different, each one requires a different process to block, requiring millions of experiments as with COVID and other deadly viruses such as Ebola, Marburg, Lassa fever, MERS, SARS, Nipah, Zika, and Crimean-Congo hemorrhagic fever. Any of them could be our next pandemic. The common cold doesn't even have a vaccination. Stopping duplication of the virus requires five steps: (1) attaching and penetrating infected cell; (2) uncoating and releasing the cell's DNA; (3) mixing the antivirus with the cell's DNA; (4) changing it into a new virus that can no longer duplicate itself; and (5) releasing the new virus to invade the next sick cell. Antibiotics and anti-fungal treatment will not stop viruses because none of them enter the cell.

Bacteria: Larger than viruses, these single-celled micro-organisms do not kill cells by exploding from within as viruses do. Instead, they live outside the cell and surround it, consuming its nutrients and starving the cell to death. Bacteria can live almost anywhere—soil, water, and living creatures. At least one nonillion bacteria are on the earth—that's 1 followed by 30 zeros.

Much of the Earth's biomass is comprised of bacteria, some good, offering protection against diseases and aiding with digestion in the gut. Others, not so much. Bacteria cause many types of diseases, ranging from mild skin irritation to lethal pneumonia. Among the more dangerous diseases caused by bacteria are tuberculosis, anthrax, tetanus, leptospirosis, pneumonia, cholera, botulism, strep throat, gonorrhea, gastric ulcer, diphtheria, and bubonic plague.

Stopping Bacteria: Antibacterials such as penicillin and cephalosporin kill bacteria outright by directly attacking the bacterial cell wall, injuring the cell so that the bacteria can no longer absorb the cell's nutrients.

Fungi: More complicated than bacteria and viruses, fungi have cells and are closer in structure to animals than the other two. People and animals with weak immune systems can get sick when spores from fungi, such as yeast and mold, affect living bodies. Like bacteria, they surround cells and consume their nutrients. With only about 300 types of fungi, they cause skin infections such as ringworm and athlete's foot. Bacteria can also collect on fungi.

Stopping fungi: Antifungal cures, both oral and topical, surround the cell and weaken the cell membrane to force the fungus to leak out, thereby stopping reproduction.

Parasites: These creatures can kill human cells by biting off chunks of cells until cells die. Parasites come from mosquitos, worms, leaches, bed bugs, lice, fleas, etc. They cause illnesses such as malaria, sleeping sickness, Chagas, Toxoplasmosis, Giardia, toenail fungus, yeast infections, and jock itch.

Stopping Parasites: Hydroxychloroquine can kill the parasite thereby preventing malaria, some types of lupus, and rheumatoid arthritis, but it does not kill viruses or bacteria. Ivermectin also kills parasitic organisms by paralyzing their muscle/nerve systems but again does not kill viruses or bacteria.

Before diseases can be stopped, their structure and behavior must be determined. Simply put, viruses invade the cell, exploding from within; bacteria surround the cell, starving it to death; fungi puncture the cell; and parasites take bites out of the cell, sucking out the nutrients. What works for one doesn't work for the others.

"The highest form of ignorance is when you reject something you know nothing about." – Wayne Dyer

Vaccinations

Each state sets requirements for vaccinations, going back to the nineteenth century, and all states have some mandates. As of July 18, 2018, all 50 states and DC require vaccinations for diphtheria, tetanus, and pertussis (whooping cough)—all bacterial—as well as virus-caused polio, measles, and rubella. Most states also require vaccinations for mumps, chickenpox, and hepatitis A & B, all caused by bacteria or viruses.

Since the COVID pandemic began, the FDA has issued nearly 100 warnings regarding fraudulent claims of cures. The snake doctor always appears where money is to be made.

It's a fine thing when someone tells me I am unreasonably scared of a deadly virus when that same person is scared of black and brown people, LGBTQ people, immigrants, women with good jobs, Obama Care, higher wages, vaccines, voting by mail, laws protecting our air, water, and earth, windmills and electric cars, face masks, and voting by mail.

Saving Our Marine Life

For the past 30 years I have made my home among people who make a living from the yield of the sea and the need to protect it. We can still save our marine life by 2050 with interventions. Although rising temperatures, pollution, and acidic water are killing the coral reefs and decimating our ocean life, there is hope. We have the skills and expertise to restore vital marine life by saving and replacing any losses to our seagrass, saltmarshes, mangroves, coral reefs, kelp, oyster reefs, fisheries, megafauna, and the deep sea. Time, however, is running out. For example, our coral reef will by gone in thirty years without intervention. When that happens, we will have no more time to save anything.

In his last two years in office, Trump's elimination of almost all environmental regulations "indefinitely" were those that had nothing to do with the pandemic. No penalties for breaking the rules, no need for reporting any problems. Big business just has to say what they do relates to the pandemic. An "open license to pollute," wrote former EPA administrator Gina McCarthy. Trump removed federal protections for over half our nation's wetlands and millions of small streams, rivers, wetlands, ground water, and endangered species. No more restrictions on methane leaks, chemical and fossil fuel pollution, and unsafe oil drilling. Joe Biden reversed many of Trump's damaging changes. Not a minute to waste.

California Poppy

I found this lovely volunteer growing throughout my yard. Believing it was an Arizona poppy, I had a long debate with Nel, and she won. The magical internet explained it was a California poppy. Maybe next time . . .

Shy Particle Points to Undiscovered Physics

This discovery reminds us that the knowledge of physics allows us to understand how things work such as light bulbs, engines, paints, brains, cathedrals, earthquakes, tornados, DNA, and black holes. The muon, an elementary subatomic particle similar to the electron but 207 times heavier, may be a tiny particle but has the giant potential to upend our understanding of the subatomic world and reveal an undiscovered type of fundamental physics.

The More We Know—Lightning

Scientists have found that lightning bolts and, surprisingly, subvisible discharges that cannot be seen by cameras or the naked eye produce extreme amounts of the hydroxyl radical and hydroperoxyl radical. Vital to the atmosphere, the hydroxyl initiates chemical reactions and breaks down molecules like the greenhouse gas methane.

Reversing Spinal Cord Injuries

Northwestern University researchers have developed a new injectable therapy that harnesses "dancing molecules" to reverse paralysis and repair tissue after severe spinal cord injuries. Researchers administered a single injection to tissues surrounding the spinal cords of paralyzed mice. Just four weeks later, animals regained their ability to walk.

Science Does Not Lie

Since the advent of COVID, many people accuse scientists of lying. We do know, however, information changes with additional knowledge; scientists present the facts as they discover them. It's like the way we absorb our environment. Our "truth" changes when we experience more.

Coffee, for example, was once good for us; then it wasn't. Decaf coffee was then better; then it wasn't. Etc. The automobile combustion engine developed from one cylinder to electric, but each change or improvement did not mean the last discovery was wrong. The job of science is to find the truth and a way to make it useful with available research tools at the time. We have so much more out there to learn—and accept until we don't.

Quarantine

Isolation seems to be on the wane, and I'm looking for the positive from the past year. Even the great Bard wrote *King Lear* while quarantined during one of the bubonic plagues. Sir Isaac Newton came up with his theory of gravity during another bubonic plague. Edvard Munch managed to paint one of his masterpieces, "Self-Portrait with the Spanish Flu," during the influenza outbreak of 1918. Salvator Rosa painted "Human Frailty" during the Black Plague after he lost a son. If companies producing the virus are willing to "jab" everybody in the world for free, that would be the greatest human accomplishment of all. The world's greatest masterpiece.

"The Important thing is to never stop questioning." - Albert Einstein

Mark Twain once wrote, "Be careful about reading health books. You may die of a misprint."

Homo Sapiens Evolution

According to science, mammals have evolved big brains after big disasters. So says a large study revealing the way relative brain size of mammals changed over the last 150 million years. Brain mass data was used to measure 1,400 living and extinct mammals using endocranial volume data from the skulls.

"We've overturned a long-standing dogma that relative brain size can be equivocated with intelligence," says Kamran Safi, a research scientist at the Max Planck Institute of Animal Behavior and senior author on the study. "Sometimes, relatively big brains can be the end result of a gradual decrease in body size to suit a new habitat or way of moving—in other words, nothing to do with intelligence at all. Using relative brain size as a proxy for cognitive capacity must be set against an animal's evolutionary history and the nuances in the way brain and body have changed over the tree of life."

The study further explained that most changes in brain size occurred after two cataclysmic events in Earth's history: the mass extinction sixty-six million years ago and a climatic transition twenty-three to twenty-four million years ago. Brain to body size does not depend on the evolution of intelligence, explained Planck. Rather, it may indicate a more general adaptation to large pressures from the environment that go beyond intelligence.

Elections Don't Make People Smart

I have been listening to an incredibly famous man who gave us very weird and very deadly advice: "So, supposing we hit the body with a tremendous—whether it's ultraviolet or just very powerful light. And then I said, supposing you brought the light inside of the body, which you can do either through the skin or in some other way. Sounds interesting. And then I see the disinfectant where it knocks it out in a minute. One minute. And is there a way we can do something like that, by injection inside or almost a cleaning?" He also tweeted, "Hydroxychloroquine is a cure for Covid." It is not. Hydroxychloroquine kills parasites that cause malaria, lupus, and rheumatoid arthritis. COVID is caused by a virus and not a parasite. And last, "You don't need a mask to slow the spread of coronavirus."

And this man ruled the world for a while. And still might again.

As Mark Twain would say, "We have the best government money can buy." As for me, I know a machine that spreads the best cure I know. There is a manure gun spreader can shoot a 30 -foot by 40-foot stream of fine crap, hopefully covering all the liars.

"Don't bother walking a mile in my shoes; that would be boring. Spend 10 seconds in my head; that'll freak you right out."

- Hans Asperger

It must be painful to believe historians, scholars, and scientists have spent their lives lying to you, but you will believe a TV star who has spent his life in fraudulent behavior and lying as your source for truth.

May 2021

Roller-Coaster Flight of the Bald Eagle

I watched a jubilee of bald eagles, at least 15, soar and tower overhead, catching thermals over the bay most of the day. They slowly made their way to the Yaquina Bridge and back upriver again, their hollow bones and eight-foot wingspan helping them easily stay aloft.

It's chinook salmon and steelhead season, and they could be hunting. Or just having fun.

Monogamous birds, building and raising their offspring together, they may be getting ready for the mating season in a ritual in which the pair climb high, clutch talons together, and cartwheel through the sky as one.

This guy sat there for a very long time, just staring back at me. I think it would be fun to be able to turn my head without turning my body. Maybe yoga? Or a contortionist who revels in freaking me out.

Everybody Matters

"You may think that you are completely insignificant in this world. But someone drinks coffee from the favorite cup that you gave them. Someone heard a song on the radio that reminded them of you. Someone read the book that you recommended and plunged headfirst into it. Someone smiled after a hard day of work because they remembered the joke that you told them today. Someone likes themselves a little bit more because you gave them a compliment. Never think that you have no influence whatsoever."

– Christina Makeyeva

Fishing in the Yaquina River

Blessing of the Fleet

I had a grand time sitting on my perch over the river watching it all. I have photos. I know, I know, no surprise there.

The Newport Fisherman wives will again sponsor a strong tradition, its community ceremony honoring local fishermen and their families.

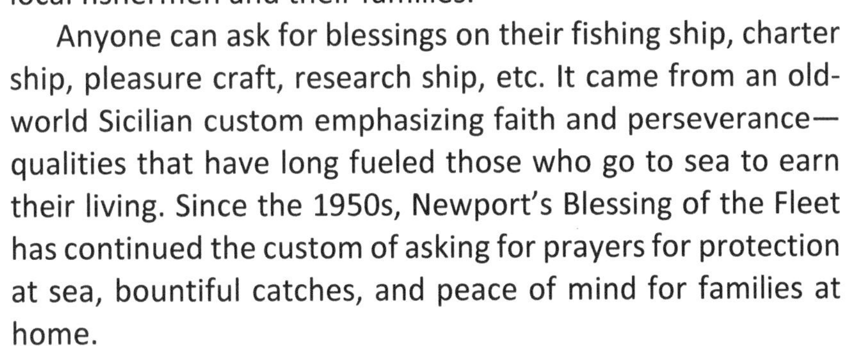

Anyone can ask for blessings on their fishing ship, charter ship, pleasure craft, research ship, etc. It came from an old-world Sicilian custom emphasizing faith and perseverance—qualities that have long fueled those who go to sea to earn their living. Since the 1950s, Newport's Blessing of the Fleet has continued the custom of asking for prayers for protection at sea, bountiful catches, and peace of mind for families at home.

Chocolate

The idea of chocolate lost in the climate change breaks my heart. It's my last major addiction aside from a love of living. Did you know that between 20 percent and 30 percent of our world's cacao trees are annually dying? And it takes twenty plus years to produce new and, hopefully, tougher varieties.

Maybe hope is on the way: I read that scientists found a gene controlling the flowering of the cacao tree that may help us accelerate the research needed to find the solution. The more we know.

Money Tree

I bought a money tree just because I liked the name. I also thought its seeds would be shaped like coins. Not true. That one is called the money plant, also known as the silver dollar, honesty, and moonwort. So, if it doesn't drop coins, why a money tree? The story comes from an old legend of a poor man who, when praying for money, found a strange plant. Believing it was an omen, he took it home and made a pot of money selling plants he raised from the seeds. So, he named it the money tree. Maybe money does grow on trees.

Legend tells us the money tree also brings us prosperity, helps balance and ground us, and creates positive energy around us. They have five or six leaves on every stem, although occasionally it may have seven leaves, which means those who own one should be extra lucky.

I bought a house plant about 10 inches tall and found out they grow to seven feet. Good thing I have an eight-foot ceiling. I also did not realize until I stared long enough to see I had actually bought four trees braided together as one. But the tree died so I don't have to worry about how much it grows.

Pro-Birth

"I do not believe that just because you're opposed to abortion, you will be pro-life. In fact, I think in many cases, your morality is deeply lacking if all you want is a child born but not educated, not a child housed. And why would I think that you don't? Because you don't want any tax money to go there. That's not pro-life. That's pro-birth. We need a much broader conversation on what the morality of pro-life is."

— Sister Joan Chittister

Sign on a Restaurant Door

MASK REQUIRED FOR SERVICE. Do not pout. Do not whine. Do not argue. Do not harass the employees. Do not spout conspiracy theories or regurgitate misinformation you got from your dumb uncle on Facebook. This isn't political; it is basic health and safety. Do not choose to be the reason the rest of the world is laughing at us.

"I forgot it in my car." Well, go get it.
"This is unconstitutional." No, it's not.
"This is a hoax." You're an idiot.

Gene Editing

So many good things did emerge from the tragic 2020 year. Telemedicine made life much easier, and scientific discoveries regarding our health were amazing.

Gene editing now uses enzymes to target a specific DNA sequence and cut into the strands to remove existing DNA and insert DNA replacements.

To be able to tell someone faced with enduring a lifetime of pain such as sickle cell that they can now be cured is miraculous.

Gaslighting is when someone hurts you, then blames you for being hurt.

Gaslighting

The term gaslighting came into popularity in the last decade although it's been around since the 1938 British play called *Gas Light* made into the 1944 movie.

Current popular use is the politicians' manipulation and abuse by giving a false narrative to mislead others, who then doubt their own perceptions and therefore get upset or even disoriented. Common terms, sometimes from people we trust and/or love, which make us doubt our own sanity:

You're being insecure.
You're too emotional.
Stop making things up.
That never happened.
Stop being dramatic.
Stop imagining things.
You're overthinking it.
You're being paranoid.

People who harm you will blame *you* for it.

I am always in awe of our ever-changing sunrises on the Yaquina River.

"THOSE WE LOVE DON'T GO AWAY.
THEY WALK BESIDE US EVERY DAY."
-Alex Maclean

Like the petals of a flower
Or the heart warmth of giving,
We should be so grateful
For the amazing gift of living.
– Miranela Reks

June 2021

Neskowin Ghost Forest

My friend Ann Hubard is traveling again, this time to the Neskowin Ghost Forest. Unusually extreme low tides have uncovered the ancient forest on the Oregon Coast. These 100+ decaying stumps of Sitka spruce trees first appeared during the powerful winter storms of 1997-98. Originally 200 feet tall, they carbon-date at about 2,000 years old.

Geologists theorize the Cascadia subduction zone earthquake in 1700 felled the trees, and the land dropped, allowing the ocean to rush over them and bury them in the sand.

An excellent day trip from Newport, Neskowin is fifteen miles north of Lincoln City at Milepost 98. Park in the public lot at the Neskowin turnoff and head for Proposal Rock across the creek. The stumps are south of Proposal Rock, named when in 1900, Charles Gage proposed to Della Page.

Politics:

Loss of Democracies

It is a sad fact that, historically, democracies have never survived. According to the 2021 Freedom of the World Report, the last fifteen years has seen global freedom for 75 percent of our global countries on the decline from both the cruelest dictators to democracies such our own. Even in our own time, we have witnessed loss of democracy as dictators took over Libya, Syria, Iraq, Afghanistan, Yemen, Congo, Colombia, and Vietnam. So many of the major safeguards protecting our democracy have been whittled away by corporate greed that few of us have found ways to fight back.

Liberals are easy to ignore because conservatives assume we won't fight back. We don't want to fight back. We don't think the world owes us anything because it was here first, and we should take care of it. We don't want to hurt others. We don't think we have the answers for anyone else and are pleased to find satisfying answers for ourselves. We think everyone should be free to find our own way in this world as long as we don't hurt or diminish anyone else in our pursuit. Let me repeat that. As long as we *DON'T HURT OR DIMINISH ANYONE ELSE.*

We think everyone has value and should be helped to reach whatever reasonable positive goal they set for themselves. We believe in our constitutional rights for ALL in "Life, Liberty and the pursuit of Happiness."

I repeat. No one should be denied these rights. No one. Yet here we bleeding-heart liberals sit, contemplating our navels as the old saying goes, waiting for the final drop of the guillotine.

Politics:

Liberals Are Wimps and Proud of It

We don't want to overthrow a government. We don't want to fight. We are not angry enough; we don't hate enough. We want peace, to feel safe and loved. We want everybody to have a chance to get a good education or training to get their dream jobs, a home and family. We want everyone to get their shots so that we are all protected and can go about doing all the things we need to get done. But here we are, at war to protect our democratic way of life, a war we are going to lose because enough violence and hate from those willing to destroy anything to get what they perceive as freedom will win over the peacemaker every time. It is hard to accept that that the rules, regulations, and laws that, by protecting each of us from the other, provide the only freedom we get.

Yaquina River Dock

Card to Parent

I was a media specialist for two-thirds of my thirty years in teaching and looked for ways to help teachers. One of my projects was giving them cards to mail to parents complimenting their child on an achievement. One teacher who sent out the cards came into my office and sat down across from me. She said, "I sent one of your cards and the girl came in this morning with tears in her eyes. "I graduate this year," she said. "In all those years this is the first time any teacher ever said something nice about me." The teacher and I sat quietly for a while, both trying to hold back our own tears.

Always help someone. You might be the only one who does

Pecking Orders

Don't think your backyard feeder is utter chaos. Although the term pecking order started with hens, all birds have them. Even other animals. If you ever watched a herd of cows, the pecking order rapidly becomes obvious. But back to birds. Not only do they have pecking orders within the species, they also have them among species. For those of you who enjoy watching birds, here's the hierarchy with the crow on top:

Crow
Grackle
Red-bellied woodpecker
Starling
Blue jay
Robin
Red-winged blackbird
Mourning doves
Cowbird
Cardinal
Sparrow
Downy woodpecker
White-breasted nuthatch
Wren
Tufted titmouse
Finch
Red-breasted nuthatch
Dark-eyed junco
Purple finch
Goldfinch
Chickadee

A research project followed the interaction of nearly 100,000 birds of 200 species.

Nobody was surprised the crow came out on top; it is considered the number one smartest animal next to human beings, the only animal next to us that can make hooked tools. More important, it can solve problems at the level of a ten-year-old.

Sea Foam

I woke up to a stream of sea foam snaking up the river for a good mile. I'm always fascinated by what we find on our Oregon beaches and rivers that is connected to the sea. Two-million-year-old fossils in a variety of ancient shell life uncovered by the shifting sand, gloriously-colored agates ground smooth, sands shifting into waves and curls often awash with piles of kelp, waves pounding rocks sending waterspouts that rise in a rainbow show, masses of Velella

and jellyfish too slippery to walk on, sunsets and sunrises with flashes of color so beautiful you want to cry, teaming sea life in all sizes, shapes, and colors.

On the beach, I watched thick swarms of mayflies for over an hour. They kept coming, always managing to fly around me. Remember when, at the beginning of rain when you watched a few heavy drops fall before you ran from the deluge? Rather than down, these mayflies came sideways.

Mayflies are an ancient insect of the dragonfly family. Although they are not dangerous, they can cause allergies and do smell like dead fish. Their only serious problem is when their dense numbers closed highways due to bad visibility.

But this post is about sea foam which I had called spindrift. Looking it up, all I found was Spindrift bottled water. So sea foam it is. To me, sea foam looks like a nice bubble bath peppered with rainbow-colored bubbles. It is really a mass of tiny living single-celled sea plants called phytoplankton, food for other sea life. The foam is created when strong winds and waves inject enough air into the phytoplankton to form bubbles pushed onto the beaches in massive pileups. It's fun to run through, but don't turn a small dog loose in it. A friend almost lost her little white poodle until it yapped in protest, and we knew where to dig.

"'The government has no business making me wear a mask,' I say, before I buckle my seatbelt in a car built to safety regulations, drive the speed limit to a restaurant built to code, eat food made in a state-inspected kitchen, and receive the Heimlich maneuver from a waiter who learned it from a mandatory workplace poster."

– Ben Rosen

The Yaquina River Bar

Too many boaters lose their lives on river bars, and our own Yaquina River bar is one of the most treacherous in the United States. My education about its danger happened just after we moved here. On a cold, cloudy, wind-slapping day, a friend came by the house and told us about a sailboat attempting to cross the bar. We gathered along the jetties with a few hundred others staring at the end.

The bad storm the day before had ripped the boat's big sail from the main mast, and it was dragging behind the boat. Ocean swells were running so high from fierce winds that the crew had to wait all night and into most of the day for a slack tide they could hopefully ride safely into the river. The 40-foot sailboat hesitated before it seemed to gather its nerve and spurt forward. When the boat hit the bar, it rolled so far down the top of the mast disappeared.

Everyone held their breath in silence until, at last, the mast popped up and the boat crested into quieter waters. Shouts, whistles, and clapping echoed across the waters. We trailed the boat up the river until it tied up at the dock. The two men on the boat jumped off, got on their knees, and kissed the earth. This was my first experience with a coastal fishing town's gathering to support those who make their living from the sea.

My own first experience crossing the bar was a non-crossing fizzled failure. I was on a whale-watching trip, heading for the bar behind the Yaquina dredge, when a huge wave blasted over the north jetty and bounced the massive dredge around like a toy. The tour boat's pilot blurted, "Wow! Did you see that?" and immediately turned the boat around. We cruised the bay instead.

My usual daft curiosity made me wonder what made the bar so dangerous. Shallower river currents slamming into the deeper ocean waters generate high waves and deep rolling troughs. Add a nasty storm with monster waves as high as forty feet leaping into the mix, and you can have disaster. These waves either roll over and smash down on a boat when it drops into the bar's tough or plow into the side of the boat, capsizing it or shoving it into the side of the jetty. Recent losses of the FV *Chevelle*, *Two Mikes,* and *Nat* fishing boats are deadly reminders of the bar. More recently, 16-foot breakers slammed the FV *Mary B II* running from a building storm and broke the older plank boat into pieces.

The Yaquina River Jetties

The jetties have fascinated me from my first glimpse while crossing the Yaquina bridge into Newport. Their purpose for jetties—establishing a reliable and safe waterway for sea-going ships. The word "jetty" was French from "jetée," meaning "thrown" which pretty much fits considering how our jetties were assembled. The U.S. Army Corps of Engineers built one-way railroads into the ocean near the Yaquina River egress. Huge boulders weighing thirty to fifty tons were hoisted onto flatcars, backed up on the rails, and dumped over-board until they piled high enough to break most waves. The rails were then ripped up, leaving behind the trestles.

Originally 2,300 feet long, the north jetty was too short to keep sand from stacking up at the mouth of the bay. With a need for deeper water for larger ships and damage from storms, it was repaired and extended six times. The 8,600-foot south jetty was completed in 1896 and was extended another 1,800 feet in 1972.

Our jetties protect a 300-foot-wide boat channel into the large harbor of Yaquina Bay. They also offer a certain amount of recreation such as surfing further down from the south jetty and bird watching, but they are also incredibly dangerous to walk on. Even though they appear safe, they have sinkholes, slippery rocks, and sneaker waves that knock people off every year, many of them drowning. Recently a young couple was washed off the South Jetty. Both of them drowned. Two years earlier, it was two young men. One lived. One did not. A year before, a 64-year-old man needed rescuing after he fell on the jetty rocks. Like a lot of things in life, you can look but you shouldn't touch.

Space Flight

Jeff Bezos, owner of Amazon.com, and his brother are the first private citizens to fly into space with no specific reason. Based in Seattle, his rocket, the *Blue Origin*, launched on July 20, the anniversary of Buzz Aldrin and Neil Armstrong's Apollo 11 moon landing in 1969. Bezos stepped down as Amazon CEO two weeks before takeoff. I do wonder about the money Bezos spent to get to space.

"Our world is not divided by race, color, gender, or religion. Our world is divided into wise people and fools. And fools divide themselves by race, color, gender, or religion." - Mohamad Safi

"Researchers have proven, scientifically, that humans are all one people. The color of our ancestors' skin and ultimately my skin and your skin is a consequence of ultraviolet light, of latitude and climate. Despite our recent sad conflicts here in the U.S., there really is no such thing as race. We are one species – each of us much, much more alike than different. We all come from Africa. We all are of the same stardust. We are all going to live and die on the same planet, a Pale Blue Dot in the vastness of space. We have to work together." - Bill Nye

Politics:

Modest Proposal

In 1729, Jonathan Swift wrote the satirical essay "Modest Proposal." The full title was "A Modest Proposal for Preventing the Children of Poor People from Being a Burthen to their Parents, or the Country, and for Making them Beneficial to the Publick."

Swift's scathing review attacked the rich who not only allowed the extreme poverty and starvation but were also the main cause. According to the satire, the best way to solve this problem was to "find out a fair, cheap, and easy method" to fatten up the children so that they could be butchered and fed to the rich.

As he put it, this would "improve the culinary experience of the wealthy and contribute to the overall economic well-being of the nation." Selling the fattened children would add income for poor parents and save the price tag for raising that child. (It's now $175,000.)

Following Swift's direction today, the government would save a fortune. Critics of the safety net complain about $40 billion in childcare, $195 billion in child-tax credits, and $48 billion in food stamps. Not to mention education and other costs for kids. Always better to stick that money in the pockets of the rich with their tax cuts than leave people in poverty.

A (hopefully) misprinted wedding reception menu went viral because it offered "__Beef __Pork __Child (under 12)" as entree choices, it isn't quite so funny in light of the 13 million (that's one in seven) of our children in the U.S. who go to bed hungry every night. I wondered if the Critical Race Theory opponents complaining about the government programs to help hungry children will now claim there is no such thing as a hungry child—or just not talk about them because it causes non-hungry people "discomfort."

Politics:

Critical Race Theory

Really? Critical Race Theory in elementary and high schools is now a real thing? Wow! How to twist white supremist bigotry into the righteous true path. I had a hard enough time when cancel culture claimed fighting oppression is an assault on freedom. For whom? What happened to the freedom for the oppressed? So, now it's not only just fine to deny freedom to any nonwhite the supremist doesn't like; it's okay to unleash bigoted cruelty on others without consequences. What happened to our constitutional guarantees of equal rights and protection for all?

Common COVID Symptoms

In England, a study of 508,707 participants examined long-lasting effects of COVID infections, referred to "long COVID" in patients with the 29 most common symptoms. Women were more affected than men, and symptoms increased with aging. Effects last many months, frequent ones being shortness of breath, loss of sense of taste, and fatigue.

A separate Norwegian study of 312 patients found that 61 percent still experienced persistent symptoms at six months, including 52 percent of 16- to 30-year-olds. Common symptoms they reported were loss of taste and/or smell and fatigue. Long COVID is a great reason for wearing your mask. And hoping others do it too, especially if they refuse to get vaccinated.

Naming Towns and Places

When traveling around my state of Oregon, I have to wonder why anyone would name a place that would evoke a variety of emotions from laughing to "Oh, gluk!" Let me give you a few examples: Timbuktu, Jennyopolis, Pochahontas, Boring, Zigzag, Clackamas, Idiotville, and Jackass Butte.

Halfway got its name when the post offices at Pine and Jim Town closed and consolidated to the Alexander Stalker ranch, halfway between Pine and Jim Town. Voila! Halfway.

The town of **Sisters** was named after three mountains side-by-side in the Cascade Volcanic Arc, a part of the Cascade Range, and located in the Three Sisters Wilderness. The mountains have other names as well. The North Sister is named Faith, Middle Sister is Hope, and South Sister is called Charity.

Riddle was named after an early settler, William H. Riddle, who arrived from Springfield, Illinois in 1851.

Drain came from its founder, Charles Drain, a politician.

Nimrod's biblical origins means a "mighty hunter." In the early 1900s, the owner of an inn called it The Nimrod, maybe advertising fishing on the McKenzie River.

Sublimity earned its name from its surroundings that left early settlers awe-struck.

Zigzag was named after the Zigzag River. The river? Early travelers supposedly crossed it by following the directions of pioneer Joel Palmer who wrote this description in his journal. "The manner of descending is to turn directly to the right, go zigzag for about one hundred yards, then turn short round, and go zigzag until you come under the place where you started from; then to the right, and so on, until you reach the base."

Wankers Corner was named after the Wanker family, who owned the country store. Not very exciting.

Cascade Volcanic Arc

Peanuts!
My friend Mr. Munk returned this morning, but the jays beat him to the peanuts again.

July 2021

Choosing Food to Eat

We are learning how flies and maybe people choose their food. Flies discriminate between sweet foods, which they prefer, and bitter ones, which they avoid. When researchers starved the flies, they found flies will eat the bitter food. Even more, they manipulated brain neurons to make starving flies select food with lower calories. Neurons are controlled by neuropeptides and dopamine; in humans these secretions give sensations of rewards. So people aren't really choosing food—neurochemistry is.

> Don't change to please others. Be you and choose those who choose you.

Fourth of July Fireworks

On this glorious morning, I'm drinking my coffee and watching the sun chase the night's shadows off Table Mountain while I muse about the coming fireworks in three days, worrying about the vulnerability of the hill I live on. Will the dry vegetation on the side of the hill catch fire this year from my neighbors' illegal fireworks? And yet I still like the fireworks. Except for last year when we didn't have any because of COVID.

I do not question the restorative benefits of faith. I do not have a problem with anyone believing in a higher authority. My problem is that faith in any religion depends on believing in a spirit we cannot see, a voice we cannot hear, and a force we cannot touch. Faith is a world with no reality checks as it hides behind symbols such as the cross, safe from criticism or any way to correct erroneous and dangerous beliefs such as white supremacy.

My Birthday

I cannot believe today is my 89th birthday. Don't say it. I've already heard so many old age jokes it's not even funny. You know the ones. At my age "getting lucky" means walking into a room and remembering what I came in for. Or this one: I'm so old that my blood type is discontinued. Or you know you're getting old when everything hurts and what doesn't hurt doesn't work. Or you're getting old when you stoop to tie your shoelaces and wonder what else you could do while you're down there. Then there's this one: old people shouldn't eat health foods. They need all the preservatives they can get. Then there's Maggie Smith's famous comment: "The trouble with getting older is that you eat breakfast every half hour." My favorite? You know you are getting old when you can't walk past a bathroom without thinking, "I might as well pee while I'm here."

There are also the birthday cards with pithy sayings such as "forget about the past, you can't change it. Forget about the future, you can't predict it. Forget about the present, I didn't get you one." My favorite? Stay positive and remember it's just another birthday. More good times are still to come. Why, just the other day I fell down the stairs and thought, "That's the fastest I've moved in years!"

So today I wish my twin brother "Happy Birthday" because he used to always call me on this day and now it's my turn. I hope he can hear me. One of my sisters-in-law and oldest niece sent me a card so that helped. I do live some in the past, mostly good memories with family and friends I am grateful to have known. And pets. My present dog is getting old with me, and she'll be my last. She's 14 now and, like me, counting the months rather than years.

If I had to admit, the worst part of growing old for me are the things that went wrong I cannot fix. I have learned to repeat "I forgive myself" until the regret is buried in my mental coffin, and I refocus on a healing image. Anything will do. The flick of a cat's tail stalking a fly. A bird bathing in the fountain outside my window. My big toe.

The best part of growing old is how grateful I am to family and friends, to everyone who looked me in the eye, smiled, and wished me a good day and meant it; who stopped to take a breath and try to fix whatever's wrong with today, because they know that yesterday is gone and tomorrow will never come.

So, thank you, dear readers, for sharing my birthday with me, and for hanging in there with me all these years. And I thank the person who walks beside me every day. Thank you, Nel. And hopefully, if the sky doesn't fall as far as the rest of me, I will be around to thank you again next year.

P.S. I'm not adding 2020 to my age. I didn't use it. And I may not use 2021 either.

Whale's Song!

Wouldn't that be something? Replacing the spendy research ship the R/V *Marcus Langseth* with a whale song. Or so Jes Burns wrote in the *Register-Guard* (February 2, 2021). By studying whale songs, scientists discovered the vibrations from fin whales can penetrate up to 1.5 miles under the ocean's seafloor and analyze them to study geologic layers for earthquake movement and faults.

Although probably never gaining the detail achieved by the presently used air guns exploring sea depths from the *Langseth*, scientists surmise the possibility that adding other types of calls such as the sperm whale with its higher pitch could gather acceptable information.

A great benefit to our oceans would be if whale songs replace the seismic air guns. We need information about our Cascadia Fault sitting 60 miles off our shores, famously dangerous for earthquakes and tsunamis, but we also recognize the danger of seismic guns, the loudest sounds made by humans, to sea life.

This gun's explosive sound can travel underwater as far as 2,500 miles. Repeated every 10 seconds for days on end, the sound destroys sea habitats, injuring and killing marine animals from zooplankton to large whales.

The *Langseth* is careful using the seismic guns, but the oil industry is not so careful in its search for oil and gas. Former Rep. Joe Cunningham (D-KY) demonstrated how extensive use of the seismic guns by oil exploration can kill nearby sea life and displace whale populations and turtle nesting habits as well as disrupting fish migration and spawning.

The Spruce Railroad – World War I

Sometimes when I wander about, I wonder what once traveled with me. One day I discovered I had walked in the same place as a famous railroad track. Actually, a ghost railroad.

In the early 1900s there were vague, barely passable roads or bridges, along the coast or over the Coast Range. The only railroad to the coast from inland for central Oregon was Hogg's railroad from Corvallis to Yaquina City which hauled people. It was abandoned in 1937.

The Pacific Coast was filled with rugged mountains and steep canyons, huge trees, and thick underbrush; it was rife with fog and mud because of an average annual rainfall of eleven feet. Not where you would expect to find railroads. And yet a railroad was built. In an unprecedented fifteen months during World War I, the entire 354 miles of railroad track was laid along the coast from Alaska into northern California to transport Sitka spruce and Douglas fir as far away as England, France, and Italy.

Of all the conifers that grew along the coast, builders preferred the Sitka spruce for building biplanes and wooden laminated propellers from the lightest, strongest, and most resilient wood because of its long and tough fibers. Bullets couldn't even splinter the wood.

Sitka spruce, it turned out, mainly grew in a wet, fog-cloaked narrow band along the Washington and Oregon coast. For ship building, the Douglas fir was preferred for the tight-knotted, non-porous close grain—wood that lasts longer than any other when exposed to water.

By 1916, the lumber industry was already going strong as were the big unions that frequently went on strike. To avoid dealing with unions, U.S. Army General Brice Pursell Disque, upon arrival in Washington D.C. on May 7, 1917, replaced loggers whose union interfered with U.S. Army soldiers. The government formed the SPD (Spruce Production Division) of 30,000 soldiers. Most of them had no logging experience, customarily carrying rifles. This time, they came carrying misery whips—two-man crosscut saws—and wore tin pants, work pants made of heavy cotton treated with oil and wax to make them fire resistant and waterproof, fashioned around the 1900s for the logging industry.

Sitka spruce are massive; the largest presently living Sitka, now in Clatsop County, is 206 feet tall and 18 feet in diameter. Men who were never before in a forest tackled them with hand-made tools. These "soldiers" also fought forest fires and built roads, railroads, and bridges. Protected from union sabotage, mill owners were most grateful to find a steady labor force of loggers and access to new roads, bridges, and railroads.

During the fifteen months that SPD operated along the Pacific coast, it moved a massive amount of 143,008,961 board feet, mostly by railroad tracks. The main tracks on the coast were 173 miles long with 181 more feet in tributaries. They built thirteen railroads in Washington and Oregon alone, six railroads in Oregon and two in Lincoln County. The 30,000 soldiers built their 230 self-sufficient camps, set two miles apart.

One of the railroad tent camp headquarters, housing 3,370 soldiers, was at Newport's South Beach, and another was set up in Agate Beach. The army also started building a sawmill in Toledo for milling the logs. Not completed during the war, logs were shipped out of Yaquina Bay to Vancouver, Washington. Another headquarters was at Camp One, south of Waldport on the corner of Camp One Road and Highway 101 and part of the Blodgett Tract consisting of 12,700 acres of old-growth trees. In the early months of 1918, SPD began the Alsea Southern Railroad to reach the South Beach log dump. Logs had to wait on tides to raft them into place, and the railroad wasn't completed until November 8, 1918, just three days before the Germans and Allies signed the armistice ending the war.

Unfortunately, not one log of the one million board feet had been shipped on the new railroad. All lumber work and construction stopped on November 12, 1918. All was dismantled, and soldiers moved on.

After the war, the Army sold Camp One, the Blodgett Tract, the railroad, and the partially finished mill in Toledo to the Pacific Spruce Corporation. The business added bunkhouses and small family bungalows, a school, a mess hall, and machine shop for work on locomotives and logging donkeys as well as a steam boiler and steam engine connected to a winch mounted on a sled. The demand for spruce slowed when frames for planes were replaced by aluminum, and accessible spruce trees were hard to find in the over-logged forest. The trestles began to break up, and Yaquina Bay sometimes became too shallow for the schooners to get to the Toledo mill. Camp One was abandoned in 1936.

Over time the march for civilization and unfettered access to the earth's bounty destroyed almost all the Sitka spruce. Today, in Oregon, the Cape Perpetua houses the last intact ancient forest, and in the Yakona Nature Preserve, only six Sitka spruce still stand.

After the Agate Beach Hotel burned in 1940, the Towne House, a restaurant, was built on the same spot. In 1979, Izzy's Pizza Parlor opened; it recently closed permanently due to COVID. The building still sits above the road that goes out to the Yaquina Head Lighthouse. I remember many years ago in one of our big storms the roof blew off Izzy's, flipped and broke into pieces in the parking lot and down the hill side, while the owner watched from down the hill. Thankfully, none of the customers inside was injured. A few cars got battered, but no one was in the parking lot. The Spruce railroad track is visible in front of the Agate Beach Hotel in the photo above.

"Instead of cleaning the house, I just watch an episode of *Hoarders* and tell myself, 'Wow, my home looks great!'"

– Anonymous

August 2021

Cabled Array 001: The Cascadia Subduction Zone

This research project almost never was. The *Marcus Langseth* was a common sight in our bay this year when she hung around OSU's Hatfield Marine Science Center dock most of January and February, returning again in May and July. I was delighted to see her there after I heard she was decommissioned, and Trump was sending her to the dust bin. Apparently, she survived Trump and teamed with our OSU Hatfield's *Oceanus* research ship on a two-month operation to create 3-D images in the Cascadia fault from the Juan de Fuca ridge to where the trench dives under the North America plate.

The *Langseth* zigzagged up the Cascadia subduction zone, firing seismic guns through the water deep into the earth of the Cascadia subduction zone for these images of the earth's interior faults, including tsunami-producing earthquakes, and magma chambers in details unmatched by any other source. This information helps predict where and how fast the earthquake/tsunami will arrive at particular places along the fault.

For several years, the fault has been scary quiet, worrying scientists that the "big" one is due although along central Oregon coast the fault seems to be releasing some pressure. Evidence reveals that parts of the fault did not rupture during the past 10,000 years because "gates" such as mountains stopped the rupture. *Langseth*'s latest imaging will find these gates and verify Cascadia has segmented, averting catastrophic earthquakes.

To catch the soundwave echoes from the firing seismic guns, the *Langseth* drags a lengthy chain of hydrophones. Because sound waves at that depth cannot be collected from such a distance, 800 seismic receivers for catching and storing the sound wave data are scattered along the ocean floor and coastal land. These instruments contain geophones and a hydrophone, recorder, floatation, and weight.

Once a location is decided, the seismometer is deployed overboard, its weight sinking it to the seafloor. After the *Langseth* passes over the seismometer, sending its sound source, the *Oceanus* recovers the seismometer and drops it again in front of the *Langseth* along the fault. Like playing hopscotch. When the *Langseth* reaches her destination, *Oceanus* recovers all the seismometers one last time and returns to homeport.

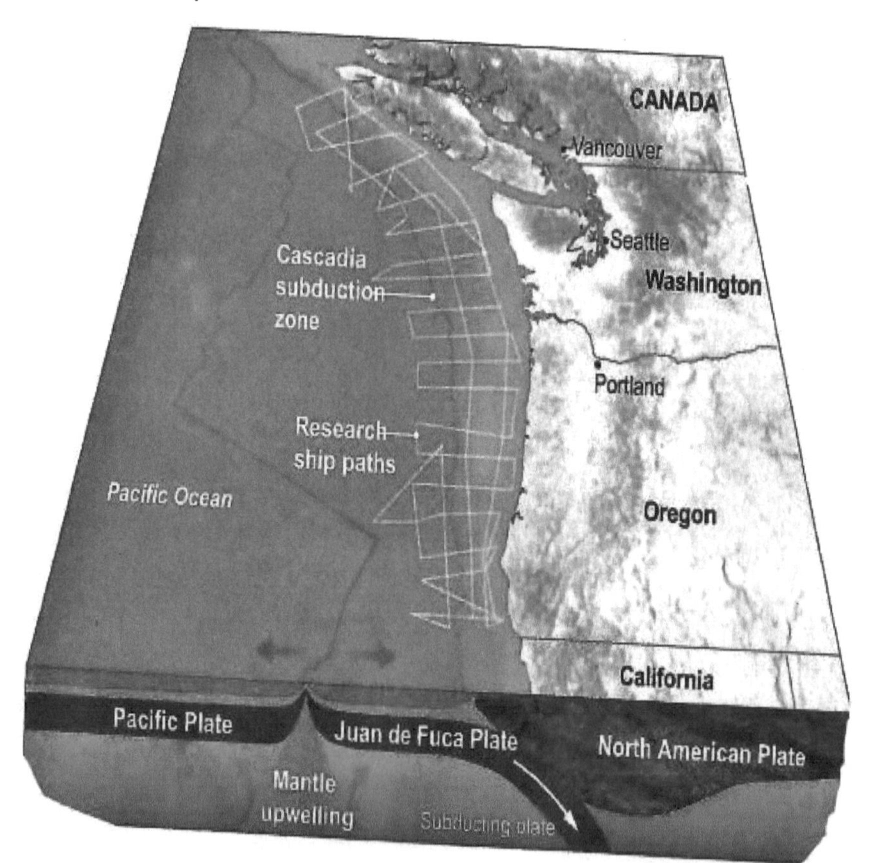

Lilies are red
and sometimes white,
Thank you for those times
admitting I'm right.

The More You Know—Origins of Bigotry

A decade after scientists discovered that lab rats will rescue a fellow rat in distress but not a rat they consider an outsider, new research pinpoints the brain regions that drive rats to prioritize their nearest and dearest in times of crisis. It also suggests humans may share the same neural bias.

Sand Labyrinths

Ann Hubard found sand drawings at the mouth of New River on the beach between Bandon and Floras Lake. She writes: "Due to the extreme minus tides, for four mornings labyrinths were drawn in the sand by a volunteer group which does this at summer minus tides. Each day it was a little different design. The man who started the labyrinths and does the designs from his head was such a happy and joyful person."

IT Integrity

We have a new visitor in our bay, belonging to Canada, the *IT Integrity* is a BHP Platform supply/ROV support ship for subsea cable repair.

Mothers! If you have a stubborn girl with fiery attitude, don't douse it whatever you do. She will be needing it.

Mother of Wi-Fi

Stereotyping can be useful when we need emergency judgments for survival, but it can lead to serious misconceptions. For example, one of the great beauties of the world was also a prolific inventor. In 1941, movie star Hedy LaMarr filed for a patent for frequency-hopping technology, providing the basis for secure Wi-Fi, GPS, Bluetooth, and cell phone technology. She offered it to the Navy which replied, "What do you want to do, put a player piano inside a torpedo? Get out of here!"

Although her invention garnered billions of dollars, her estate didn't receive any of it, but the military did finally give her credit for the invention.

Born in Austria and married in 1934 at the age of 19, she fled her domineering German munitions manufacturer husband on a bicycle in the middle of the night. She knew little English, but Louis B. Mayer noticed her on a ship to New York and hired her. Friends helped her collect equipment to experiment with her inventions while she was on the movie set. She also told Howard Hughes he should change the original square design of his airplanes to a streamlined shape, imitating fast birds and fish.

COVID-19 Vaccinations

A niece sent me an article from conservative news commentator Stu Peters about how COVID vaccinations will kill people. Too many people believe this lie, creating lack of trust and possible illnesses and/or deaths. The craziest conspiracy theory about vaccinations, however, is that the left-wing Antifa (abbreviation for anti-fascists) has a "do not get vaccinated" propaganda campaign to convince the far-right that the vaccination is deadly. Or another theory, that Democrats try to persuade people to get vaccinated, knowing they won't do anything the political party asks. Question: If the chance of death is much higher without the shot and you are against the shot, aren't you shooting yourself in the foot?

September 2021

"Feel Good" Moments

It is my unscientific belief that we stay in the world for one reason. Well maybe two. The first is the incredible drive to survive, often leading to an adrenalin rush that ends in heroic deeds. The second reason, in order to feel good and get that spurt of dopamine in our brain, we will do most anything. That's why we want to help others, want to be loved or in love one last time, want to hurt others, want to hate, want anti-depressants and other drugs, alcohol, sex, power, greed, arrogance, etc.—all and anything that helps us achieve euphoria. Rats can spontaneously release the "feel good" brain chemical "dopamine" as a reward. Consider what life might be like if we could access our dopamine at will without the need of assistance.

"Pay attention to the gentle ones, the ones who can hold your gaze with no discomfort, the ones who smile to themselves while sitting alone in a coffee shop, the ones who walk as if floating. Take them in and marvel at them. Simply marvel. It takes an extraordinary person to carry themselves as if they do not live in hell." – Danny Bunyavong

Repairing the Heart and Vocal Cords

Science has done it again. An injectable hydrogel for wound repair of the heart and vocal cords has arrived. Because the heart and vocal cords are in constant movement, finding an injectable substance strong enough to survive and repair damage such as what is caused by cancer was not possible until McGill University combined a knowledge of chemistry, biology, physics, and engineering to produce hydrogel, a biomaterial providing room for cells to live and grow.

Angela Merkel

My favorite subject in college was philosophy, especially the study of Plato, student of Socrates and teacher of Aristotle, who lived during Ancient Greece's Classical period. Plato believed that "philosophers would be the best rulers of society because they're able to understand true goodness and justice in a way that other people cannot. Because they would understand that the greatest self-benefit is living virtuously, they would act out morally and not out of self-interest."

Of all the leaders in our modern world, I consider Angela Merkel a leader fitting this description. She was a physicist with a doctorate in quantum chemistry working as a researcher before she went into politics. Belonging to the Christian Democratic Union (CDU) political party, she was the first woman chancellor of Germany.

During the eighteen years she was chancellor, she never bought cars, jets, yachts, villas, and the like; she never moved out of the apartment where she lived before she entered politics. She never had a servant, and she never divorced. Famous for wearing the same suit, she never bothered with fashion. Asked once if she had any other clothes, she answered, "I'm a civil servant, not a model." She reprimanded reporters for not sticking to the important issues. She never cried "fake news" to create suspicion and division, never fought with those who ruled before her, never got her family and friends government jobs so they could pilfer millions of dollars, never arrogantly shoved others out of the way to be out front, and never misbehaved causing stress and gossip. I could go on for pages, but you get the message.

Once named Lady of the World, Merkel built her country into Europe's largest economy and quietly ruled Germany's eighty million people with humbleness and grace. I wish her the best for the rest of her retired life and hope she will always be proud of all she achieved.

The world would be so much different if more of our world leaders followed the earlier philosophers rather than using Niccolo Machiavelli's *The Prince* (1513), also a favorite of Hitler, as a pattern. Considered the great daddy of modern political philosophy and political science, Machiavelli's treatise is about how to take and hold power through fear, violence, and divisiveness.

Washed Up Whale

A friend sent this photo of a 30-foot juvenile gray whale washed up on the Yachats beach and a likely victim of orcas. It isn't the first whale death this year on Oregon beaches. Grey whales traveling our West Coast are dying off by the hundreds. Their food supply is disappearing, and the whales, along with orcas and other sea life, are starving to death.

Everything has a moral: A guy digs through the floor of his cabin and water flows in. Other passengers are angry. But it's his own cabin, the guy argues, so what business is it of anyone else? Personal choice only goes so far when we're all on the same boat.

– An Old Jewish Tale

Politics:

Wearing a Mask

The second mask-wearing mandate has arrived in Oregon, and I still don't accept those who claim to value "freedom" over the lives of others, especially our children. Just as my freedom ends with your nose, your freedom ends with mine. Because you won't wear the mask, we have now developed a new variant killing our children. When your carelessness and apparent indifference, that you call freedom, infects others and they die, you become a murderer.

According to the new IPCC Report (Intergovernmental Panel on Climate Change) climate change is widespread, rapid, and intensifying in every climate system across the world. Changes that have never occurred in hundreds of thousands of years are now set in motion and can no longer be changed such as sea rising and warming.

Politics:

Freedom

The word has many definitions. The World Court states, "Freedom is a right." The First Amendment of our Constitution reads, "Congress shall make no law respecting an establishment of religion or prohibiting the free exercise thereof; or abridging the freedom of speech, or of the press; or the right of the people peaceably to assemble, and to petition the Government for a redress of grievances."

According to the online dictionary, "Freedom is the power or right to act, speak, or think as one wants without hindrance or restraint."

The Wikipedia uses more legalese: "In political discourse, political freedom is often associated with liberty and autonomy in the sense of 'giving oneself their own laws,' and with having rights and the civil liberties with which to exercise them—without undue interference by the state."

The Bible uses "freedom" 54 times.

Second Corinthians 3:17: "Now the Lord is the Spirit, and where the Spirit of the Lord is, there is freedom." John 8:36: "So, if the Son sets you free, you will be free indeed." Galatians 5:13-14: "You, my brothers and sisters, were called to be free. But do not use your freedom to indulge the flesh; rather, serve one another humbly in love. For the entire law is fulfilled in keeping this one command: Love your neighbor as yourself." 1 Peter 2:16: "Live as free people, but do not use your freedom as a cover-up for evil; live as God's slaves". Luke 4:18: "The Spirit of the Lord is on me, because he has anointed me to proclaim good news to the poor. He has sent me to proclaim freedom for the prisoners and recovery of sight for the blind to set the op-pressed free."

Freedom to the mathematician means we are free within boundaries. "The phase rule states that $F = C - P + 2$. Thus, for a one-component system with one phase, the number of degrees of freedom is two, and any temperature and pressure, within limits, can be attained." Other definitions:

"Freedom is the right to live as we wish." - Epictetus

"Money buys you the freedom to live your life the way you want." - Keanu Reeves

"Freedom: To ask nothing. To expect nothing. To depend on nothing." - Ayn Rand

"People seldom do what they believe in. They do what is convenient, then repent."- Bob Dylan

"For to be free is not merely to cast off one's chains, but to live in a way that respects and enhances the freedom of others." - Nelson Mandela

"Liberty is different from freedom in that freedom is primarily, if not exclusively, the ability to do as one wills and what one has the power to do; whereas liberty concerns the absence of arbitrary restraints and takes into account the rights of all involved. As such, the exercise of liberty is subject to capability and limited by the rights of others." - John Stuart Mill

My personal favorite? Sort of follows the math equation $F = C - P + 2$. I repeat: "Your freedom ends where my nose begins." Often credited to Oliver Wendell Holmes, the saying refers to the boundary within one can act but has to stop when approaching the boundary of another.

We each have our own personal space of freedom within that boundary but not within the boundaries of anyone else without permission. When you harm others, such as refusing vaccinations and thus aiding the morphing of new variants into an even bigger killing pandemic, you have invaded my personal space and placed me in mortal danger. I would like the freedom to live. Legally you may be free to do as you wish . . . how about morally?

The fact some states lock down while others don't is like designating one corner of a swimming pool where people can pee. Or worse? Not getting your covid shot is like playing roulette with a gun at your head.

NOAA *Hi'ialakai* Stripped

On March 1, 2019, I watched this ship towed and docked at the NOAA terminal. She mapped and studied coral reef health and fish stock; before the 2018 Hurricane Walaka, she was diverted to French Frigate Shoals to evacuate researchers. Now decommissioned, the NOAA ship, no longer under her own power, remains at the Yaquina Bay dock. On a rare morning when the quiet river doesn't seem to move at all, the *Hi'ialakai* leaves reflections while she waits to be sold or sent to the junk heap.

The person next to you could be working hard not to fall apart. Whatever you may say, do it with love.

Storm Watching

This scene scared me enough that I didn't know whether to run or scream. Luckily, the wave dropped and rolled, disappearing into the sand at my feet. In the aftermath of a winter storm, I took this shot at Quail Street, a few miles from my home.

These storms. usually out of the southwest, provide me with one of my favorite entertainments, storm watching, especially during king tides. These unusually high tides occur when the full moon is at the perigee, meaning closest to the earth. The power in a wave reaching as high as 300 feet generated by raging winter storms is a special show unto itself.

Coming from Arizona, I had never heard of a king tide, let alone the ocean's strong relationship to the moon and sun. Each long-lasting wave rolls around the planet as the gravitational pull of the moon and sun heave these waves back and forth and create high tides along with the huge waves which mean: BE CAREFUL on the beaches. Or just stay home during these high tides. Or rather than walking the beach on King Tide days, find a high place to watch the mind-blowing show. I cannot think of a better way to spend an afternoon than the unique experience surrounded by the spectacular show in the sound and fury of Mother Nature.

Some of my favorite places to watch—other than my living room window—are all a short drive from Newport except for Shore Acres Park, over 100 miles away but so worth it. Dress warm, and waterproof for sideways rain, I swear, climbing up pants legs and sleeves. Stay well back from the water, especially around tidal pools and beaches. Logs can roll over you in only four inches of water. Don't forget your camera and binoculars. Never, NEVER turn your back on the ocean.

Boiler Bay Park, slightly north of Depoe Bay: Giant waves crash up against the shore.

Depoe Bay: Especially exciting is the powerful Thor's Well in the center of town.

Rocky Creek, south of Depoe Bay: The bluff has a sweeping view of the ocean and the offshore rocks where waves crash and leap high in action-packed energy.

Seal Rock turnouts: The slamming and arching of foamy waves against the rocks is mesmerizing.

Devil's Punch Bowl at Otter Crest: Once a cave, the roof fell in to form a perfect bowl, allowing water to pour in through unseen openings, filling and emptying with the tide. During a storm the bowl fills, wild and foamy like a bubbling cauldron.

Cape Perpetua, south of Yachats: In Cook's Chasm, a narrow opening in the basalt, waves create a spouting horn.

Shore Acres Park, south of Coos Bay: This offers a mystical play with some of the dramatic waves hitting the cliffs rise as high as 300 feet in the air!

Or you can stay home and watch this video:

https://www.youtube.com/watch?v=fKK3nZvM_go

Beaked Whales

On OPB's "In the News" section about Science and Environment, Jes Burns wrote about a failed expedition. The malfunctioning engine on a Hatfield Marine Science Center's ship, the R/V *Pacific Storm,* turned into a big winner. The project was to find beaked whales at the famous Great Pacific Garbage Patch.

On the unplanned early return to Newport, one of the ship's audio specialists, Annamaria DeAngelis, heard a never recorded before, unknown whale song through the hydrophone they were towing behind the ship. The song stopped, and she knew the whales were surfacing to get air.

Beaked whales are so shy that six of their species have never been seen alive and are known only because their bodies have washed up on shore. They are a small whale, not much bigger and just a bit fatter than dolphins. They are rarely close to land, preferring to feed on squid and live deep in dark ocean waters.

When the R/V *Pacific Storm* and her group of students watched two elusive beaked whales finally surface, the whales were not only curious about the students but also decided to ride the waves with the ship, swimming close enough for students to collect a sample of skin with a crossbow-fired biopsy dart.

Just another proud record-breaking research moment for our Hatfield marine science students. Congratulations to you all! **https://youtu.be/wTJG3hnY5SE**

Tale of a Space Rock

Eleanor Roosevelt was heard to say . . . "I once had a rose named after me and I was very flattered. But I was not pleased to read the description in the catalog. 'No good in a bed but fine up against a wall'."

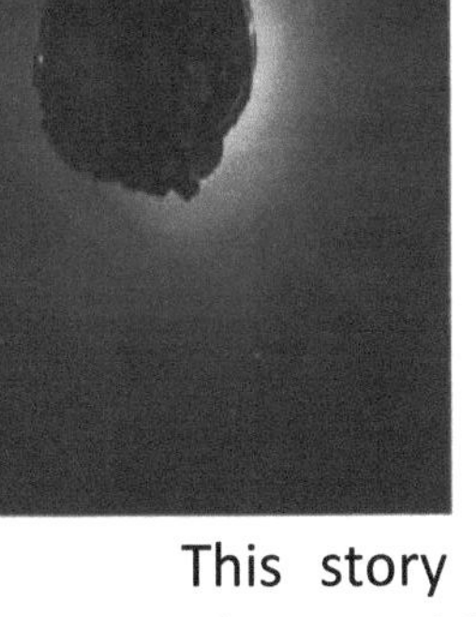

Stranger things can happen in a bed. A woman woke up with a space rock beside her. British Columbia resident Ruth Hamilton was asleep when an explosion broke through her roof, rained debris, and jerked her awake.

Hamilton jumped out of bed and found a rock about the size of her fist on the pillow next to her. People later reported a bright light followed by booms, determining the rock was from outer space.

This story was by Mindy Weisberger in *LiveScience*, October 15, 2021. Weisberger is a senior writer covering a general beat that includes climate change, paleontology, weird animal behavior, and space.

October 2021

November 2021

More about Feel Good Moments

Feeling good or pain—may be two sides of the coin. The number of drugs to help us feel good or cover pain grows each day. But what if we could trigger the feel good or pain relief from inside. Scientists are experimenting with rats to find ways to mediate these changes within the brain.

Roaming in our bodies are chemical messengers, hormones that run our heart rate, digestion, breathing, emotion, etc. Four of these hormones are our happy ones: dopamine, serotonin, oxytocin, and endorphins. Each brings us those feel good/pain relief moments in different ways and by different means.

Dopamine: Our pleasure hormone chemical often spikes into satisfied and motivating emotions, sometimes even downright giddy bubbles. It also helps us gain better coordination, improves short-term memories, and increases impulsive behavior. In reverse, low-level dopamine may cause depression, addiction, schizophrenia, and Parkinson's disease.

Serotonin: It stabilizes rather than spikes happy moods and helps us sleep, digest food, clot blood, and control impulsive behavior. Low levels, likewise, adversely affect moods, disturb sleeping, and cause digestive problems.

Oxytocin: Delivering our bonding, love, and trust emotions, the hormone appears naturally in our bodies when we engage in caring relationships, for example with lovers, babies, family, friends, and pets.

Endorphins: These pain-killing hormones are released by the brain, spinal cord, and pituitary gland in response to stressful situations, threats, or pain. We release endorphins into our bloodstream through exercises increasing our heart rate and blood circulation. Other methods to release endorphins are creating music or art, dancing, having sex or a glass of wine, eating dark chocolate, getting acupuncture, and laughing.

Drugs such as opiates, alcohol, nicotine, amphetamines, and cocaine can raise dopamine and serotonin levels, and some can block pain sensors to the brain, which is why we get addicted to them. The drug itself doesn't make us feel good or hurt less; instead they activate the chemical hormones already in our bodies. With long term drug use, other factors such as weight gain, smoking, inactivity, and binge drinking can cause drugs to be less effective by causing a chemical imbalance in the brain. When the drugs are no longer active, dopamine levels can drop below normal, causing depression, painful withdrawal symptoms, and powerful cravings.

If you don't want to wait for scientists to tell us how to control our dopamine and serotonin levels on our own, you can use the old-fashioned way. Our guts produce 90 percent of these hormones. Yogurt and nuts contain prebiotics, a type of dietary fiber feeding the good bacteria in your gut and producing serotonin and dopamine. Chocolate and nuts provide amino acids producing dopamine in brain cells. Milk, cheese, and yogurt contain tyrosine and phenylalanine that boost thinking, clarity, and memory as well as the levels of dopamine and serotonin in the body. Caffeine stimulates dopamine (waking us up) by actively interacting with dopaminergic neurons. Eating a banana can boost your mood almost instantly, containing not only prebiotics but also quercetin and tyrosine to stimulate dopamine production. Eggs have compounds tyrosine and phenylalanine which are converted into serotonin.

Amino acids, such as in fish, also increase the chemical serotonin. Spinach is rich in antioxidants, vitamins, and minerals plus tryptophan necessary to produce serotonin. Lean meats and poultry are high in the protein necessary in manufacturing dopamine and serotonin.

We can't yet give ourselves a "feel good" burst at will or lessen physical or mental pain, but we can feel better when we eat the right foods, exercise, make love, dance, get enough sleep, meditate, listen to quiet music, and maybe wander around awhile in the sun. And laugh. Don't forget to laugh. You can't feel pain when you laugh.

December 2021

COVID Mental Health Problems

Although philosophers and poets have always known we share a common mental health problem, recent studies fear it is much more prevalent and serious than depression. Some worry it's a precursor to serious mental illness. Henry David Thoreau tagged it as, "Most men lead lives of 'quiet desperation.'" T.S. Eliot described the loss of life's music as "I have measured out my life with coffee spoons."

A 15-year study by sociologist Corey Keyes, pioneer in researching positive psychology, has a following by sociologists and psychologists who dub it the neglected middle child of mental health. Called "languishing," it's that feeling between flourishing and depression, a lack of motivation, foggy thinking, aimless muddling, or just a general "meh." Corey's study, completed before the pandemic even started, determined 55 percent of U.S. workforce were in a state of languishing. Believed to be the dominant emotion in 2021, because languishing is also the most frequent symptom of long-haul COVID, I can't help but wonder how we will cope in a world of people who just don't much seem to care. Many don't even care enough to end this pandemic by getting their shots. It may be too late as the morphing into other COVID viruses are caused because people won't allow the pandemic, having reached critical, to be controlled. In the midst of a public health crisis even the Supreme Court has ruled against a mandate.

Mental healing is nothing to laugh about. You have no idea what problems others are dealing with. Regardless, it is no joke.

A famous quote by psychotherapist Virginia Satir goes: "We need 4 hugs a day for survival. We need 8 hugs a day for maintenance. We need 12 hugs a day for growth." It was a sad day when we were no longer allowed to hug our students to say we care – likely the only one they would get that day!

Preventing Covid

Sharks may save us. Science has found a protein in the immune systems of sharks known as VNARS. They believe it can not only prevent the COVID-19 virus from infecting us, this protein can also stop any of its variants. Get your shots anyway because this preventative cure is still a long way from your arm.

In another miracle, Trump is finally telling everyone to get their shots. He may have realized the majority of dying people are his followers who refuse the shots. I think he knows that by late 2021, 95 percent of COVID-19 deaths are among the non-

vaccinated. In counties that Trump won, the vaccination rate is 35 percent. And the spread in deaths between those who got their shots and those who did not rapidly grows. Republican rebellion against the vaccinations has reached the point of no return and they are still killing each other.

Crabbing Invasive Species

What an excellent way to make an invasive species beneficial: eat it. And just in time as two days ago the crab boats left their moorings to drop crab pots along the coast at their favorite hunting spots. Although they seek the Dungeness crab, an invasive crab, known as the Green Crab, now churns our waters. A native to Europe, this crab began invading the West Coast in the late 1980s. They became so aggressive at replacing other crabs that Canada listed it as one of the ten most unwanted species in the world.

The bad part? This crab digs up and eats the eelgrass, destroying ecosystems relied on by other sea creatures including other crabs. They also eat clams, oysters, and mussels. The good thing? Many gourmets regard green crabs as better than the Dungeness. The fun part? How about getting rid of them by trying new recipes such as Leek and Green Crab Croquettes. Or Green Crab and Mushroom

Risotto. Or Green Crab Stuffies. Or Green Crab Rangoon. Or scores of other recipes.

Another best part is that, during the next three months, I get to watch the lights from the crab boats far out to sea as they head for home with (hopefully) a full belly in their hold. Then the unloading begins as crabs are removed from the boat with a crane, packed into huge crates, loaded onto semi-trucks, and hauled away.

> **"Men fight for liberty and win it with hard knocks. Their children, brought up easy, let it slip away again, poor fools. And their grandchildren are once more slaves."**
>
> **– D.H. Lawrence**

The Great Pacific Garbage Patch

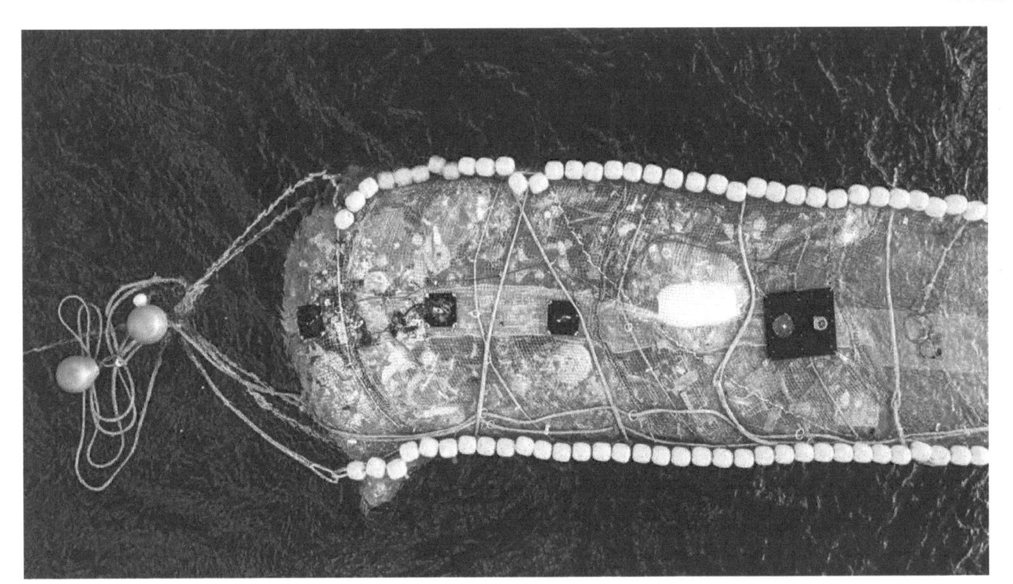

All the trash we put into the ocean is frightening, the reason many devices have been invented to pick up this ocean trash with just as many failures. Maybe until now with a new trash picker-upper named Jenny. Much like trawl fishing, this device, a U-shaped funnel net half-mile long, is attached to a boat at each end. With one swipe the net can remove 20,000 pounds of plastic bits. That's 0.000025 percent of the 80,000 tons already there. Developed by the non-profit group called Ocean Cleanup, Jenny intends to remove 90 percent of the Great Pacific Garbage Patch by 2040. Quite a feat considering this floating cluster of plastic bits covers an area twice the size of Texas.

Even worse, the trash pile, caught in one of the two circling currents in the Pacific Ocean known as a gyre, continues to rapidly expand. As do the number of plastic bits that settle on the ocean floor. Did I mention the trash pile keeps growing? And this trash pile is one of five in the oceans. All together they contain 297 million tons—and that was in 2016!

Science couldn't care less what you believe. It is what it is.

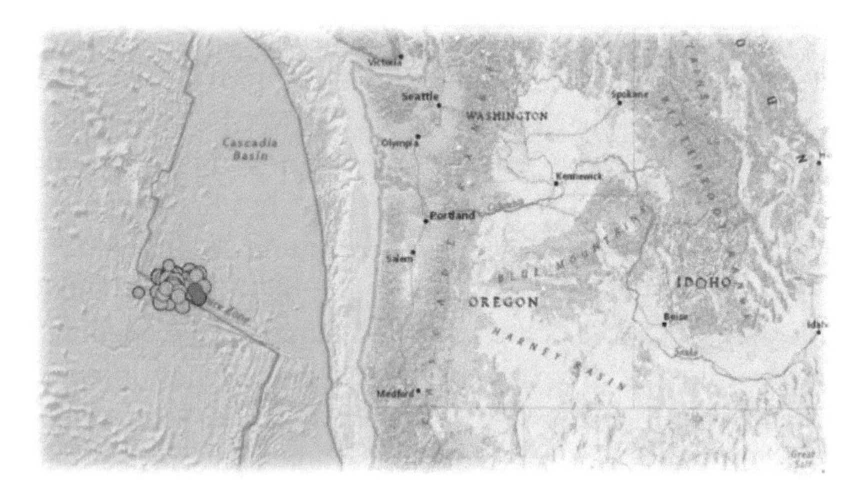

Earthquake Swarm

According to the U.S. Geological Survey, a swarm of more than 50 earthquakes hit the Cascadia fault at a magnitude of 4.0 to 5.8 on December 8 and 9, 2021. They all occurred in the Blanco Fault Zone, a well-known area for shaking. Generally, scientists agree these swarms do not foretell a big one so if you feel a shake, go back to sleep.

The Cascadia Subduction Zone, 70 to 100 miles off the Pacific Coast shoreline, is a fault that runs 600 miles from northern California to British Columbia. In the last 10,000 years, it has been the cause of 41 earthquakes from 190 years to 1,200 years apart.

Aliens from Space

Researching scientific discoveries, especially those about the human condition, fascinates me as do all discoveries that might be useful somewhere sometime. For example: A group of astronomers have found a new way of searching for alien civilizations. Someday someone from earth will likely meet an alien. Hope we find friendly ones first.

The James Webb Space Telescope

Christmas Day, filled with football and food, also revealed history in the making—the launching of a telescope designed to detect light emitted 13.8 billion years ago at the dawn of the universe. This extraordinary telescope might change everything we know about the universe. Maybe we'll even see the hand of God.

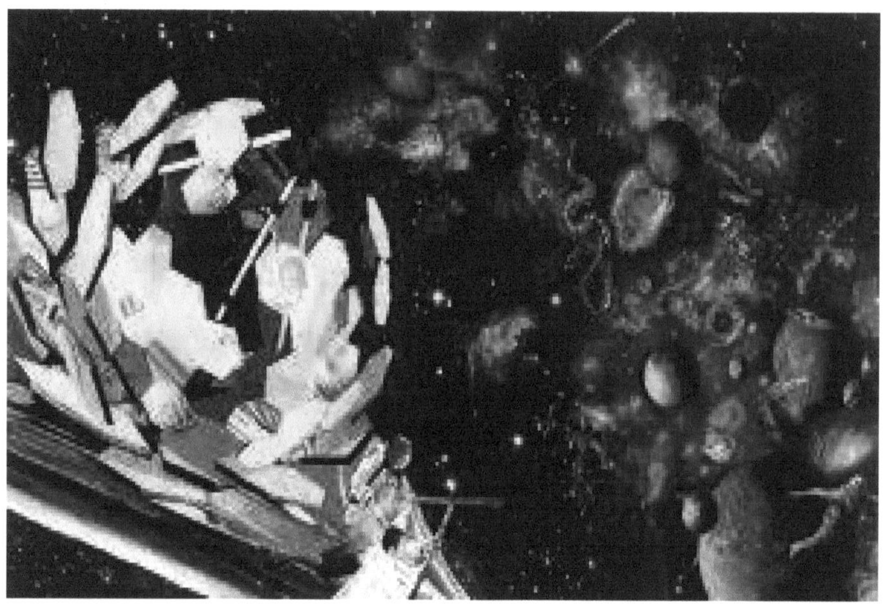

"It is the mark of an educated mind to be able to entertain a thought without accepting it."

– Aristotle

It's in the Water

For all the really stupid behavior, at least we have two excuses for it. The first is long-haul COVID with symptoms covering anything you can conjure. The second? Lead poisoning reduces IQ by impairing brain development and lowering cognitive ability. Even though lead pipes were outlawed in 1986, the pipes already in the ground were allowed to remain.

Three decades later, an estimated 15 to 22 million Americans still cook with and drink tap water entering their homes through lead pipes owned by various public and private entities. Then there's the air we're breathing. More than half of the Americans alive today were alive before 1996, when leaded gas was outlawed. Which means we all inhaled a lot of lead. A neurotoxin, lead erodes brain cells when it enters the body through air or water.

Therefore we have no safe level of exposure at any point in life. So, the next time you observe stupid behavior or get caught up in it yourself, blame it on lead. That's what I do!

Another exhausting year is finally ending as the pandemic continues to rage. Thing is, I don't know whether to go out and get ice cream or commit a felony. I'll decide in the car.

2021 was like walking across an intersection on the green light and getting whacked by E.T.

Epilogue – 2022 – A New Dawn

I'll tell you how the Sun rose –
A Ribbon at a time –
The Steeples swam in Amethyst –
The news, like Squirrels, ran –
The Hills untied their Bonnets –
The Bobolinks – begun -
Then I said softly to myself –
"That must have been the Sun!"

But how he set – I know not –
There seemed a purple stile –
That little Yellow boys and girls –
Were climbing all the while –
Till when they reached the other side –
A Dominie in Gray –
Put gently up the evening Bars –
And led the flock away –
- Emily Dickinson

"Life is a gift and every day is an opportunity to share your gift with others. Don't be grateful, be fabulously grateful."— Val Uchendu

Yaquina River's famous Table Mountain from the Knothole

When it's my time, at my funeral I would like a bouquet of red carnations placed on my casket. And just before you lower me, toss the bouquet to any person who has not had the COVID shots so that I can see who's next.

Cat vs. Bull: Who Imitates Whom?

After a couple of bats at the bull, my cat Latte stopped to wash her face. What's the old saying? When in doubt, wash. Then nap.

Politics:

Another New COVID Variant

From the first U.S. COVID case in February 2020 to the first vaccination in December 2020 we were hit with wave after wave of variants known as Alpha, Beta, Gamma, Delta, Lambda, Mu, and Omicron (also called BA.1, BA.2, and BA.3), more contagious than COVID. Hopefully, with only 24 letters in the Greek alphabet, we have only 17 to go. Then there's 26 letters in ours . . . So far each variant has often been more virulent, more contagious, and the shots less effective than the last.

We ignore these waves, returning to our old lives for the sake of our children and paying the bills. Businesses that cater to crowds such as restaurants and bars reopen along with millions of other contact businesses such as stores and offices. Many places don't even require masks and distancing, mainly because our Supreme Court ruled January 13, 2022, against most restrictions.

All because what some people on the far-right call freedom the right to refuse vaccinations while they deny freedom to others by increasing death sentences to millions with no end in sight.

This year for Christmas all you anti-vaxxers are getting ~~dictionaries~~ science textbooks.

Humankind Moving from Type 0 to Type 1 Society

Although we seem intent on destroying our world (greed can do that), we still hope to fix it. Or hope something will come along to fix it for us. There's that word again—hope. Toward that end, scientists have given us a glimpse into the future. In 1964, Soviet astronomer Nikolai Kardashev came up with a scale in 1964, a way to measure the "big picture." Basically, our survival depends on how much usable energy we can collect and store. Although we have harnessed enough energy in fossil fuel and water deposits to power an industrial explosion in the last century, we still have so much more energy potential on this earth we have yet to access.

Scientists such as Carl Sagan, Neil deGrasse Tyson, and Michio Kaku use the Kardashev scale to chart our progress—or lack of it. While searching for signals from extraterrestrial life, Kardashev determined three classes, starting with Type 1; the chart has since been extended to 5 types. Carl Sagan listed us still at Type 0.7.

Type 1: Humans control and store all earth's energy including volcanoes, earthquakes, weather, and some energy from the sun.

Type 2: Humans control all of the sun's power. They can create megastructures such as Dyson Spheres, an energy absorbing and storing device encircling the sun. The ability to control and store such energy also protects humans from becoming extinct.

Type 3: Humans are galactic travelers, hopping from star to star across the galaxy, capturing energy and colonizing planets. Humans will likely morph into highly advanced cyborgs with mechanical prostheses as the human body would no longer be practical. Kardasgev did not go beyond Type 3, but other theorists did.

Type 4: These travelers control the energy of the universe. This advanced species could live inside black holes and be powerful enough to change space/time construct or control the laws of thermodynamics.

Type 5: This species manipulates the universe any way they wish. They control a compilation of universes as they hop about, absorbing many forms of matter in space/time. They are the new gods. Sound loony bin crazy? Not really. Compare the infinitesimal growth of the last 4.5 billion years compared to the explosion in advancing civilization during the last 450 years.

In some ways we have reached Type 1 with satellites and the internet opening communications throughout the world. Air flight made the world physically accessible, and we're learning to harness renewable energy from sun, wind, and water.

In populating outer space, however, Neil deGrasse Tyson compared the size of the earth to other objects in the universe by comparing our achievements to maybe three-fourths of an inch to the moon. Mars is still a mile away. Yet we are a long way from stone tools and weapons used by roaming warring hominins with little to no social structure to political and social systems plus learning to access and use large deposits of energy.

What blocks us from greater achievement, however, is the tribal win or lose mindset in which one country takes from another country so that they both lose. Darwin's theory is survival of the fittest, but ultimately survival of the friendliest moves us into collective societies consuming energy to help each other to not only survive but also to flourish.

The freedom embraced by democratic societies for exploration, inventing, and entrepreneurship does not do well in closed autocratic societies. Until we all agree on a global economy in which liberal democracy and free trade are ruled by all the people worldwide in fair elections, we will never achieve Type 1 civilization.

Is it possible other life forms have already reached Type 1 and above? Consider the Fermi Paradox, a question posed by Enrico Fermi, "Where is everybody?" There are as many galaxies drifting around up in our sky as stars in the Milky Way. The European Space Agency estimates the number at about 1,000,000,000,000,000,000,000,000 (or 10^{24}) stars. There is a possibility that for every grain of sand on Earth are 100 Earth-like planets. Because the universe is approximately 13.8 billion years old and the Earth is only 4.542 billion years old, logically other life forms may have existed long before our Earth was even cobbled together. Still, organizations like SETI that have searched for alien life for years now, found nothing . . . Yet.

When this is over,
May we never again take for granted
A handshake with a stranger
Full shelves at the store
Conversations with neighbors
A crowded theater
Friday night out
A taste of communion
A routine checkup
A school rush each morning
Coffee with a friend
The stadium roaring
Each deep breath
A boring Tuesday
Life itself.
When this ends,
May we find
That we have become
More like the people
We wanted to be
And may we stay
That way – better
For each other
Because of the worst.

- Laura Kelly Fanucci

This is not the end. You can find the continuation of our writings here:

Sue Hardesty: https://www.facebook.com/sue.hardesty2

Nel Ward: https://nelsnewday.wordpress.com

Contributors

Sue Hardesty (author/photographer): Life in rural Arizona where her mother enjoyed prospecting and her father farmed and ranched shaped Sue's life during the 1930s and 1940s. Her college degree in English after a few years of exploration led her to teaching in high school before becoming an audiovisual specialist in high schools. At this time, she developed her interest in photography, and her interest in reading and teaching literature was the background for her having published four novels, two nonfiction books, and two short stories. (Sue's first novel disappeared after problems with computers in the 1980s.) After 27 years working in education, Sue retired to the Oregon Coast with Nel. She now writes an eclectic Facebook page, the inspiration for *Through the Knothole.*

Nel Ward (author): Growing up in rural Nebraska, Nel graduated from a small college before pursuing graduate work at the University of Kansas and Arizona State University. For 21 years, she taught English in both secondary schools and higher education before finishing that career as a high school librarian for ten years. Nel's work in professional organizations led to involvement in state and national teaching and librarian organizations, both on committees and in publishing articles. After retirement, she continued these endeavors along with editing books, writing book reviews, and posting on her political blog.

Nel and Sue together: Meeting in 1969, Nel and Sue have spent their 50+ years as partners working on many projects. In the early years, they developed educational programs, wrote pamphlets and media textbooks, and created evaluation systems for media centers. After their retirement, they opened and operated two B&Bs, a bookstore, and then a small publishing company while flipping houses that they remodeled. Love of good food and the delight of a new project led them into writing and editing *the butch cook book* also doing the layout and illustrations. And of course, taste-testing the recipes. Nel and Sue have also been politically active with involvement in the local chapter of NOW and PFLAG.

Ann Hubard (photographer): Ann describes herself as a "former juvenile delinquent" and "now a retired attorney." After growing up on the beach in Virginia, she attended college in California during the 1960s civil rights movement. After traveling, she attended law school in Oregon before working at Legal Aid representing low-income people and then coordinating citizen review boards who heard cases of foster children for the state judicial department. Partnered with Taylor West for over 30 years, she married "the love of my life" in 2015. As "outdoor enthusiast, political activist, vegetarian, and amateur photographer," Ann takes pleasure in exploring urban streets, hiking, and snowshoeing, sometimes continuing her travels throughout the world.

More Thanks

Art: Rick Chambers, 51; Maud Frances; 116; Laurence Hardesty, 115; Wallis Nash; 2; Betty Santavicca, 85; Harold Williams, 114.

Photography: Sally Boyle - 33, 34, 103;
Chuck Forinash - 83;
Sue Hardesty - Verso, ii, 4-10, 13-17, 21-32, 36, 38, 42, 44, 46, 48, 51-52, 55, 58-61, 63, 65, 67-68, 70, 74, 78, 86, 96-97, 103, 105, 107, 110, 116, 119, 122-123, 125, 127-128, 138-142, 147, 156, 158-159, 163, 167, 169-170, 177, 181, 183-184, 188, 191, 199-200, 205-206, 216-217;
Ann Hubard - Verso, 4, 12, 15, 22, 34, 39, 73, 75, 82, 93, 98, 119, 145, 158, 151-152, 169-170, 186, 183, 185-186, 200;
Lincoln County Historical Society - 3, 12, 21, 33, 54, 67, 79, 109, 172;
Mark Moore – 33;
NOAA - 81, 91, 124;
Nancy Shogren – 69;
Caroline Wheeler - 47, 215.

Sources

Books

Bill Gulick. *Roadside History of Oregon*. Mountain Press, 1996.

Robert Hadlow. *Elegant Arches, Soaring Spans: C.B. McCullough, Oregon's Master Bridge Builder.* Oregon State University, 2001.

John B. Horner. *Days and Deeds in the Oregon Country: Ten-minute Stories from Northwest History.* J.K. Gill, 1928.

Lewis A. McArthur. *Oregon Geographic Names*. Oregon Historical Society, 1982.

Wayne O'Neil. *Man & The Sea: Shipwrecks of Southwest Washington and Northwest Oregon, 1792-1949*. Midway Printery, 2013.

Richard L. Price. *Newport, Oregon: 1866-1936: Portrait of a Coast Resort*. Lincoln County Historical Society, 1975.

Elizabeth Rusch. *The Next Wave: The Quest to Harness the Power of the Oceans (Scientists in the Field)*. Houghton Mifflin, 1999.

J.E. Stembridge, ed. *Pathfinder : The First Automobile Trip from Newport to Siletz Bay, Oregon, July, 1912*. Lincoln County Historical Society, 1975.

Websites

2.amazonaws.com
academic.com
alternet.org
allaboutbirds.org
aquariumvillage.org
aquarium.org
abiotech.eu
atlasobscura.com
bbc.com
bing.com/images
beachconnection.net
britannica.com
businessinsider.com
cbsnews.com
commondreams.org
cnn.comcbc.ca
cato.org
citeseerx.ist.psu.edu
climate.columbia.edu
cdc.gov
chateaudevin.org
ceoas.oregonstate.edu
climate.gov
dailykos.com
depositphotos.com
dfw.state.or.us
digitalmedia.fws.gov
dreamstime.com
edweek.org
earthsky.org
elpasotimes.com
oregonlive.com
entomologytoday.org
fernbank.edu
feedingamerica.org
flickr.com
futurism.com
facebook.com
fallenheroesmemorial.com
freedomhouse.org
geocaching.com
gettyimages.com
grist.org
healthline.com
hummingbird-guide.comilo.org
ijpr.org
istockphoto.com
imdb.com
interactiveoceans.washington.edu
insider.com
jstor.org
katu.com
kerrynewberry.com
kodiakmaritimemuseum.org
livescience.com
lighthousefriends.com
lincolncountymuseum.org
marine.ucsc.edu
myjewishlearning.com
media.defense.gov
msnbc.com
microchemlab.com
medicalnewstoday.com
nakamotoforestry.com
nationalgeographic.org
nationalgeographic.com
nature.com
natureworldnews.com
nps.gov
nbcnews.com
ndependent.co.uk
newportoregon.gov
news.jardinemotors.co.uk
newslincolncounty.com
newsweek.com
nhm.ac.uk
noaa.gov
nrl.navy
nyebeach.net
nytimes.com
oceanconservancy.org
oceanobservatories.org

ocean.washington.edu
offbeatoregon.com
ohs.org
oldsaltblog.com
oldoregonphotos.com
opb.org
oregon.gov
oregoncoasthistory.org
oregondigital.org
oregonhikers.org
oregonhistoryproject.org
oregonlive.com
oregonstate.edu
owlcation.com
pacwaveenergy.org
pdxhistory.com
pinterest.com
pgpf.org
pixabay.com
pixnio.com
phys.org
portofnewport.com
postalemployeenetwork.com
preparednessadvice.com
presidency.ucsb.edu
publicdomainpictures.net qz.com
qz.com
raitoinc.com
rawpixel.com
rd.com
readersupportednews.org
reaganlibrary.gov
researchblog.duke.edu
reuters.com
roadtrippers.com
saltydogboatingnews.com
savethepostoffice.com
sbpdiscovery.org
sciencedaily.com
seapowermagazine.org
seattlepi.com
ship-technology.com
statesmanjournal.com
statnews.com
teamunify.com
telegraph.co.uk
thegailygrind.com
theguardian.com
thenmusa.org
thenewsguard.com
thenmusa.org
theweek.com
time.com
timeout.com
timeline.com
traveloregon.com
tripsavvy.com
troop245.org
truthout.org
uaf.edu
unols.org
uscg.mil
visittheoregoncoast.com
vocal.media
urbandictionary.com
usatoday.com
washingtonpost.com
washington.edu
wbur.org
whalespoken.wordpress.com/
wikihow.com
Wikimedia.org
wikipedia.org
wikisource.org
wikiwand.com
whoi.edi
wimp.com
workboat.com
yachatsnews.com
yakonaoregon.org
youtube.com

Index

Acknowledgments

"It takes a village ...." So begins the African proverb, now sometimes considered a cliché, about raising a child. The same expression refers to putting together this book, a village of both local folks and the far-reaching new and old friends and family responding to Sue's social media. The comments were funny, kind, informative, and enlightening. Although these statements haven't been included in the book, we want to acknowledge Teresa Atwill for her welcome information (sometimes corrections!) from her connections to research at Hatfield and NOAA; Jane Cothron and Jackie Lambert for their dry humor; and new friends such as Rici Peterson for her curiosity.

Our gratitude goes out to wonderful photographers who brought our words to life, especially Ann Hubard who generously offered all her images from the past decades and provided the cover photograph of our cherished bridge. Art came from local places—hillsides, murals, and works of local artists—as well as from Sue's father and his friends.

More thanks go to our nieces and nephews who keep us in contact with their lives as well as friends from long ago in our teaching careers, beloved students and other teachers who also found us on Wikipedia. Sue still remembers them, especially Tex (Lyle Goins) who helped set up Sue's classroom lesson that went disastrously wrong (Teacher's fault). He forgave her. We even reconnected with a visitor to our bed & breakfast who stayed with us almost 30 years ago.

Part of our village sent serious and funny cartoons and quotes included in the social media posts and the book. The most prolific, Donna Silver, began as a dogsitter and ended up being a dear friend. Others encouraged us in organizing, editing, and completing the books such as MaryKay Dahlgreen. She has a bay view and emails Sue to ask about arriving ships. Additional contributions came from the community of authors who interacted with Sue's social media.

Scholars and other brilliant thinkers provided food for thought, and a best part of our village is our publisher, Lori Lake, who tirelessly worked on the final layout after we had sent her the rough draft with its organization. We appreciate her patience and willingness to make all the changes we kept requesting.

Hopefully, readers will enjoy our village.

—Sue and Nel

love

CPSIA information can be obtained
at www.ICGtesting.com
Printed in the USA
BVHW060240020223
657351BV00001B/3

* 9 7 8 1 6 3 3 0 4 2 3 3 9 *